# The Darkness of the Present

MODERN AND CONTEMPORARY POETICS

# The Darkness of the Present

POETICS, ANACHRONISM, AND THE ANOMALY

STEVE McCAFFERY

The University of Alabama Press · Tuscaloosa

Copyright © 2012
The University of Alabama Press
Tuscaloosa, Alabama 35487-0380
All rights reserved
Manufactured in the United States of America

Typeface: Minion Pro and Eurostyle

Front cover photograph: "Lunar Eclipse," © Faris El-khider |
Dreamstime.com
Cover design: Michele Myatt Quinn

∞

The paper on which this book is printed meets the minimum
requirements of American National Standard for Information
Sciences—Permanence of Paper for Printed Library Materials,
ANSI Z39.48-1984.

Library of Congress Cataloging-in-Publication Data

McCaffery, Steve.
The darkness of the present : poetics, anachronism, and the
anomaly / Steve McCaffery.
     p. cm. — (Modern and contemporary poetics)
   Includes bibliographical references and index.
   ISBN 978-0-8173-5733-7 (quality paper : alk. paper) — ISBN
978-0-8173-8642-9 (ebook)
   1. Poetics. I. Title.
   PN1042.M37 2012
   808.1—dc23
                                        2012015849

For Karen
sharing "the oneness of language as infinite syzygy."

# Contents

**9**

Difficult Harmony: The Picturesque Detail in Gilpin, Price, and Clark Coolidge's *Space* 149

**10**

The 'Pataphysics of Auschwitz 167

**11**

The Instrumental Nightingale: Some Counter-Musical Inflections in Poetry from Gray to Celan 185

# Illustrations

# Acknowledgments

I want to offer my sincere thanks to the editors of the books and journals who first published earlier versions of some of the materials in this book. Chapter 11 appears for the first time in English. Chapters 3 and 9 appear for the first time in print. All other chapters have been revised, expanded, or modified.

"Cacophony, Abstraction, and Potentiality: The Fate of the Dada Sound Poem," *The Sound of Poetry/The Poetry of Sound*, eds. Marjorie Perloff and Craig Dworkin (Chicago: University of Chicago Press, 2009): 118–28, 310–14.

"Corrosive Poetics: The Relief Composition of Ronald Johnson's *Radi os*," *PreTexts* 11. 2 (Fall 2002): 7–23.

"Transcoherence and Deletion: the Mesostic Writings of John Cage," *Etudes Anglaises: Littérature et Philosophie* 59 No. 3 (Summer 2006): 329–340.

"A Chapter of Incidents," *Errata: The Cultural Production of Accidents, Errors, and Unforeseen Events*, special issue of *Public: Art/Culture/Ideas* 33 (Fall 2006): 64–73.

"From Muse to Mousepad: Informatics and the Avant-Garde," *Phrasis: Studies in Language and Literature*, 49.1 (Fall 2008): 168–192.

"Parapoetics and the Architectural Leap," *Architectures of Poetry*, eds. María Eugenia Díaz and Craig Douglas Dworkin (Amsterdam and New York: Rodopi, 2004): 91–108. Revised ed. in *Contemporary Poetics*, ed. Louis Armand (Evanston: Northwestern University Press, 2007): 321–47 and 372–76. 2nd revised ed. in *A Time for the Humanities*, eds. James J. Bono, Tim Dean, and Ewa P. Ziarek (New York: Fordham University Press, 2008): 161–79.

"'To Lose One's Way' (for Snails and Nomads): the Radical Labyrinths of Constant and Arakawa and Gins," *Architecture Against Death*, special issue of *Interfaces: Image Texte Language* 21/22 (Winter 2003): 113–144.

"The 'pataphysics of Auschwitz," *William Anastasi's Pataphysical Society: Jarry, Joyce, Duchamp and Cage*, eds. Aaron Levy and Jean-Michel Rabaté, Contemporary Artist Series No. 3 (Philadelphia: Slought Books, 2005): 24–31.

"Le Rossignol Instrumental: Inflexions contre-musicales dans la poésie de Gray à Celan," *Le Rossignol Instrumental: Poésie, Musique, Modernité*, trans. Piotr Burzykowski, eds. Jean-Pierre Bertrand, Michel Delville, and Christine Pagnoulle (Leuven & Paris: Peeters Vrin, 2004): 91–138.

"Interpretation and the Limit Text" was first presented in an earlier version at the "Transgressing Boundaries and Strategies of Renewal in American Poetry," conference at the Universidad de Salamanca, Spain, May 2000.

The Darkness of the Present

# Introduction

## Linearity, Anomaly, and Anachronism:
## Toward an Archaeology of the New

Many of the chapters in *The Darkness of the Present* started life on emergent occasions, the details of which can be consulted in the acknowledgements section. Some have appeared in earlier versions and these I have chosen to update; accordingly most are substantively revised and altered (mainly by amplification). As such, they might seem to present a farraginous façade and can certainly be read independently. They are linked, however, by a common preoccupation reflected in the title of the book. In many ways these chapters underscore the interlacement—even perplication—of an odyssey of two well-known, abused, and disabused concepts: the anomaly and the anachronism and the way their empirical emergence works to unsettle a steady notion of the "contemporary" or "new." I judge my attempts in this regard against the backdrop of one of Jerome McGann's arresting apothegms: "Out of scholarship comes the advancement of learning, out of criticism, its arrest" (*The Point is to Change It* xv). The turbulation of the past in order to arouse the imp of anachronism is a critical appropriation of the scholarly and results at times in juxtapositions that might seem mobilized along Reverdy's theory of the image: a chance convergence of vastly distant periods and proclivities. Hopefully, however, the studies in this book contribute to a genuine poeticology of the anomaly and the anachronism, and in so doing engage the past and the present as both metaleptic and chiasmic, by which the contemporary is historicized at the same time as the historical finds itself contemporized.

Collectively the book challenges the validity of historic models of supercession and offers a variety of investigations into undeclared and even uncanny affiliations. It also strives to present historical articulations that disconcert the urge to literary periodization and disciplinary partition. In many ways the book was written in awareness of Derrida's caveat against periodization: "The *post-s* and *posters* which proliferate today (poststructuralism, postmodernism, etc.) still surrender to the historicist urge. Everything marks an era, even the decentering of the subject: post humanism. It is as if one again wished to put a linear succession in order, to periodize, to distinguish before and after, to limit the risks of reversibility or repetition, transformation or permutation: an ideology of progress" (*Point de Folie* 137). Derrida's statement is in broad concurrence with Bergson's own emphatic rejection of the linear nature of time and its supporting logic of succession—for Bergson the present and the past are coexistent. Where McGann envisions a historical model that proposes a past that has not yet happened, I activate a model along Bergsonian and Derridean lines in which a past leaps into the now (*Black Riders* 156). In its investment in bringing to light unexplored connections, the book also situates the radical geophilosophy that Deleuze and Guattari outline in *A Thousand Plateaus*. Friedrich Schlegel famously declared that "[a]ll self-sufficiency is radical, is original. . . . Without originality, there is no energy of reason and no beauty of disposition" (256). *The Darkness of the Present* questions this intimate connection of originality and autonomy by calling up the necessary insistence of the unacknowledged precedent and the already belated "new." The new is always a milieu of multiplicities where echo sometimes meets a magnet that pulls heterogenesis to the past or propels the past forward. In the process this book repositions certain texts in genealogies different from those they are traditionally and customarily assigned to. As well as broadening ancestral series, this book aims to invoke historical rumblings whose sediments collectively work to muddy the clarity of the notion of "contemporary" in a chronological manner recently articulated by Giorgio Agamben, for what is the contemporary if not "*that relationship with time that adheres to it through a disjunction and an anachronism*"? (Agamben *Nudities* 11). This sentiment is not that dissimilar to Charles Olson's bold claim that "the work, the real work of the future has already been done" (*Charles Olson at Goddard College*) or Lyotard's tenet that "every occurrence is a recurrence, not at all in the sense that it could repeat the same thing or be the rehearsal or the same play, but in the sense of the Freudian *Nachträglich,* the way the first offense touches our mind too soon and the second too late, so that the first time is like a thought not yet thought while the second is like a not-thought to be thought later" (*Peregrinations* 8–9). Whereas Shakespeare famously has Brutus hear a clock strike, the anachronisms I present frequently remark the return of the repressed, the forgotten, and the unacknowledged, of what Agamben calls the darkness of the present, a phrase I have adopted in my title; it marks the volatility of origin famously noted by both Heidegger and Foucault. Phrased differently, the judgment of a text as being in-

novative is ineluctably confronted by the fact of the anachronic. Indeed, to eluci-
date an anachronism is to reimagine a historic momentum that is quantum in its
trajectory; as a result this book seeks to offer fresh perspectives on the contemporary as a condition that is partly reiterative and refractive.[1] No anxieties of influence are argued, nor any revisionary ratios proposed, but rather the focus is the
surprising appearance of predecessors, of a text before a text sufficient to complicate the notions of contemporary and innovation. At its most rhetorical, this
book contributes to what might be called an "Archeology of the New," insisting
on an absolute, chiasmic dynamic to both categories "present" and "past."[2] Figured more playfully, it can be regarded as assembled positions arrived at by treat-
ing time not as unidirectional but as palindromic. (This rescues time from theology, physics, and metaphysics alike to locate it in the literary and the tropic.)[3]
I hope further that this book rises to McGann's challenge "to change it: the Archive, our thinking about the Archive" (ibid. xix).

The term *anomaly* was born from a split etymology: the first was a correct
derivation but the second came from a misprision. The Greek *anomalia* refers
to the rough, uneven, irregular, to *an-omalos*, that which lacks smoothness. The
alternative, inaccurate derivation traces the word *anomaly* to *a-nomos*: without
law, or outside the law. I employ both these senses in the book as well as its more
customary, current sense (itself taken from anatomy) that indicates something
unusual and uncustomary, a deviation from the typical, that is to say from the
majority of texts within a certain class. While avoiding Geoffroy Saint-Hilaire's
degrees of anomaly (in ascending degrees of severity: varieties, structural de-
fects, heterotaxy and monstrosities) the book presents instances of exceptionalities.[4]

Chapter 1 examines the emergence of the Dada sound-poem in 1916 as a generic anomaly, a veritable poetry without words that jettisons one of the hitherto
indispensable elements of poetic composition: meaning. Drawing heavily (and
of necessity) upon the diaries of Hugo Ball (the sound-poem's self-proclaimed
inventor), the chapter examines *lautgedicht's* two telic intensities (the mantic and
the individual) and suggests that it seems correct to interpret the *lautgedicht* as
an extreme form of lyric expressionism. Considered as such, the sound-poem offers proleptically one answer to Alain Badiou's question to the French intellectual Jean Borreil, "How can we adapt speech to a series of disasters?" (*Pantheon*
149). Detailed examination of the sound-poem's ephemeral history, however, reveals that it invests not in the sonic and non-semantic *per se* but rather offers a
radical theory of the poetic image as a collective mnemonic provocation—what
Ball himself names the "grammalogue." In this respect the *lautgedicht* can be

fruitfully compared to Pound's theories of the *Imagiste* and Vorticist images that date from the same decade. Ball's innovation is further undermined when measured against Mallarmé's own project of the "essential" word, whose bias toward connotation gains it intimate comparison with Ball's grammalogue. Additionally, the chapter puts forth some of the psychophysiological theories of Ball's age (Cesare Lombroso's, Worringer's, and Wundt's), which demonstrate that Ball's psycho-anthropological interests and Dada's general fascination with irrationality and insanity should be seen as less anomalous than commonly thought and simply typical of the period.

As well as questioning the general validity of periodization in its first part (specifically modern and postmodern), chapter 2 specifically questions the normative positioning of Ronald Johnson's *Radi os* as an exemplary postmodern text of deletion, the realization of a "corrosive" poetics. *Radi os* is a treated text, a poem exhumed from a different poem: Milton's *Paradise Lost* whose twin inspirations Johnson claims were the structured inaudibility in Lukas Foss's *Baroque Variations* I, and William Blake's "infernal" method of relief etching. This chapter argues for a diachronic connection that traces *Radi os* well beyond Blake's compositional method to the poetics advanced in Geoffrey of Vinsauf's *Poetria Nova*, an early-thirteenth century treatise that inflects a chronologically distant notion of the modern. This second chapter also introduces a discussion of transumption and metalepsis that can be taken as synecdochal of the book's entire thematic orientation: an attempt to render problematic the precise notion of the contemporary by adopting a metaleptic approach to linear, sequential history. In discussing Johnson's deletional method of composition, I introduce a theme of "negative creation" that is developed in the succeeding two chapters from variant interpretational perspectives.

Chapters 3 and 4 offer two conjoined considerations of the systematic chance-generated compositions of Jackson Mac Low and John Cage. Chapter 3 addresses the hermeneutic problems facing any reader of Mac Low's *Words nd Ends from Ez*, a text systematically excavated from Ezra Pound's *Cantos* for the express purpose of exhuming the authorial name embedded in Pound's epic. Mac Low's method might be likened to the willful production of fragmentation, the revelation or return of letters to their material base as the building blocks of language, stripped for the most part of content. Accordingly, the trenchant unreadability of Mac Low's poem makes it a poetic text easier to talk about than actually read (a facility pertinent as well to the conceptual, uncreative writing of Kenneth Goldsmith considered in chapter 6). Following the lead of Umberto Eco, I approach Mac Low's poem by way of information theory and utilize the latter as an interpretive strategy within aesthetics to uncover a new angle of approach to the poem as an organized system governed by fixed laws of probability in which "redundancy" is virtually zero and whose criterial rules are not those of grammar, reference, and signification, but rather pertain to mathematics and statistical recurrence.

Chapter 4 considers the mesostic (medial-acrostic) writings of John Cage as posing a similar interpretational anomaly: how does a reader negotiate a treated source text whose procedural method yields incoherent phrases with minimum semantic reward (a question that recurs in chapter 9 where I consider some of the minimal poems of Clark Coolidge)? In Cage's writing, the anomalous is understood not merely as a species of limit-text (that kind of limit that is frequently attributed to Ball's poetry without words, Stein's *Tender Buttons,* Joyce's *Finnegans Wake,* and Mac Low's *Words nd Ends from Ez*) but as inherent in Cage's staging of a curious relationship to coherence. The mesostics (like Johnson's *Radi Os* and Mac Low's radical reorganization of Pound's *Cantos*) are in part a product of textual erasure, yet unlike *Radi Os* (which is the result of its author's conscious textual sifting) Cage's mesostics are systematically chance-generated. The result is a largely incoherent text developed through a highly coherent method. Where most critics of Cage's "writings through" *Finnegans Wake* have dwelt on the order of secondary meanings in Cage's systematic chance method, I choose to conceptualize the paradox of a coherence within incoherence via the concept of transcoherence, seeing this as an order imposed upon, yet never totally controlling, textual cognitive dissonance.

Chapter 5 (and its two brief codas) address anomalous interpolations of bibliographical content into textual codes and considers the materiality of composition and the significance of the single copy. Laurence Sterne's *Life and Opinions of Tristram Shandy, Gentleman* (the subject of this chapter) is arguably the most formally egregious anglophone text of the eighteenth century; its formal outrages render it both anomalous to its age and prescient of the innovative novels of the twentieth and twenty-first centuries. Rather than view Sterne's novel as exemplary, post-modernist fiction *avant la lettre,* I choose to scrutinize a particular anomalous aspect of its material format: the marbled leaf manually inserted at pages 169–170 in volume 1 of the first and subsequent early editions. After a brief discussion of the history of marbled paper, I trace a recessional dynamic from Sterne's marbled page and the painted marble of Tristram's own "unimmaculate" conception back to the Quattrocento Annunciation paintings of Fra Angelico, where painted marble functions as a trope of disfiguration. As well as developing this diachronic trajectory, the chapter can also be read as a defense of singularity and the exceptional in resistance to the erosive force of concepts that support generalities (a topic discussed in more detail in chapter 10). The first coda compares the marbled page in two different (yet contemporary) editions and documents an anarchy of the singular at play, an odd phenomenon pertaining to one specific copy of one of the world's most anomalous books. By demonstrating how the faulty assembling of a book can generate a different yet plausible reading, this chapter registers as a historical (and singular) *lalangue,* an inassimilable excess in the remainder and an example of creative misunderstanding. The second coda discusses Mina Loy's "Brancusi's Golden Bird" as a poem that advances not only a theory of poetic minimalism and essence, but also a strategy of disfiguration and inversion that turns Didi Huberman's theory of Fra Angelico's paintings of the divine insemination on its head, replacing painted marble with polished brass and inverting the entire choreography of the incarnation.

Chapter 6 shifts the focus from anomalies of the material text to engage three different contemporary responses to information overload and thus explore the fate and possibilities of poetry in a hyperspatial age. In the Flarf Collective (a group of contemporary American poets brought together by online social networks) there is an evident updating of Modernist collage that exploits new digital modes of accessing material. The practice of "flarfing" or "Google sculpting" involves a renegade use of search engines to generate odd phrases akin to extreme collage and the disjunctive texts of Language writing. I offer Bill Kennedy's and Darren Wershler-Henry's *Apostrophe* as a more sophisticated intervention into digital technologies. By actually designing software to intercept formal grammatical patterns within search engines, *Apostrophe* proffers a piratical-bardic synthesis of human and machine. The bulk of the chapter discusses an inverted and more extreme form of negative poetics than those found in Ronald Johnson's, Cage's, and Mac Low's practices of textual deletion: Kenneth Goldsmith's anomalous practice of uncreative writing. In his 2003 project *Day,* a verbatim transcription of all words, numbers, and characters in a single issue of the *New York Times,* Goldsmith not only resuscitates the old scribal practice of the Middle Ages so highly praised by Johannes Trithemius, but also radically challenges the validity of any creative composition in the current ethos of information and creative overload. Conceptual writing of this kind both abnegates the creative production of texts and licenses the modality of boredom and the banality of transcription as it ushers in the epoch of the post-readerly text and the transformation of a readership into a "thinkership." The chapter also discloses precedents to many of Goldsmith's conceptual projects but remains mindful of the fact that Goldsmith has never claimed his work to be original (a confession that led Marjorie Perloff to the concept of "unoriginal genius"). I do not consider Goldsmith's conscious appropriations (the appropriative practice of Andy Warhol, for instance) but rather focus on less familiar resuscitations, unknown to Goldsmith, such as the unpublished diaries of Robert Shields and Tobias Smollett's fastidious noting of a year's weather in Naples. While Goldsmith's repudiations of aesthetic and creative criteria rehabilitate the Kantian model of reflective taste, resuscitate Nietzsche's transvaluation of all values, and indicate a paradigm shift from the poetics of Language writing, I argue for an atavistic summoning of archaic symbolic action from the data and digital archives that saturate our world.

Although references to architecture occur periodically throughout this book, chapters 7 and 8 are both largely devoted to the subject. Wittgenstein famously compared language to "an ancient city: a maze of little streets and squares, of old and new houses" (*Philosophical Investigations* 8e) and Sherwood Anderson wrote of a postmelancholic, neglected city of words rebuilt and recast by Gertrude Stein. The intimate bond between architecture and writing dates beyond such twentieth-century commentaries, back at least to Pindar's sixth Olympian ode; increasingly I've come to believe that poetry and architecture are the unacknowledged sister arts. A critical rethinking of this classical theme (that places poetry and painting together as mutual prostheses supplying the other's lack) seems urgent given the collapse of mimesis and image as contemporary poetic paradigms. Through considerations of space (cosmic, public, private, and historic) and of language (as critical attractor, manipulator, game, proxy, and obdurate materiality), contemporary poetics and architecture might convolve toward, if not hybridity, then certainly cross-pollination.

Chapter 7 is divided into three uneven sections. The first section of this chapter offers a "soft" manifesto on parapoetics as well as examples and possibilities for a hybrid practice. Proposing a new virtual discipline, a poetics emancipated from the historical burden of genre, discreetness, and predetermined areas of *poeisis,* this section envisions a state in which architects and poets initially explore under the aegis of an undetermined concept: parapoetics. Section II offers a critical analysis of the frame, teasing out its general pliancy and topological quirkiness that allows it to be compared to the nonlinear thermodynamic phenomena of dissipative structures; the section challenges both artists and thinkers to reverse the conventional function of frames and deframe interiorities in a way that forges a relationship to the external that opens up the internal to the outside. Section III concludes chapter 7 with a few speculative suggestions for areas of parapoetic investigation.

Wittgenstein also famously claimed that language is a labyrinth of paths: "You approach from *one* side and know your way about; you approach the same place from another side and no longer know your way about' (*Philosophical Investigations* 82e). Chapter 8 picks up this theme of labyrinthine disequilibrium to examine its architectural implementation by a Situationist architect, Constant, and in the post-ontological, procedural architecture by Arakawa and Madeline Gins. This chapter argues that a precedent to the latter's work can be found in the directionality and unitary urbanism of the Situationist–architect Constant's *New Babylon*. While *New Babylon* was conceived at roughly the same time as Olson's projective verse and open field composition (1950), Arakawa and Gins' *Reversible Destiny* project was developed alongside the emergence of Language writing and its theories of post-referentiality, antinarrative and semantic disjunction (since 1980). Arakawa and Gins offer the first truly post-ontological approach to action and habitat, their controversial mission being to realize human eternity and mandate a legal proscription of death. Although Arakawa and Gins unwittingly resuscitate as their general desideratum Parmenides' "truth" that things exist eternally, I hone my focus in on their proposals for purposeful disorientation and disequilibrium as a way back to human resensitization, especially in their plans for a multiple labyrinth. Following a brief history of the classic, Minoan, unicursal labyrinth, and the later maze, I align Arakawa and Gins' multiple labyrinth with Constant's precursory labyrinths. Both offer trenchant alternatives to the plethora of functional architectural projects that ideologically articulate affiliation with consumer and commodity capitalism. Towards the end of the chapter, I link Arakawa and Gins' mandate to cheat death and literally become immortal to the condition of biopolitics that Giorgio Agamben forcibly argues justifies both "base life" and the emergence of the concentration camp. (This topic is also revisited in the penultimate chapter). It is in the name of bare, naked life that biopolitics exercises its power and in which democratic materialism appears in its most essential manifestation.

Chapter 9 considers some of Clark Coolidge's early poetry found in his 1970 book *Space*. Rather than regard these poems as either influenced by American Abstract Expressionism or prescient of the disjunctive, hypotactic compositions of Language poetry, the chapter demonstrates their cogent, "anachronistic" apposition with the eighteenth-century aesthetic theory of the picturesque. Indeed, the chapter renders the latter as a "present investment" (to use Charles Bernstein's term) and in doing so moves to habilitate Nathaniel Mackey's critical efforts to break out of predetermined cultural categories through purposeful readings across the African American and Euro-American avant-gardes aimed at reaching a broader historical horizon. Where Mackey seeks creative kinships and affinities across ethnic and regional boundaries I offer a trans-historic reading across three centuries. The picturesque partook of its "new" through a radical rupture of the dominant aesthetic doublet of the beautiful and the sublime as well as through its theory of variety: the detail (as outlined by William Gilpin and Uvedale Price) opens up the horizon to envision a poetics of the rough and irregular. The chapter moves on to present this new poetics of the irregular that inflects the condition of infancy, and inflection that equally summarizes the vanguard trajectories of the twentieth and twenty-first centuries. To wish infancy and to desire to recover a state outside of adult parlance, a state before language, is less the exception than the norm in many texts. Indeed, the evidence I enumerate of numerous attempts to escape the regime of the signifier are sufficient to constitute a literary counter-tradition.

Chapter 10, though relatively short, offers the radical axis of the entire book (at one point, after initialing calling the book *Exceptionalities,* I considered this chapter's name, "The 'Pataphysics of Auschwitz: Poetics, Anachronism, and the Exception," as a title for this book.) This chapter explores Jarry's science of 'pataphysics, which was conceived amidst the hilarities of the Banquet Years as the science of imaginary solutions that governs the rules and laws of the exception rather than the norm. After a panoramic parade of unrecognized 'pataphysicians and a brief consideration of 'pataphysics as a potential weapon against metaphysics, the chapter picks up the tenor that concluded chapter 8 by examining the implications of 'pataphysics in the light of the Nazi–jurist Carl Schmitt's theory of sovereignty. A disturbing affinity is proposed between Jarry's science and the Nazi justification for the Final Solution, endorsed on January 20, 1942, at Wannsee. Converting an "imaginary" into a "final" solution, Nazi ideology in part is shown to be 'pataphysical in its preoccupation with the state of the exception. The chapter concludes interrogatively: how do we engage this conjunction in a way other than non-causally?

The final chapter puts forward a historical account of music and musicality in poetry from the mid-eighteenth century to the mid-twentieth century; this might be best considered as a modest contribution to critical historiography, provoked by my readings in the human-animal relationship and my reflections on Adorno's statement in his *Negative Dialectics* of the ethical burden bestowed on all artistic endeavor after Auschwitz. I note intimations of a paradigm shift, then an insurgent counter-aesthetics emerging in some key poetic texts of the mid-eighteenth century. An earlier preoccupation with the musical gives way to an interest in insect sounds and initiates what might be called an apophatic turn in the acoustic paradigm. An anomalous genealogy emerges that links the pre-romantic poetry of Thomas Gray and William Collins to the avant-garde accomplishments of the Dada sound-poem, the Italian Futurist *parole in libertà,* and, via a short concrete poem of Eugen Gomringer's, to the fate of all creative practice after Auschwitz.

While composing the volume, I have chosen where I deemed the situation appropriate to recirculate occasional passages from earlier publications into fresh and different contexts and mark a continuity in some of my thinking. What I present are pen-trials in thinking whose scholarly sediment is necessary but secondary to a more expansive and, let me say it, *poeitic* meditation on the grand conjunction of past, present, and future that Walt Whitman predicted in his original preface to *Leaves of Grass.*

I have many people to thank. I thank Anne Lecercle for first introducing me to the work of Georges Didi Huberman. I also thank Marjorie Perloff, John Higgins, Michel Delville, Sascha Bru, Jean-Jacques Lecercle, Craig Dworkin, María Eugenia Díaz, John-Michel Rabaté, Louis Armand, and Aaron Levy who facilitated the publication of early drafts of some of these chapters. I thank my colleagues James J. Bono, Tim Dean, and Ewa P. Ziarek for their kind invitation to participate in the University at Buffalo Humanities Institute's inaugural conference, from which the present chapter 10 is distilled; I thank Carrie Tirado Bramen as well for her seminal discussions on the urban picturesque. My deep thanks also to the two anonymous readers of the manuscript whose incisive comments allowed me to improve vastly on the first submitted version. I also must thank the series editors Hank Lazer and Charles Bernstein for their peer friendships, warm support, and positive reception of this manuscript, as well as Dan Waterman and Kevin Fitzgerald at The University of Alabama Press for their relentless efficiency in matters of style. My gratitude extends as well to Sophia Canavos and James Maynard for helping me with the illustrations in three of the book's chapters and to Piotr Burzykowski for his French version of chapter 11, the language in which this chapter first appeared.

Finally, my ongoing gratitude to Karen Mac Cormack for her prompts, challenges, and perceptive suggestions as well as her unwavering support of all my endeavors, illuminating my own moments of darkness and to whom I dedicate this book.

# Cacophony, Abstraction, and Potentiality
## The Fate of the Dada Sound Poem

First let me offer a necessary prolegomenon. This chapter relies heavily upon quotations from Ball's diary—which was published posthumously (in abridged form) as *Flight Out of Time*—for precisely the same reason as Ball's fellow Dadaist Hans Richter relied upon it. As Richter elucidates:

> I shall often quote from Ball's diaries, because I know of no better source of evidence on the moral and philosophical origins of the Dada revolt which started at the Cabaret Voltaire. It is entirely possible that any or all of the other Dadaists . . . went through the same inner development, but no one but Ball left a record of these inner conflicts. And no one achieved, even in fragmentary form, such precise formulations as Ball, the poet and thinker. (14–15)

Notwithstanding Richter's trust, *Flight Out of Time* presents an interpretative challenge in being both compiled retroactively and published posthumously. Taking his personal diary entries between 1910–21, Ball started revising them in 1924 (after the emotions and incidents described had settled into a reflective distance) and *Die Flucht aus der Zeit* (*Flight Out of Time*) was finally published in 1927. A second edition appeared in 1946 with a forward by Ball's wife Emmy Ball-Hennings. It is important to emphasize the fact that *Die Flucht aus der Zeit* was assembled from the controlling, executive viewpoint of Ball's new conversion to Catholicism (Michel 1). For the earlier Ball, during his Zurich days (the focus of this chapter), God was not dead but reified in the profiteering plunder of German capitalism and supported ideologically by a state apparatus that included religion. Ball had already launched a scathing attack on the conflation of Christianity and capitalism in his pre-Dada poem *"Der Henker"* (The Hangman) where Christ is born as "the god of Gold" and lives as "the god of lustful greed" *(der Christenheit Götzplunder)* (quoted in Steinke 79).

## I. Prelude

> *No sound is dissonant that tells of Life.*
> —Coleridge

The sound poem is the last of three rapid developments within the performative poetics of Zurich Dada that appeared between late March and June 1916. Marcel Janco, Richard Huelsenbeck, and Tristan Tzara introduced the simultaneous poem (a genre invented by Henri Barzun and Fernand Divoire) at the same time as Huelsenbeck inaugurated his quasi-ethnographic "negro songs."[1] Both types were launched at Hugo Ball's newly established Cabaret Voltaire on March 30, 1916 along with Ball's own contribution (some poems without words) on June 23, 1916. In the simultaneities, such as Tzara's inaugural "The Admiral is Looking for a House to Rent," sound, text, discrepant noises, whistles, cries, and drums interweave in a sonic version of collage. Interlocution collapses into a texture of promiscuous parlance and polylogue at the same time as linguistic fragments, in French, German, and English, intersect and combine into efficacious new amalgams. (It's surely no coincidence that the three languages utilized are respectively those of the three combatants in the Great War and most fitting to a performance in quadrilingual Switzerland.) Although, as a collective manifestation, the simultaneity attains the status of a *gesamtkunstwerk* only by way of a parodic valence, it nonetheless brings about that desired confluence and border blur of song, noise, music, and dance that Dick Higgins christened "intermedia" in the 1960s.[2] Ball has left a succinct definition of the simultaneous poem: "a contrapuntal recitative in which three or more voices speak, sing, whistle, etc., at the same time in such a way that the elegiac, humorous, or bizarre content of the piece is brought out by these combinations" (Ball 57). Ball is also sensitive to the more somber, existential implications of this cacophonous, combinatorial genre. To his mind it represents "the background—the inarticulate, the disastrous, the decisive [expressing] the conflict in the *vox humana* with a world that threatens, ensnares, and destroys" (ibid.)[3]

Huelsenbeck conceived his *chants nègre* as whimsical abstractions designed to evoke the rhythms and "semantics" of African songs. As stereotypical and racist as Vachel Lindsay's 1914 poem "The Congo" (Huelsenbeck's versions mix phrases of calculated nonsense, each refrain ending with the phrase "umba umba"), they gained limited authenticity when Huelsenbeck substituted an authentic African song for happy senselessness (retaining, however, his beloved end-refrain). The *chant nègre* took on a genuinely ethnopoetic dimension when Tzara incorporated fragments of authentic African songs culled from anthropology magazines that he read in Zurich.[4]

From its very inception the twentieth-century sound poem has been shrouded in contradiction and uncertainty. There are at least two antecedents to Ball's "invention:" Christian Morgenstern's "Das Grosse Lalulà" (1905) and an untitled piece by Paul Scheerbart (1900). Indeed, a German or Swiss audience would have been familiar with the basic form of Ball's "poetry without words." Scheerbart's begins:

> Kikakoku!
> Ekoralaps!
> Wiao kollipanda opolasa

Morgenstern published his poem in his immensely popular *Galgenlieder (Gallows Songs)* and called it a "phonetic rhapsody." It opens:

> Kroklokwafzi? Sememmemi!
> Seiokronto-prafriplo;
> Bifzi, bafzi; hulalemi:
> Quasti basti bo . . .
> Lalu lalu lalu lalu la![5]

The sound poem's "historical" origin and definition, however, are generally attributed to the German poet *émigré* Hugo Ball, who first performed his own samples on June 23, 1916. He recorded his definition of the new genre on the same date in his diary: "I have invented a new genre of poems, 'Verse ohne Worte' [poems without words] or Lautgedichte [sound poems], in which the balance of the vowels is weighed and distributed solely according to the values of the beginning sequence" (70). It is tempting to theorize the *lautgedicht* as Ball's voluntary abnegation of meaning, a splendid and festive nihilism designed to discover a self outside the limitations of reason and semantics. Yet neither the logic of the phoneme (Ball's chosen unit of composition) nor the poet's own recorded reflections support such a judgment. As I hope to demonstrate, Ball's sound poem is thoroughly grounded in historical sense and awareness. It was not, however, formulated as a response to Symbolism, nor to Dada's ambient competing avant-gardes of Cubism and Futurism, but rather as a response to, and a refusal of, the contemporary state of discourse under early twentieth-century capitalism. In addition, it emerged in a time of much non-poetic speculation about the powers of vocal sound.

The life and death of the sound poem can be constructed around a sequence of incidents and reflections that occurred over a brief period of time. To understand Ball's invention beyond a merely formal synopsis requires an investigation of his motives, activities, and state of mind both on and prior to June 23, 1916. His departure from semantic verse was certainly influenced by his own involvement in the emerging German expressionist theater and by his pre-Zurich studies of Chinese theater. Demoralized and traumatized by the horrors of actual combat, Ball came to realize the catalytic possibilities to effect revolutionary change through theater by way of expressionistic exaggeration.[6] Directed to the subconscious, this new theater develops a code of the festive, with archetypes and loudspeakers used to by-pass realism (Ball 9). Less atavistic than transcultural in its propensities, the new theater draws heavily on Chinese and Japanese sources. Ball believed that especially Chinese theater preserved a mantic character—a trait he carried over into his own sound poetry.[7] A diary entry for April 2, 1915 is of especial interest precisely because of its implicit comparison of actual war to the theatrical representation of battle:

> When a general receives orders for a campaign into distant provinces, he marches three or four times around the stage, accompanied by a terrible noise of gongs, drums, and trumpets and then stops to let the audience know he has arrived.... the holy man sings and grabs the leader of the Tartars by the throat and strangles him with dramatic crescendos. The words of the song do not matter; the laws of rhythm are more important. (Ball 16)

Here Ball is obviously intrigued by the inflexion of singing into the representation of violent physical conflict and the concomitant downplay of semantic value within the song to the paramount importance of rhythmic law; this is a patent blueprint for the *lautgedicht*.[8]

There is clearly a forcefully political dimension to Ball's sound poem. To understand some of its ramifications we need to bear in mind the climate of Europe and Zurich in particular. At that time Zurich was a city in a neutral nation surrounded by the carnage of a mad war of attrition. We must also look at an important event that took place in Zurich. In March 1915 Walter Serner—Ball's friend and future Dadaist—joined the staff of *Der Mistral,* a self-styled "literary newspaper" whose editors, Hugo Kersten and Emil Szittya, launched a prescient attack. This attack was aimed not at the current military conflict *per se,* but rather at the linguistic structures of the bourgeois institutions—religion, law, and politics, the current linguistico-cultural industry—collectively responsible for a "grammar of war." To supplement this editorial policy (so anticipatory of Foucault's work on discourse and the critique by Language poetry of language, narrative, and referentiality in the 1970s) poems were included and chosen on the basis of their deliberate undermining of grammatical and syntactic norms— hence the appearance of Apollinaire's *calligrammes* and Marinetti's *parole in libertà* (Witkovsky 421). Ball was unquestionably sympathetic to this agenda. In fact, when he arrived in Zurich from Berlin in May of 1915 he had hopes of collaborating with Serner on *Der Mistral,* though those aspirations failed to reach fruition. Similar to the work featured in *Der Mistral,* Ball considered his own sound poem as a frontal attack on the contemporary condition of instrumental language. Ball had previously been involved in radical publishing ventures. Prior to his flight to Zurich he had published in Franz Pfemfert's left-wing periodical *Die Aktion* and in October 1913 had himself founded with his companion Hans Leybold the short-lived *Revolution.* Ball quotes the French historian Florian Parmentier who linked the crisis in independent creative existence to a collusion between democracy and journalism, a collusion whose origin Ball traces back to Rousseau.[9] Indeed, the origin of Ball's existential unrest dates to well before the war. As early as 1913 he reflects on a life "completely confined and shackled" by an unremittingly compartmentalized world in which serialized existence binds human beings to a monstrously predictable and repetitive functionality. The antidote he offers is resolutely non-futuristic and a surprising anticipation of Georges Bataille's theories of heterology and general economy: "What is necessary is a league of all men who want to escape from the mechanical world, a way of life opposed to mere utility. Orgiastic devotion to the opposite of everything that is serviceable and useful" (3–4). I find it significant that at this time Ball directs his ire and invective at the dehumanizing rhythms of the machine: it is this target that marks Ball's radical dissent from Futurist valorizations. Whereas in a few years Ball will inveigh against the language of journalism, in 1913 he offers a savage analysis of the material implications of the printing press itself:

The machine gives a kind of sham life to dead matter. It moves matter. It is a specter. It joins matter together, and in so doing reveals some kind of rationalism. Thus it is death, working systematically, counterfeiting life. It tells more flagrant lies than any newspaper that it prints. And what is more, in its continuous subconscious influence it destroys human rhythm. . . . A walk through a prison cannot be so horrifying as a walk through the noisy workroom of a modern printing shop. (4)[10]

(It's sobering to compare Ball's account of the state of the work of art in an age of mechanical reproduction with Benjamin's more famous document.) Before the horror of war and its incomprehensibility, Ball reacts to the horrors of the machinic imaginary, and this reaction is carried over into wartime. Indeed Ball emerges as the paramount Dada Luddite, writing in late 1914 after returning from a visit to the Belgian front, "It is the total mass of machinery and the devil himself that has broken loose now" (10–11). Later in a June 26, 1915 entry he claims an ontological and tactical confusion lies at the root of the war: "The war is based on a crass error. Men have been mistaken for machines. Machines, not men, should be decimated" (22).

## II. June 1916 and After

Ball's diary entry for June 24, 1916 (previously incorporated into the program notes for the June 23 performance) proclaims, in manifesto-like fashion, the theory of his sound poem: "In these phonetic [sic] poems we totally renounce the language that journalism has abused and corrupted. We must return to the innermost alchemy of the word, we must even give up the word too, to keep for poetry its last and holiest refuge. We must give up writing second-hand: that is, accepting words (to say nothing of sentences) that are not newly invented for our own use" (71).[11] This passage is remarkable for its synthesis of clarity and obfuscation. It carries a lucid call to praxis, yet at the same time petitions a vague mystery and prophylaxis. To neologize in order to innovate? Most certainly. Lyric neologism arises from a disgust with human words as historically sedimented, culturally debased phenomena; while entering history neologisms do not convey history as their burden.[12] The move is not without precedent, for Ball follows in the footsteps of the Russian Futurist poets Khlebnikov and Kruchenykh whose practice of *zaum* (transrational language, to which Ball had been introduced by Kandinsky) produced texts and phrases of deliberate incomprehension.[13] (It was the zaumniks' insight to realize that which is inexpressible in words is expressible through sound, thereby undermining Wittgenstein's claim in the *Tractatus* that "What we cannot speak about, we must pass over in silence" (6.54). *Zaum* also anticipates Joyce's portmanteaux poetics employed throughout *Finnegans Wake* and lauded by Eugene Jolas in 1948 as the new language of the future.)[14] As well as marking a stark reversal of his earlier beliefs in the dangers of neologism (Ball had recorded on 25 November 1915 that "Each word is a wish or a curse. One must be careful not to make words once one has acknowledged the power of the living word") it advances a poetics of bold individualism one consequence of which is an indirect critique of German ideology (49). For in reverting to the phoneme and to the force of haptic, pathic affect, Ball removes the very possibility for such propositional constructions and narratives on which any national language must be constructed. If Tzara's simultaneous poetry dismembers and collages national languages, Ball's *lautgedicht* effectively destroys them.[15]

So far so good, but major questions now arise: What is "the innermost alchemy of the word"? And where is, let alone what is, poetry's "last and holiest refuge"? Ball's critical vector slides at this point from social disgust into a rhetorical enigma, a vague spiritual poetics, and a veritable poetical theology. Indeed, the *lautgedicht* surpasses any socio-linguistic critique of the contemporary, ambient conditions in the warring, secular world and encapsulates the very spiritualization of politics, sounding the redemption of the word via the power of abstract phonematicity.[16] Ball offers an alchemical poetics of alembication by which the word, in being pulverized, is preserved as a higher distillate through refinement from its semantic dross. He summarizes his achievements five days prior to the first performance of the *lautgedicht*: "We have loaded the word with strengths and energies that helped us to rediscover the evangelical concept of the 'word' (logos) as a magical complex image" (68). Clearly by June 18 Ball had worked out not only a new genre of acoustic poetry but also a new theory of the image, one carried not by words but by phonemic rhythm, an image Ball himself calls a "grammalogue." (It is difficult not to think of Pound's own contemporary modification of the poetic image in which the image is uncoupled from a pictorial paradigm and redefined as an emotional and intellectual complex in an instant of time alongside Ball's comparable conversion of the image into a sonic shorthand for a mnemonically charged acoustic force.)

Jeffrey Schnapp speculates (somewhat unsuccessfully in my judgment) on the precise nature of the *lautgedicht's* alchemical potential, seeing in it a "generative mode of expression that, tapping the innermost alchemical powers of the word, renders unfamiliar worlds familiar by means of semantic [*sic*] units that are simultaneously words, pictures, and incantations" (4). A less esoteric explanation lends itself via the logic of phonemic articulation itself. The abstract, vocable string registers a confluence of negation and potentiality, transforming denotation into an unpredictable, indeterminate vertigo of connotational possibilities. Ball himself seems aware of this:

We tried to give the isolated vocables the fullness of an oath, the glow of a star. And curiously enough, the magically inspired vocables conceived and gave birth to a *new* sentence that was not limited and confined by any conventional meaning. Touching lightly on a hundred ideas at the same time without naming them, this sentence made it possible to hear the innately playful, but hidden, irrational character of the listener, it weakened and strengthened the lowest strata of memory. (68)

Here, as elsewhere, Ball shows himself susceptible to the same intoxication by analogy that patinated Marinetti's futurist poetics, yet the gist of his assertion is clear: the sound poem is *not* a departure from semantics as such but rather from the doxa of conventional meaning. Indeed, the mantic power within the *lautgedicht* creates a semantic condition in which meaning is *potentialized* and in that way becomes *unconventional.* This is not a commitment to Cratylism (that ancient belief that a word possesses a natural relation to the thing it designates) but it certainly represents a significant move towards a radical conative poetics grounded in irrational, infantile, and primary forces. Ball strives for that magical center Auden speaks of in his "Homage to Clio"; but where Auden's great poem testifies to the failure of visual paradigms, Ball's *lautgedicht* registers as an assertion of sound's capacity to transcend the visual and situate the phenomenal and imaginary in a mantic space of indeterminate intellectual and mnemonic eruptions. By introducing difference into continuity, the phoneme inflects the sonic with the haunting potential of meaning. The quotidian issue raised by any phonetic, non-semantic poetry is precisely this: what happens to meaning? And the answer is quite clear: phonetic poetry has a repositional rather than negative effect upon meaning; it situates the semantic order elsewhere, where meaning lurks in its own potentiality. Indeed, one of the central questions arising in both the *chant nègre* and the phonetic *lautgedicht* is how to discern an abstract, senseless sound poem from authentic xenoglossia when both are interchangeable and equally efficient in creating the desired "cabaret" effect.[17]

The sound poem's innovative status is further complicated by the fact that Ball's distillation of the word continues Mallarmé's 1886 proposal in *The Crisis of Poetry* that separates two distinct verbal orders: the one of immediate and unrefined words and the other of the "essential" word. The *lautgedicht* enjoys the identical connotative power of the word that Mallarmé aimed for: the ideal suggestion of an object. One is thus left questioning whether Ball actually broke away from the tenets of symbolist poetics or actually enriched them by adding an abstract method onto a poetics already geared to suggestion. The constitutional paradox at the heart of the *lautgedicht* is readily apparent: by eliminating precise denotation, the connotational potential of the phoneme and phonemic string—as well as its susceptibility to stirring the irrational and mnemonic strata in the addressee—is maximized.[18] Like Scheerbart's and Morgenstern's texts, Ball's poems read and sound like extreme attempts at creating the effect of "another" language rather than the abstract acoustic constructions so evident in Raoul Hausmann's untitled "kp'erioUM lp'er" and the *letterklankbeelden* poems by Theo van Doesburg.[19] They carry a strong propensity to ignite mental associations and sensory stimulations. Moreover, in some of his six *lautgedichten*, the title frames the poem within a mimetic project; "Elefanten Karawane" (Elephants Caravan) is a clear example of this. Ball himself acknowledges the onomatopoeic intention in the poem to evoke "the plodding rhythm of the elephants" (Ball 71).

ELEFANTEN KARAWANE
jolifanto bambla ô falli bambla
grossiga m'pfa habla horem
égiga goramen
higo bloiko russula huju
hollaka hollala
anlago bung
blago bung
blago bung
bosso fataka
ü üü ü
schampa wulla wussa ólobo
hej tatta gôrem
eschige zunbada
wulubu ssubudu uluw ssubudu
tumba ba- umf
kusagauma
ba—umf[20]

The appeal to instigated depths of primordial memory adds a genuine complexity to the sound poem; this is the significant aspect of Ball's poetics.

Significant but not egregious, for the psycho-anthropological thinking Ball inherits marks his grammology more typical of the times than exceptional. His theory of regression and deep memory finds support in the work of Cesare

Lombroso (1835–1909) whose own theories on the relation of creativity to dementia shifted consideration of mental illness from that of a disease of the brain to that of a disorder of the mind. In his 1864 *Genius and Madness* (a book that Ball did not read until August 1916 and hence could not have been a direct influence on his poetics), Lombroso records his examination of the creative output of 107 patients and concludes that creativity in dementia produces work bearing a striking resemblance to artworks from earlier evolutionary times—what Lombroso refers to as "primitive cultures."[21] (Lombroso's atavistic theory is in broad concurrence with Wilhelm Worringer's 1908 study *Abstraction and Empathy*, a book that influenced Kandinsky's thinking on the parallelism of modern and tribal; this train of thought remains a basic tenet of contemporary ethnopoetics.[22]) Lombroso's and Worringer's dual influence helps explain the common fascination among several Dadaists with the creative possibilities of irrationality and insanity; it also sheds light on the masks and songs of tribal cultures that informed the *chants nègre* and pervaded Dada.[23]

In retrospect, Ball feels a close affinity to this nascent ethnopoetics of the irrational as the following passage makes clear:

> The new theories we have been advancing [the *lautgedicht* or Dada at large?] have serious consequences for this field. The childlike quality I mean borders on the infantile, on dementia, on paranoia. It comes from the belief in a primeval memory, in a world that has been supplanted and buried beyond recognition, a world that is liberated in art by unrestrained enthusiasm, but in the lunatic asylum is freed by a disease." (Ball 75)

There are, however, more direct Germanic precedents. As early as 1836, Wilhelm von Humboldt had insisted on the penetrating powers of phonetic sound upon the nervous system, as well as emphasizing the important role of the subconscious processes in linking sound to meaning.[24] For his part psychophysiologist Wilhelm Wundt (1832–1900) had theorized as early as 1900 the existence of both *Lautbilden* (sound pictures whose acoustic impact precipitated involuntary visual effects in the listener's mind) and *Sprachlaute* (expressive sounds involving facial, internal, mimetic, and pantomimic movements).[25]

## The Swoon and the Aftermath

Ball left a vivid record of his famous first (and last) presentation of the *lautgedicht* in which he recalls his mental and emotional transmogrification during the per-

formance. After describing his dramatic entrance onto the cabaret stage in darkness, dressed quasi-ecclesiastically in a cardboard Cubist costume, with claw
hands and a blue and white striped "witch doctor's hat," immobile (because of
the costume) and therefore carried, he recalls:

> I do not know what gave me the idea of this music, but I began to chant
> my vowel sequences in a church style like a recitative and tried not only to
> look serious but to force myself to be serious. For a moment it seemed as if
> there was the pale, bewildered face in my cubist mask, that half-frightened,
> half-curious face of a ten-year-old boy, trembling and hanging avidly on
> the priest's words in the requiems and high masses in his own parish. The
> lights went out, as I had ordered, and bathed in sweat, I was carried off the
> stage like a magical bishop. (70)

I find it hard not to be skeptical of this image of the forty-year-old Ball's regres-
sive epiphany on that Zurich night in June. The dubious may rightly place Ball's
magical bishop scenario on a par with Coleridge's strategic fiction of the Person
from Porlock.[26] Notwithstanding the factual uncertainty of his psychosomati-
cally induced state, the condition described accurately corresponds with Ball's
general theories of primordial memory and the complex imbrications of the
child and the irrational. Renouncing one type of institutional codification, Ball
returns involuntarily to another: the Catholic Church. Ball predicts that in the
conditions experienced in the world around him, art "will be irrational, primitive, and complex; it will speak a secret language and leave behind documents
not of edification but of paradox" (49). This adds an achromatic dimension to
the *lautgedicht;* Ball's grammology reveals itself to be also a cryptology. There
is yet another dimension that further convolves the actual intentions of Ball's
sound poetry; it is implicit in his final pre-Zurich diary entry: "If language really
makes us kings of our nation, then without doubt it is we, the poets and thinkers, who are to blame for this blood bath and who have to atone for it"(36).[27] The
*lautgedicht* does not offer to humanity a soteriological solution but rather gestures towards an alliance of penitence and creativity. Ball's poetic mission is
atonement, the assumption (not the renunciation) of the burden of guilt for a
senseless war, and the *lautgedicht* is Ball's penitential method.

I conclude with a brief consideration of a couple of passages from Ball's now
famous "First Dada Manifesto" of July 14, 1916, which simultaneously introduced and closed the brief history of the *lautgedicht* and mark, I believe, Ball's
final break with Dada: "How does one achieve eternal bliss? By saying dada. . . .

With a noble gesture and delicate propriety. Till one goes crazy. Till one loses consciousness. . . . Dada m'dada. Dada mhm'dada da" (220–21). Of all Zurich Dadaists, Ball alone elevates the playful name of Dada to the level of a mind altering mantra. Jonathan Hammer insists that Ball constructs the repeated phoneme as a password in order to gain "access to the ineffable meditation" (quoted in Schnapp 13). If that is the case, then Ball's Dada was not a movement but a shibboleth appropriated as the tetragrammaton of a new century. Ball writes, "I will serve to show how articulated language comes into being. I let the vowels fool around. I let the vowels quite simply occur, as a cat meows. . . . Words emerge, shoulders of words, legs, arms, hands of words. Au, oi, uh" (Ball 221). I find it hard not to read into this curious dramaturgic equation of words to body parts (surely one of the strangest equations of body to language ever conceived) a reference to the creation of the Golem, that being infused with the illusion of existence, a simulacrum of rabbinical creation out of the four elements and destined to serve man in a better way than language. Ball's *lautgedicht* with its grammological power finally turns out to be a language homunculus.

I believe this passage marks the end of Ball's belief in the *lautgedicht*. In 1917, he will continue his fascination with magic; he will also meditate on the relationship of the mantic to ascetic individualism. Magic will become for him "the last refuge of individual self-assertion, and maybe individualism in general" and "the final result of individualism will be magic" (Ball 96, 99).[28] This is a far cry from the collective jubilation that signifies the spontaneous community of the simultaneous poem. It is perhaps Victor Markov in "The Principles of the New Art" (1912) who is most prophetic when it comes to the inner alchemy of Ball's creative-mystical state: "Where concrete reality, the tangible, ends, there begins another world—a world of unfathomed mystery, a world of the Divine. Even primitive man was given the chance of approaching this boundary, where intuitively he would capture some feature of the Divine—and return happy as a child" (quoted in Janacek 42). Perhaps no other Dadaist wrote himself into the history of the avant-garde in such a brief space of time and with such a meager contribution. Ball's career remains a testimony to how a conative poetics of the self—linked fundamentally to collective memory and made manifest in the form of incantatory phonemes—can find an end in solipsism and enigmatic soliloquy. The *lautgedicht*, Ball's creation and gift to Dada, proved to be an ephemeral moment in an equally transient movement: ultimately, he left both behind. Although two of the *lautgedicht* found their way into his fantasy novel *Tenderenda the Fantast*, Ball's total legacy to the new genre is a mere six poems plus a handful of equally short statements (most of which this chapter has supplied). On June 18,

1921, long after his departure from Dada, Ball recalls an almost Pauline experience, a Christian abduction-through-interpellation that parallels his swoon
as the magical bishop: "When I came across the word dada, I was called upon
twice by Dionysius. D.A.—D.A." (Ball 210). It may be coincidental that D.A. are
the first two letters on the road to spelling out "DAMASCUS," the road to which
proved the locus of Paul's conversion, but it is not coincidental that these are the
initials of that most famous of Neoplatonists, the sixth-century Dionysius the
Areopagite, about whom Ball was subsequently to write in great detail in his *Byz-
antine Christianity.* Ball's theologization of the avant-garde is complete, poetry
is atonement not critique, articulate language is a homunculus, and for the poet
of the *lautgedicht* "DADA" becomes "BYE-BYE."[29]

# Corrosive Poetics

## The Relief Composition of Ronald Johnson's *Radi os*

This chapter is divided into two separate but related parts. The first revisits the over-theorized matter of periodization to take issue with the accuracy of the label "postmodern" in its specific application to much recent North American poetic practice; the second examines Ronald Johnson's 1977 *Radi os* as a complex intertextual enterprise whose mode and implications extend beyond the literary into both philosophical issues and the practice of everyday life, as well as beyond imputed "postmodern proclivities" into an unwitting resuscitation of a thirteenth-century poetic. The term *postmodern* has acquired a fashionably unproblematic currency as a buzzword of our time; it is the powerful and ready term that encapsulates our contemporary condition. Yet there remains essential research to be done on the broad theme of the prefix. As the precise registration of an addition *before* to mark a having passed *beyond,* "post" carries a semantic import and ineluctable janiformity that implicates it in that broad historicizing agenda that Derrida has noted: "It is as if one again wished to put a linear succession in order, to periodize, to distinguish before and after, to limit the risks of reversibility or repetition, transformation or permutation: an ideology of progress" ("Point de Folie" 324).[1] Postmodern hardly generates consensus as a descriptive term for a cultural condition. Defined variously as the advent of the simulacrum and the hyperreal (Baudrillard), as a consequence of the logic of late capitalism (Jameson), the general collapse of efficacious master narratives in the broad condition of Western knowledge (Lyotard), and as a paradigm shift from epistemology to ontology (McHale), postmodernism remains stubbornly elusive, heterogeneous, and paradoxical. Notwithstanding the differentials, this term for our current period has been intransigently ensconced within contemporary conceptual presuppositions since the 1970s.[2]

An added complication springs from the emigration of *postmodern* from its broad cultural designation to one that offers descriptions of a multiplicity of art discourses and frequently takes the form of a catalogue of stylistic devices. Thus Charles Jencks co-opts the term to designate a strain of architectural practice emerging in the 1970s that takes the form of a quasi-historicism formulated upon a schizophrenic crossing of discrete codes, resulting in a double coding of modern and traditional. The appreciator, or depreciator, of postmodern architecture encounters numerous instantly recognizable features and predilections: a rejection of austerity with a resultant use of ornament, a preference for non-primary pastel colors, a mixture of heterological quotations from styles of other periods, and a general proclivity to pluralism, complexity, and hierarchical collapse. This latter feature of postmodernism does not elude a longstanding theological resonance. Indeed, Jenks' architectural postmodernism, with its defining collapse of hierarchy, unwittingly inflects the central paradox of Christianity: the mystery of the Incarnation. As Meyer Abrams summarizes:

> [The New Testament] is grounded on the radical paradox that "the last shall be first," and dramatizes that fact in the central mystery of Christ incarnate as a lowly carpenter's son who takes fishermen for his disciples, consorts with beggars, publicans, and fallen women, and dies ignominiously, crucified with thieves. This interfusion of highest and lowest, the divine and the base, as Erich Auerbach has shown, had from the beginning been a stumbling block to readers habituated to the classical separation of levels of subject matter and style. (Abrams 115)

Similarly, Michael Camille points to the habitual heterogeneity and hierarchical collapse of medieval reading: "The concoction of hybrids, mingling different registers and genres, seems to have been both a verbal and visual fashion for élite audiences" (13).

Unlike literary postmodernism, yet similar to Language poetry, architectural postmodernism developed out of an intense semiotic awareness and a belief in the contingent nature of meaning. Distinguishing between modern from postmodern architect is the conscious approach of postmodernism to architectural practice, which it takes as a language developed upon the perceptual codes of its makers and users. For her part, Linda Hutcheon has defined postmodern writing as primarily a practice of irony, formal and thematic reflexivity, and a deliberately paradoxical use and subversion of conventions, with its quintessential genre being prose historiographic metafiction.[3] But where exactly (if ex-

actly) does postmodern emerge in the twentieth century? Kenneth Rexroth locates a "postmodern sensibility" in Eugene Jolas' *Transition* enterprise but claims
Robert Desnos to be "the first 'postmodern' intellectual in 1925," a claim that
renders subsequent discussions somewhat atavistic.[4] However, Charles Olson
is the first American poet to have called himself postmodern, a characterization subsequently endorsed by critic Charles Altieri and somewhat modified by
Ralph Maud to an "archaic postmodern."[5] Critical attention was first drawn to
the term's poetic application through a key interventional document: Don Allen's then controversial anthology *The New American Poetry* (1960), which first
brought to wide attention a generation of practitioners that subsequent scholars (and Allen too in the revised 1982 edition of the anthology) would claim to
be postmodern. Sparse though not devoid of female poets, the anthology included (among several others) work by Paul Blackburn, Charles Olson, Robert
Creeley, Denise Levertov, Barbara Guest, Robert Duncan, Gary Snyder, and Jack
Kerouac. In 1966 Harry Levin applies the name "postmodern" dismissively to
a contemporary "anti-intellectual undercurrent" opposed to those "Children of
Humanism and the Enlightenment" who Levin refers to as "the moderns" (271).
Four years later Herbert Schneidau constructs a Heraclitan, yet equally oppositional, template that specifies the modernist mission as a search for the formal
fusion of fixity and fluidity, thereby inscribing the postmodern as a Dionysian
consecration of flux. Schneidau announces the new poetry to be apocalyptic
rather than avant-garde, one that is directed toward demolishing all hierarchic
distinctions between high and low culture and erasing any difference between
art and life, a mission, I might add, embraced more than half a century before by the European and New York Dadaists.[6] Leslie Fiedler writing in 1971
concurs with Schneidau's apocalyptic placement of the new poetry but draws a
more affirmative conclusion. The "New Mutants," as he calls them, successfully
freed themselves "from all vestiges of the elitism and Culture Religion" that he
judged as typifying the modernist ethos (403). In the same year Richard Poirier
applauds "the dislocating, disturbing impulses" in contemporary writing that
challenge the very core of "literature as a humanistic impulse" (xv). The critical squabbles around *postmodern* accumulated through the 1970s until in 1980,
when Ihab Hassan speculates that it is "a term that may now have outlived its
awkward use" (91). Having questioned the usefulness of the term, Hassan proceeds to analyze, with neither critical nor diagnostic rigor, two crucial features
of a postmodern episteme: indeterminacy and immanence (ibid.). This perlustration is not exhausted; suffice to say that all these critics agree that a qualita

tive rupture between two periods occurred circa 1960 with postmodernism's embrace of anarchy and its celebration of flux and hierarchic dissolution in a concerted challenge to a broadly liberal humanist enterprise. James Breslin indicates the deleterious consequences of such partitioning:

> To conceive of twentieth-century poetry as divided into two unified but distinct periods is to draw a very schematic map indeed; it also raises a lot of knotty theoretical and practical questions. How, for example, did the first of these stable unities change into the second? The whole sense of history as a dynamic process is lost by dichotomizing twentieth-century poetry into two static periods. (57)

Ironically such allegedly postmodern criticism repeats in its analyses and interpretations the fundamental gesture it imputes to modernism, namely a strenuous effort to disprove and break away from the thinking of the past.

Charles Altieri likewise accepts a periodic dichotomy between the modern and postmodern but constructs a different formulation, contextualizing the rupture in the wider framework of English —romanticism. (Certainly the apocalyptic strain that Schneidau and Fiedler note and calls for a neo-romantic genealogy from Ginsberg back through Whitman and Blake to the Bible lends credence to his framing.)[7] For Altieri the postmodern poetries of the 1960s parallel the concurrent shift in philosophical interest away from aspects of mind and cognition toward the type of immanence found in the work of Heidegger and the later Wittgenstein. Like the latter two thinkers, postmodern poets "argue that the poet can never reach a satisfactory relationship with his world, or even with his mind's relationship to the world, if he constantly reflects on the acts of imagination as themselves constitutive of value" (Altieri 22). Altieri considers imagining "non-Christian sources of immanent value" to be a key challenge in this postmodern *zeitgeist* (79) and, in the work of Robert Duncan and Gary Snyder, he sees "a radical faith in the aesthetics of presence as the ground for a postmodern religious attitude" (128). The list of poets Altieri considers postmodern is telling: Denise Levertov, Charles Olson, Frank O'Hara, Gary Snyder, Robert Duncan, and Robert Bly—precisely those poets in Allen's anthology rejected in the 1970s and 1980s by Language writing in the latter's concerted critique of voice, referentiality, and presence.

My purpose is not to question Altieri's discrete insights into the writings of the individual poets he discusses but rather to underscore the problematic consequences of gathering their heterogeneous approaches under the collective banner of postmodernism. Even if we were to accept that term as an efficacious label for a cultural period, one is still faced with the fact that it (postmodernism) remains incommensurate to its practical subsets. Indeed, the specter arises of a particular line of interrogation that is synecdochal for the entire issue: if Frank O'Hara, Charles Olson, and Robert Bly are postmodern, then what are John Cage, Susan Howe, Barrett Watten, Lyn Hejinian, Clark Coolidge, Kenneth Goldsmith, and Bruce Andrews? How do we accommodate the poetry and poetics that arose in the late 1970s in direct opposition to the voiced, lived, and so-called postmodern poetry of the 1960s? Altieri offers no discussion of the impact of both Saussure and structuralism on North American poetics and the later ramifications of post-structuralism and feminism. According to his circumscriptions, postmodern poetry—a poetry of immanence as well as an outcome of an embraced aesthetics of presence—precedes May 1968 and does not reflect the impact of continental European thinking referred to initially as structuralism and the linguistic turn and later under the collective noun "theory."[8] Even laying aside the problematics of these styles of periodization, the question persists whether or not modernism and postmodernism need be either supercessionary or mutually exclusive. In architecture, Charles Jenks denies the efficacy of such stable cultural partitioning as in his reading of Venturi and Rauch's Brant House in Greenwich (1971) where an attempted historicism, by way of allusion, collapses into non-historicism owing to the extent of the distortions (88–89). Jencks detects in the building a modernist sensibility articulated onto a postmodernist theory.

This hybrid form certainly assists us in engaging Ronald Johnson's deceptively simple *Radi  os* as a poem that tangibly reconnects with the radical romanticism of William Blake and continues the characteristically modernist practice and techniques of fragmentary collage evident in Pound's *Cantos* and Eliot's *The Waste Land*. In it, the apocalyptic "anarchy" and the aesthetics of presence of 1960s postmodernism give way to a dialogic poetics of intertextuality and paragrammatic exhumation whose contemporary theoretical roots can be traced to Roland Barthes' "The Death of the Author." In this essay, Barthes' concept of the *scriptor* offers a ready and coherent theory for an impersonal poetics of techniques and recombinant materials and thereby an antidote to the dominant "workshop" confessional and self-expressive writing. Johnson himself refers to *Radi  os* as "a cosmology of the mind and of a sort of Blakean exploration of the imagination written on top of Milton but with Milton's words" (Alpert 556). Put less grandiosely, *Radi  os* is a poem found among words and phrasal passages in the opening four books of Milton's *Paradise Lost*. In formalist terminology, it applies a specific device of "finding and extracting" to epic material and fore-grounded in the poem's transparent mode of production. Guy Davenport calls Johnson's compositional process one of "sifting": "The poem we are reading is still Milton's but sifted." As well as sifting a new text into existence, *Radi  os* fur-ther presents an unfamiliar text within a text, one that is present in *Paradise Lost* but imperceptible via orthodox methods of reading. However, *Paradise Lost* does not escape a destructive (as well as deconstructive) element; given this, *Radi  os* is correctly placed within a tradition of deletional poetics.[9] Somewhat surpris-ingly, it is a philosopher, Emmanuel Levinas, who teases out the cognitive and symbolic implications of the method. Ruminating on Michel Leiris' composi-tional practice of erasures *(biffures)*, Levinas, in a comment apposite not only to paragrammatic composition in general but specifically to Johnson's Blakean method as well as Cagean transcoherence (discussed in chapter 4), maintains that thought: "is originally word-erasing—that is to say, symbolic. And because thought is symbolic, ideas can hook up with one another and create a connect-ing network . . . [which] owes its value not so much to the fact that it connects one thought to another but rather to the fact that it guarantees the presence of one given thought *within* another" (146).

An author's note and dedication to Robert Duncan as well as an afterward by Guy Davenport accompany the text proper of *Radi  os*. Johnson's prefatory remarks to the book set the compositional method of the poem in a cultural context of two inspirations: one of acoustic inaudibility, the other of material removal. The day before buying his 1892 edition of *Paradise Lost* in Seattle, John-son listened to Lukas Foss's *Baroque Variations I*, "On the Larghetto of Handel's Concerto Grosso, Op. 6, No. 12." Johnson quotes Foss's own notes on the piece: "Groups of Instruments play the Larghetto but keep submerging into inaudi-bility (rather than pausing). Handel's notes are always present but often inau-dible. The inaudible moments leave holes in Handel's music (I composed the holes)."[10] The second inspiration involves an intimate connection to a radical romantic by way of a gift. Johnson writes that *Radi  os* "is the book Blake gave me (as Milton entered Blake's left foot—the first foot, that is, to exit Eden) his eyes wide open through my hand. To etch is 'to cut away,' and each page, as in Blake's concept of a book, is a single picture." It should also be mentioned that Johnson had read Zukofsky's *A* (14), which is a similar composition from Milton by means of aeration.[11]

How does etching "cut away" and what exactly was Blake's process? Among several graphic experiments Blake made, the most important was his sortie (from

1788 onwards) into relief etching. Although Blake himself left no detailed information of the process, we have John Thomas Smith's legendary account. According to Smith, Blake received the method from his deceased brother Robert in a visionary image. Blake followed Robert's advice for the production of the *Songs of Innocence and of Experience* and the subsequent illuminated books, "writing his poetry and drawing his marginal subjects of embellishments in outline upon the copper-plate with an impervious liquid, and then eating the plain parts or lights away with aqua fortis considerably below them, so that the outlines were left in stereotype" (Smith 461). Rather than cutting away, relief etching involves a physical removal by means of corrosion.[12] Although it is a far less economical method than regular engraving, Blake seems to have been attracted to relief etching by its symbolic resonance. In *The Marriage of Heaven and Hell,* relief etching emerges as a ready symbol for dispelling the Cartesian illusion of a mind-body dualism. As Blake writes, "the notion that man has a body distinct from his soul, is to be expunged; this I shall do by printing in the infernal method, by corrosives, which in Hell are salutary and medicinal, melting apparent surfaces away, and displaying the infinite that was hid"(39).[13] This too is Blake's response to Locke's *tabula rasa,* which loses all metaphoric power in Blake's pristinely material inversion into the pre-corroded surface of a copper plate. Johnson's choice of Milton's epic is apt and additionally reinforces the Blakean bond. As well as producing watercolors and drawings for *Paradise Lost, Paradise Regained, Comus,* "l'Allegro," and "Il Penseroso," Blake also wrote and etched his own *Milton,* a lengthy critical meditation on the poet-regicide (completed in 1804); earlier he rewrote *Paradise Lost* in the form of his own epic poem, *Vala, or a Dream in Nine Nights* (itself a rewriting of Edward Young's popular *Night Thoughts).* Henry Crabb Robinson recalls a conversation with Blake in which the subject turned to *Paradise Lost:* "I saw Milton in Imagination and he told me to beware of being misled by his *Paradise Lost.* In particular he wished me to shew the falsehood of his doctrine that the pleasures of *sex* arose from the fall. The fall could not produce any pleasure" (quoted in Bentley 416).

*Radi os* then is the product of a corrosive poetics, a relief composition received by Johnson as Blake's gift to him that transposes Blake's graphic method into typographic textuality, burning away large areas of the surface text with the aqua fortis of Johnson's own imagination.[14] Utilizing his source poem as a lexical supply and applying a process of selected deletions and excavations, Johnson arrives at his own poem: a reduced, alembicated form of *Paradise Lost.* The inside front cover of the book lays bare this precise mode of production:

> OF MAN'S ~~first disobedience, and the~~ fruit
> ~~Of~~ that ~~forbidden~~ tree ~~whose mortal taste~~
> ~~Brought death~~ into the World, ~~and all our woe,~~
> ~~With loss of Eden, till one greater~~ Man
> ~~Restore us, and regain the blissful seat,~~
> ~~Sing, Heavenly Muse, that, on the secret top~~
> ~~Of Oreb, or of Sinai, didst inspire~~
> ~~That shepherd who first taught~~ the chosen ~~seed~~
> ~~In the beginning how the heavens and earth~~
> Rose out of Chaos: ~~or, if Sion hill~~
> ~~Delight thee more, and Siloa's brook that flowed~~
> ~~Fast by the oracle of God, I thence~~
> ~~Invoke thy aid to my adventurous~~ song,
> ~~That with no middle intends to soar~~
> ~~Above the Aonian mount, while it pursues~~
> ~~Things unattempted yet in prose or rhyme.~~
>                           (italics added)

Sight should not be lost of the fundamental negativity involved in this method, a production through *loss*. The *sous rature* effect of the above paratext does not appear in the body of the poem proper where the deleted passages are removed entirely to offer a highly spatial and decentered page of terse and attenuated juxtapositional relations. (Davenport refers to the poem as "Milton *imagiste*" [200].)

> O
>
>               tree
>        into the World,
>                     Man
>
>
>
>              the chosen
>
>
> Rose out of Chaos:
>
>
>
>              song,

A study of the semantic changes and significances in *Radi  os* is beyond the scope of this chapter on genealogy and method, but suffice to say that through such deletion (from Milton's 121 words to Johnson's 13 in the instance above) *Radi  os* is the literal expenditure of Milton's text. If the poem inscribes itself into a transcendentalist tradition by testifying "in a most modern way, to a most unmodern harmony, the poem becoming a transcendentalist allegory of Paradise Regained on the grounds of its loss," as Andre Furlani claims (75), it is even more so exemplary of Bataille's notion of the poem as "the least degraded and least intellectualized form of the expression of a state of loss [and signifying] in the most precious way, creation by means of loss" (120).

Literary history may eventually place Ronald Johnson's *Radi  os* in an august line of confessional poetry; if it does so it will be compelled to specify the anomalous nature of this confession as the meta-textual appearance (not the return) of the repressed, for *Radi  os* records a text turned against itself. By way of a retinal tracking and excavation of a latent other poem, *Radi  os* "quotes" the inaudible Milton, the Milton that is not Milton's, thereby bringing to textual apposition Rimbaud's famous claim that "I is an Other" linguistically reformulated as "this text also holds an Other." Johnson's poem does not relate to *Paradise Lost* parodically by setting up a parallel space, but rather induces spaces within a space through a selective deployment of reading. At first glance each page of *Radi  os* offers its reader the initial visual impression of a pull to orchestrated coherence and a counterpull to a spatially emphasized fragmentariness (the result of Johnson's self-imposed constraint of leaving the mined phrases in the identical place as they appear on the page in his 1892 edition of *Paradise Lost*). Moreover, retaining the original position of Milton's words bestows on Johnson's poem those qualities of cosmic and spatial vacuity that Valéry notes in Mallarmé's *Un Coup de Dés:* the sense that "space itself truly spoke, dreamed, and gave birth to temporal forms" (Valéry 309). In the space of the deletions "silences [assume] bodily shapes" and evanescent ideas appear "as beings, each surrounded with a palpable emptiness. . . . There in the same void with them, like some new form of matter arranged in systems or masses or trailing lines, [coexists] the Word!" (Valéry 309). In both poems, white space functions not unlike the *eon* of Parmenides permeating and participating in all it supports, encloses, and fills.

Received as a gift from Blake, this textual etching conveniently situates Johnson's poem in an august lineage of imaginative commentary. Indeed, Guy Davenport in his forward to the book waxes rhapsodically of *Radi  os* being "a meditation, first of all, on grace. It finds in Milton's poems [*sic*] those clusters of words which were originally a molecular intuition of the complex harmony of nature whose eyesight loops back to its source in the sun, the earth, the tree, our cousin animals, the spiraling galaxies, and mysteriously to the inhuman back of empty space." Notwithstanding Johnson's confessed Blakean heritage, *Radi os* can also be read through a supplementary theorization. I have written elsewhere on the congruity of Johnson's compositional method with Michel de Certeau's analyses of the practice of everyday life; to consider the poetic method of *Radi os* as a logic of action implemented within the less romantic notion of a contemporary tactical, consumer poetics opens the poem to a more quotidian contextualization.[15] Corrosive poetics then emerges as a tactical, borderline activity, manipulating the matrix of *Paradise Lost* in order to realize a negative production of detours, erasures, and new articulations. Meaning is coupled to a shifting materiality of language such that a new text, *Radi os,* is "read" into existence by way of insinuated and unconventional itineraries that produce innovative redirections and perversions of the original text. In this "poached" text, the empirical reader (Ronald Johnson) becomes a tactician and an incommensurate user who infiltrates and changes a prior message, thereby radically altering the historic, "pragmatic" function of the given words.

Cultural studies long ago called into question the inviolate paradigm of the original and turned attention to the indeterminate deployment of cultural artifacts—an issue taken up in chapter 6.[16] Johnson comes close in *Radi os* to realizing Barthes' tantalizing dream of "a pure writer who does not write" (*New Critical Essays* 53). Less writing *per se,* the poem comprises a precise transcription of a tactical reading: a type of production within consumption that subjects the object "consumed" to a non-discursive operation. (As such, Johnson's important contribution to the sociology of reading should not be overlooked.) Existing latently as an unrecognized configuration within Milton's "different" *Paradise Lost, Radi os* does not emerge as a poem until released through Johnson's written reading. Sharing the same logic and economy as the paragram, the poem registers as a sub-phenomenal aspect of Milton's epic, which both contains and represses it.[17] Johnson's tactical-consumer poetics help us rethink writing without appeal to a psychologistic model of heterogeneous orders or Bloomian anxieties of influence. Neither the conscious nor unconscious need be petitioned to support the tactic's insinuation and manipulation of an imposed system, or the unsettling of textual stability by way of a reading that invades a text in order to play among its signs according to the laws of a different power. In showing that *Paradise Lost* is not an indestructible and monumental structure but a simulacrum in its own appearance, the very promise of a self-effacement,

*Radi  os* seems to capture both the philosophical and canonical relation of Johnson's and Milton's respective texts. If we compare Johnson's tactical production with that status of poetic genius demanded by Bataille to be "not verbal talent [but] the divining of ruins secretly expected, in order that so many immutable things become undone, lose themselves, communicate" (*Inner Experience* 149) as well as to Bataille's own equation of substance as "a provisional equilibrium between the spending (loss) and the accumulation of force" (ibid. 15) with the consequent evanescence of stability, then we see how *Radi  os* can be thought to exist as a latent, unrecognized configuration within the "substance" of *Paradise Lost*. Not emerging as a poem until released at the time of Johnson's written reading, *Radi  os* stands as the sub-phenomenal aspect of the Miltonic epic that both contains and represses it. Johnson, however, recovers the negativity of the tactical to production, allowing paragrammatic play to push the system containing it to new levels of complexity. It is precisely such a recovery that endorses *Radi  os* as an intrinsic schedule in reading Milton's epic as well as ratifying how this negativity may be reaffirmed and meaning equated with the experience of a loss of signification, for both the paragram and the tactical reader register as the elusive and repressed elements inside the conventional laws of reading. Moreover, Johnson outlines a democratic method of textual excavation that not only reveals his source text to be infinitely exploitable but also his own *Radi  os*. Thus, Nicholas Lawrence has recently generated his own *Par Se Lot* and *Adi os*.[18] In what follows I wish to consolidate my earlier dispute with a modern-postmodern divide and trace an errant genealogy of Johnson's method that challenges Davenport's assessment of *Radi  os* "as a signal act of the postmodernist period" and also reveals Johnson's method to be anachronistic (196).

Medieval. Metalepsis. Modernity. I use this literate alliteration to introduce a final question: Can we read Johnson's "corrosive" poetics through the trope of metalepsis to interrogate the precise dynamic propelling his poetic method in *Radi  os*? By way of a complication, let us turn to a relatively unknown document in poetics, Geoffrey of Vinsauf's *Poetria Nova* (ca. 1210). Through this ancient text, with its remarkable prescience of Johnson's method of written reading, we can articulate a richer genealogy than a postmodern circumscription allows, a genealogy that links Johnson's corrosive poetics to an early thirteenth-century concept of "modernity." Geoffrey's poetic manual advocates a practice of scriptural renewal, a verbal art based upon a rewriting of prior writing and whose implications extend far beyond poetic pedagogy. Indeed, as the creed of the *Poetria Nova* makes clear, the act of writing is a perpetual rejuvenation of past writings.[19] Toward the end of his treatise Geoffrey offers both Seneca and Sidonius as worthy writers to be copied but attaches to his praise a significant qualification: "Both authors, it is true, deserve honor; but which should I follow, the former or the latter? Since freshness is a source of great pleasure, and sameness of manner wearies us, I shall not be like the latter, nor yet like the former; I shall not be exclusively either diffuse or concise; rather, I shall be both concise and diffuse, *becoming both of these by being neither*" (82, emphasis added). A radical poetics of modernity is at stake in Geoffrey's stance, a poetics that approaches antecedent texts as the necessary raw material for rewriting, not for superseding (Geoffrey's term for the old is *caduc,* a nuanced word that also means "obsolete.")

The *Poetria* commences with an ostensibly laudatory address to Pope Innocent the Third, the phraseology if not the idiom of which instantly reveals itself to be subversively singular: "Holy Father, wonder of the world, if I say Pope Nocent I shall give you a name without a head; but if I add the head, your name will be at odds with the metre" (15). Let's pause and reflect on this amazing opening. Pope Nocent, "Papa Nocenti," (and bear in mind that *nocens* translates as "harmful") becomes "innocent" (Inocent) by a simple transposition of the final letter. The origins of this name game are clearly Cratylian; however, a significant discursive metamorphosis occurs in the passage sufficient to commit it to a major impropriety. As Alexandre Leupin elucidates: "What the distorted name suggests, then, is that Innocent III is not viewed according to some proper historical dimension external to the text. In fact, the opposite is true: in the course of Geoffrey's 'un-'innocent name game, the pope loses his autonomy as a figure outside the text and becomes (through *transsumptio*) an example of the poet's doctrine of poetic demonstration" (33). By a ludic cephalism—a de-capitation followed by a re-capitation—the proper name of the pope, the pope external to the text, indeed the text's very addressee, is introjected into the text's autonomous reflexivity. Moreover, this transpositional action upon a single letter is, if not entirely aphonic, pre-eminently retinal—the outcome of a reading (like Johnson's) and analysis of mobile written parts. The *Poetria* lauds sight as the major sense of aesthetic judgment: "the eye" affirms Geoffrey "is a surer arbiter than the ear" (26). Leupin contextualizes this optic, lettristic playfulness within a more profound agenda, thereby accomplishing nothing less than a radical reversal of theological *doxa* on the matter of the written sign: "[I]n Geoffrey's practice of scriptural renovation, the letter is implicitly linked to life and the spirit to death . . . . Contrary to well-known biblical wisdom . . . the *Poetria's* doctrine proposes that ancient tradition relives only in its rewriting: this is how medieval literature in general reverses the tenets of theology" (27). Geoffrey's position, as a subject of modernity, becomes clear in his understanding of transumption as the renewal of, not a break from, the old *(caduc)* into the new. He figures this metalepsis as the paradoxical doublet of "old youth" *(puer senex),* "the one who renews the obsolete by giving it a new inflection or an unprecedented appearance" (quoted in Leupin 26).

Among a cornucopia of rhetorical devices in Geoffrey's *Poetria* the one of *transsumptio* enjoys a preferential status; not really a trope proper, it designates a certain protosemantic movement that governs all tropism as the very transition between two tropes. Geoffrey lauds *transsumptio* as the "genus omnibus" of tropes and specifies its dynamic as *"Scilicet improprium vocum status et peregrina / Sumpto verborum"* ("the changed meaning of the words and their wandering application") (quoted in Leupin 24). Earlier, Quintilian elucidated transumption's consequential complexities when subsuming it within the class of metalepsis, describing its performance as "a displacement of meaning from one alien base to another, so that the concept of proper location or property is nowhere implied" (ibid.). Putting aside the startling poststructural ramifications evoked by this passage, let me insist that the operation of *transsumptio* as *metalepsis* is basic not only to Geoffrey's own sense of poetic modernity but also to the governing dynamic behind Johnson's corrosive poetics. As I have pointed out, relief-writing involves a wandering elsewhere, a beckoning to another place, a movement to another displacement—what Quintilian calls "a kind of intermediate step between the term transferred and the thing to which it is transferred, having no meaning in itself, but merely providing a transition" (Leupin 24).

Geoffrey offers a further trope to describe this poetic method: that of "combing" a text. "Now, I have provided a comb: if they [compositions] are groomed with it, whether in prose or verse, they will gleam with elegance" (86). Leupin draws attention to the intimate nuance of Geoffrey's Latin, specifically to the close phonic alliance of "combing" *(pectere)* and "looking" *(spectare)* (34). Bearing in mind Geoffrey's predilection for the dynamics of single letters (seen already in the case of the un-innocent pope), Leupin's perception is not fanciful. Johnson combs Milton's text to disentangle his own text hidden inside it. (The temptation to read this as an Orphic staging of a subterranean Eurydice awaiting exhumation by Orphic charm is a theme I will pick up on toward the end of this chapter.) Framing a historical parallel as anticipatory and prescient is one thing, but to assert an actual causal connection is an entirely different matter, and by no means a simple procedure. However, I believe Johnson's own zeal to historically contextualize *Radi os* within a diachronic descent through Blake to Milton warrants this expanded genealogy. Wittingly or not, Johnson's practice *is* the practice of the medieval *poetria nova.*

Geoffrey of Vinsauf would no doubt have readily accommodated *Radi os* within the popular medieval genre of the *Speculum*, which "claims to be no more than the faithful reflection of another space or another text" (Leupin 36). *Radi os* is precisely such a space mirrored in the other space named *Paradise Lost*. Geoffrey would also note in *Radi os* his own unorthodox—even deconstructive—version of the *Speculum* by which "the mirror becomes the absent locus of the transformational power and autonomy of poetic language" (ibid.). Residing within the poetic economy that *Paradise Lost* offers, *Radi os* reflects no more than the possibilities available within Milton's initial economy: the revelation *per se* of an auto-alterity. This specular theme now reflects us back to William Blake and relief etching by way of a pedestrian summary of copperplate preparation: the engraver's, not the poet's, primal scene.

As we have noted, Johnson focuses in his introductory note on the corrosive power of Blake's gift to him. What is burnt, however, is a highly reflective surface: nothing less than a metal mirror. Before etching or engraving could begin, Blake would have had to perform (or have had performed for him) a number of preliminary activities. After beveling the edges of the plate and rounding the corners in order to minimize any creasing, the next step would be to polish the plate by a process called "burnishing."[20] The penultimate stage involved polishing the plate with a fine chalk to remove any grease and then a final, circular rubbing with a steel burnisher. It is more than probable that Blake is referring to this tedious preparation in the following passage from plate 65 of *Jerusalem*:

> . . . intricate wheels invented, wheel without wheel:
> To perplex youth in their outgoings, & to bind to labours in Albion
> Of day & night the myriads of eternity that they may grind
> And polish brass & iron hour after hour laborious task!
> (216)

Highly polished in preparation for engraving, Blake's copperplate takes on the medieval quality of specularity. Geoffrey describes his own poetics of refinement as an aesthetic labor acted upon raw material (terms equally applicable to both Blake's and Johnson's): "This is my method when I am laboring to polish words: I chide my mind, lest it linger in one place, for the quiet of standing water makes it stagnant" (86). Does not Johnson's paragrammatic method involve a similar refusal to let reading stagnate in a customary linear itinerary? In relief etching refinement is effected on an empty but polished surface, a natural material which, as Leupin insightfully notes, "is already a mirror; even before art intervenes it has undergone the polishing indispensable to its reflective capacity" (37). Blake's gift to Johnson is specular in a further way; it is a double *speculum*, a process both corrosive and inversional that requires the text inscribed on the copperplate to be written in the form of a mirror image in order that the plate prints correctly. Serendipitously, Leupin's estimate of the 1210 *Poetria Nova*, and Geoffrey of Vinsauf's own contemporary modernity, accord perfectly with Ronald Johnson's 1977 text *Radi os:* "Here, the ancient or the obsolete takes on a new luminosity, and the lost paradise of old poetic words is recaptured in modernity's most dazzling mirror" (38).

## Coda

What of Johnson's choice of title? Guy Davenport steers his own reflections toward the first three letters: *Radi* pluralized to *Radii*, "lines outward from a center," conveniently situated the poem within a vast solar poetics (202). The reading gains some plausibility concurring precisely as it does with Johnson's own claim that *Radi os* indicates "Radiant things of light all the way through" (O'Leary 575). Opening with a circle, the poem's videocentricity and photism are evident throughout. Moreover the identical circular letter that occurs within the title suggests radiating lines from a multiplicity of circular *Os*. Yet in his forward Johnson claims each page to be a single picture, thereby complicating the work's sequential flow, a flow additionally exacerbated by the absence of pagination. In effect *Radi os* is a series of page-plane suspensions, susceptible to discontinuous and discrete reading (thereby unwittingly connecting it to a broad picturesque tradition to be discussed in chapter 9).[21] Each page, in the manner of a concrete poem and other non-linear poetries, offers itself as a temporally indeterminate textual space (each can be engaged as a locus of meditation for any length of time). Yet if we pursue that different thread of evocation suggested by contracting the title's letters, we arrive at *radios*, those quintessential instruments of musical and vocal disembodiment. Radios complicate our reception of *Radi os* as either a predominantly solar or ocular text, born from a retinal sifting of a source. It introduces a forcibly vocal inflection, a disturbing, ghostly sounding, a disembodied voice in the guise of the dead Milton that is radiophonically present not beneath, not behind, but in the form of the aerated constellations that comprise *Radi os*. It is hard to deny the similarity of this residual, sifted Miltonic voice to those dead souls heard through the static of a car radio in Cocteau's great 1950 film *Orphée*. (The allusion to Cocteau's film appears less fanciful if we recall that Johnson was an avowed Orphic ever since reading Elizabeth Sewell's

*The Orphic Voice* and incorporated the first page of *Radi  os* into his magnum opus *ARK* in the section BEAMS 21, 22, 23, *The Song of Orpheus*).[22] In his 1995 interview with Peter O'Leary, Johnson admits to excavating the myth of Orpheus and Eurydice midway through his sifting of Book II, admitting further that the section "The Song of Orpheus" was and still is himself (574). Johnson was certainly familiar with Cocteau's handling of the Orphic (see Alpert 583) and in fact identified with Orpheus for a minimum of twenty years. Read then as an Orphic text of empowerment, descent, loss, and death, *Radi  os* puts forward a figure of the author as the mythic partner of Eurydice. Johnson makes text move, wedding music (words) to light (the white page), and descends into the Satanic realms to subdue an epic poem by its partial deletion. He further looks back to a Tiresian construction: towards his androgynous Eurydice-Milton. But it is not Orpheus (Johnson) who is torn to pieces by the Maenads, but *Paradise Lost* whose words (not head) float down the river still singing. Sound and touch are, of course, the two modalities of blindness, and blindness was the physical condition under which Milton dictated his *Paradise Lost*. A sunless *Radi  os* indeed.

# Interpretation and the Limit Text

## An Approach to Jackson Mac Low's
## *Words nd Ends from Ez*

It would be perfectly in order to approach Jackson Mac Low's poem *Words nd Ends from Ez* (*WNEFE* hereafter) as an exemplary text of neo-picturesque detail, embodying the variety and fragmentariness that forms the central core of picturesque poetics (outlined in chapter 9); it would be equally pertinent to examine the affinities between Mac Low's work and Ronald Johnson's method of corrosive reduction in his *Radi os,* discussed in chapter 2. However, I wish to examine Mac Low's poem through a different non-aesthetic matrix in a discussion that can be considered a prelude to the longer chapter on John Cage that follows this one. Long ago in *Democratic Vistas,* Whitman called for a Hegelian bard, the supercessionary spirit of Homer and Shakespeare who, in a confluence of poetry, spiritualism, and science, "will compose the great poem of death" (82). I wish to argue that Jackson Mac Low's *WNEFE* is arguably American poetry's extreme achievement in "death-writing." Mac Low reads *The Cantos* mechanistically and systematically to radically unsettle its complex sign economy, eliminating vast sections of the work and then, like Eliot's Fisher King, shoring together numerous textual fragments that, in Mac Low's case, consecrate and celebrate the name of Ezra Pound. A profoundly authorless text, *WNEFE* simultaneously effects the death of Pound's epic and the exhumation of Pound's name.

Pound's view of the fragment might be deduced from his Confucian beliefs that structure the relation of parts to a whole. As Peter Makin comments:

The metaphysic of the Confucian *Chung Yung* or *Unwobbling Pivot . . .* is that things are not heaps of contingent dust-drift, but have essential principles, which are durable; which are part of an overarching tendency or Principle in the universe and which, being a shaping and therefore good principle operative in man as in other things, a man may come to under-

stand. This metaphysic is all about the relation between wholes and fragments. The mosaic is not its little glass and gold-leafed fragments; the Virgin shines down from the apse at Torcello when, or if, half of the fragments
that make her have fallen. (235–36)

Whether or not the original *Cantos* shine through in *"virtu irraggiante"* is not to
be debated here; suffice to say Mac Low's strategic method might be likened to
the willful production of fragmentation, to the revelation or return of letters to
their elemental material base as the building blocks of language for the most part
stripped of content. Such a comparison, however, would be superficial and would
do great disservice to the full extent of Mac Low's achievement, for *WNEFE* is
a highly structured and constructed text. However, the "destroy-to-exhume"
procedure does not result in a *nembutsu*—that sacred meditation on the name
of Amitabha Buddha perfected in Japanese poetry—and though Pound's dic-
tum via Basil Bunting that *"dichten = condensare"* seems uncannily apposite to
Mac Low's reductive textual achievement, the actual outcome is far from constructive. Indeed, the poem offers itself to its readers as an uncompromised application of a veritable poetics of demolition. That, of course, need not be taken
negatively, as Walter Benjamin reminds us a demolition site is often a source
for teaching a theory of construction (*The Arcades Project* 95). Mac Low's oxymoronic economy of creation-through-destruction fittingly accords with Benjamin's description of the angel in Paul Klee's painting *Angelus Novus*, who per-
ceives a "single catastrophe that keeps piling wreckage upon wreckage" hurled
"in front of his feet" (*Illuminations* 257). In Klee's new angelic manner, Mac
Low pulverizes *The Cantos,* reducing them to a systematic, engineered paradox.

   Less dramatically, we might situate the text as part of some Oulipian corpus
in what Serge Gavronsky estimates to be the final formalist hurrah. Mac Low
utilizes a strict procedural method of text generation, the diastic chance selection method (hereafter DCSM). Related to the acrostic, the DCSM is a procedure designed specifically to facilitate a systematic reading through a text in
order to isolate certain letters that repeatedly spell out a "theme" or "index"
name. *WNEFE* records a reading through *The Cantos* in which the theme name
isolated is that of Pound himself. The defining feature of the method concerns
the placement of the letters that spell out the eponymous name. Each letter must
occupy in the new poem a location that corresponds to its placement in the actual name. Mac Low thus tracks successive letter strings that begin with an "e";
then he locates word strings with a "z" in the second position in the string; next
he finds words strings with "r" in third place; following this, he identifies word

strings with "a" in the fourth place; then he locates words string with "p" in the first place, and so on. Additionally, in this poetics of placement rather than of place, line-breaks and stanza demarcations are strictly determined by the original position of punctuation marks in *The Cantos*. (Mac Low speaks of the verse form of *WNEFE* as being a "projection" of Pound's punctuation and versification.) Involving exclusively a poetics of perception, with perception understood in Ombredane's sense as the deformation of an object in which the object varies according to the position of the perceiver (Eco 81), Mac Low declines a hermeneutic engagement of *The Cantos* in favor of a "search and deformation" form of reorganization. Doubtless, the DCSM challenges the basic premise of why and how we read, promoting, as it does, the letter over the word as the basic organizational unit of composition and presenting as an end product a poem of linear disequilibrium organized around the theme name and beyond which semantic degradations are dispersed.

In *Reversible Destiny* (their ambitious project on the architectural body) Arakawa and Madeline Gins (some of whose architectural work is discussed in Chapter 8) offer their germane concept of the perceptual landing site: "The body initially embraces terrains by covering them with paths" (66). Territorialization implies flagged facilities for movement, and pathways in turn facilitate landing sites. As Gins and Arakawa explain:

> Wherever a perceptual landing site occurs, a guiding or engaging bar might be placed, marking off the zone of occurrence. As well as locating areas to which direct perceiving has been guided and with which it has engaged, guiding or engaging bars repeatedly guide perception back to themselves or out beyond themselves. Guiding or engaging bar versions of things, in effect, schematize the objects from which they are reduced and on which they are based. (34)

*The Cantos* provide Mac Low with a variety of perceptual landing sites, thereby offering an event fabric for reading-perceiving activities. Within an infinite number of possible engaging bars, Mac Low chooses a single one from the diastic chain, effectively arresting the potentially infinite movement of incommensurate paragrammatic flows.

The diastic exhumation of Pound's name also produces a ricochet effect in the surrounding textual area. The eponymous name chain—like "the dark petals of iron" that self-organize to form the rose in the steel dust of Canto LXXIV— enjoys a syntactic, organizing power as a teleological terminal to be instantly repeated. But like the return of the repressed, these index name letters induce uncanny configurations around themselves, precipitating extreme cognitive disruptions that decommission conventional methods of reading. Although ordered and restrained by the axial structure, the poem nevertheless resonates as a linear disequilibrium; there is a parsimonious quotient of meaning assembled, as if magnetically, around the theme name and beyond that disperses semantic degradations.

Whereas Ronald Johnson sifts through *Paradise Lost* with aesthetic discrimination, Mac Low implements a profoundly non-aesthetic law, a rubric of pursuit, capture, and revelation that is entirely indifferent to reflective taste. Unlike conceptual writing (to be examined in chapter 6), Mac Low demolishes Kantian taste with a vengeance. It is as if, resisting Celan's call to "wandering words," Mac Low produces an uncompromising procrustean encoding whose chiasmic consequence is frequently a near obliteration of meaning entirely for the sake of a rule-determined textual reorganization. (For instance, because of the presence of the statistically rare letter *z* in the eponymous name, it is guaranteed from the outset that *Words nd Ends from Ez* will involve a severe truncation of the source text.)

But if this explains the mechanism and cultural impact of Mac Low's method, it falls far short of offering a satisfying hermeneutic engagement with the work's defiant edifice of words, part-words, and letters. Indeed, the majority of critical writing on Mac Low, like that of his affiliate practitioner of systematic stochastics John Cage (the subject of the next chapter), focuses either on the post-ontological and ethical issues of this type of composition, or the implications of the methodological procedure (for example, its Zen Buddhist inspiration or its underlying paragrammatic character). Certainly, Mac Low's detailed explanations of his chance procedural methods, which usually accompany his works, encourage such an approach. However, any attempt to subject this limit text to normative hermeneutic encounter leads to enormous, even insuperable difficulties. What hermeneutic strategy is available, or even feasible, when we attempt to negotiate the following sample of patterned textual shards? How do we engage these newly exposed topographical features? How do we interpret the following verbal and sub-verbal confection that opens the work?

En nZe eaRing ory Arms,
Pallor pOn laUghtered lain oureD Ent,
aZure teR,
un-

tAwny  Pping  cOme  d oUt  r wiNg-
joints,
preaD Et aZzle.

spRing-
water
ool  A  P.

(11)

A reader brings to any text an acquired "horizon" of experience including habits, assumptions, and inclinations, and these collide with the demands that a
text makes on the reader (Eco calls this a transactional rapport). Mac Low demands his readers suspend assumptions and comply with the requirements of
his own method, one of which is that we negotiate a perception with a reading
in that there are words we can read alongside letter stimuli that are eruptive and
semantically unsatisfying. Of course, macro-interpretations can be readily formulated; Charles Bernstein's jacket blurb, for instance, offers a condensed allegorical reading that is revelatory of some of the major socio-cultural implications of the work's specific intertextuality. Bernstein also clearly offers a general
impression of the book as a valid contribution to the readerly history of *The
Cantos*:

> At an allegorical level, *Words nd Ends from Ez* exorcizes the authoritari-
> anism that underlies *The Cantos*. Mac Low's "objective" text-generating
> procedure foregrounds much of the "free-play" that remains the most sa-
> lient feature of *The Cantos*. Yet *Words nd Ends* is less a countertext to *The
> Cantos* than an act of homage and a topographical map of features of the
> work otherwise obscured by its narrative thrusts. By purging *The Cantos*
> of any remnant of montage, *Words nd Ends* reveals a purer, inhering para-
> dise within Pound's poem.

On a similar allegorical level we might read *WNEFE* as an instance of symbolic
action by the Jewish poet Mac Low against his anti-Semitic master, or equally
as an attack on the modernist canon. Yet such readings distance the text itself
from any close encounters.

At this point readers might recall Ellsworth Snyder's highly perceptive comment that Mac Low's texts prevent a "suffocation by content" (116–117) and then
ask what exactly is presented to a reader when freed from that suffocation? Mac

Low himself offers the productive concept of events in sound and language, and at least one reader of *WNEFE*, Karl Young, stresses the poem's performative potential (Young 134).[1] However, rather than treat *WNEFE* as a performance in remission, I want to stay with its intransigent materiality and the unmitigating rigor of its rule-generated syntagms in order to investigate the possibilities of strategic engagement.

In the rest of this chapter I want to follow the lead of Umberto Eco's polemical attempt to utilize information theory (IT hereafter) as an interpretative strategy within aesthetics. In "Openness, Information, Communication," the lengthy third chapter of *The Open Work,* Eco outlines certain possibilities for aesthetic address through the categories of IT. From the outset, it's crucial to bear in mind that IT evaluates quantity not quality and that Eco is attracted precisely to its fundamental inappropriateness as a judge of aesthetic phenomena. IT comprises a complex of mathematical rules used to measure the transmission of units of information from a source to a receiver. This transmission could be between a human and machine, a machine and a human, a machine and a machine, or a human and another human. Naturally the latter transmission is the one that pertains to art. For this reason Eco restricts his use of IT to an interhuman transmission, insisting that when the source and target of a message are both human, then IT becomes a theory of communication (66). Strategically, Eco maintains some of the categories of IT (order-disorder, noise-signal, and information-meaning) while jettisoning its algorithmic system. However, he insists that when we consider the relationship of message to the human receiver, questions of information become questions of communication. He writes, "Once the signals are received by a human being, information theory has nothing else to add and gives way to either semiology or semantics, since the question henceforth becomes one of signification" (67).

IT treats messages as organized systems governed by fixed laws of probability. Language itself is an improbable event that establishes its own chain of probabilities; for example, standard uses of the English language dictate that a verb will be preceded by a subject and followed by a predicate, or that a word containing three consonants in a row will be followed by a vowel. Messages, however, are always susceptible to disorder, unpredictability, or wanderlust—what IT designates as "noise." To counter this disorder, messages are wrapped in a surplus of repetitions called "redundancies." Linguistically speaking, fifty percent of communicated language is redundant, nothing more than a restatement using different words of the message being communicated. In this light, we can consider *Words nd Ends from Ez* as an organized system governed by fixed laws of probability in which "redundancy" is virtually zero. The message is no more than the single theme name, whose systematic repetition is the sole but constant redundancy. Moreover, it is highly significant that Mac Low's method of text generation has an entirely quantitative as opposed to qualitative base. It's a matter entirely of establishing a system of predictability and fixing a method of organizing linguistic information latent in the source text. (It's because of this latent presence that we cannot meaningfully speak of this work as an "un-writing" of *The Cantos*.) It appears then that IT is highly appropriate to an understanding of *WNEFE*; I say this because its structure and production is primarily a reorganization of Pound's *Cantos* according to certain statistical determinations in which the semantic dimension is a secondary effect, outcome, or casualty, of the applied diastic law.

Mac Low's poem raises the relevant hermeneutic issue of how meaning relates to information. Arguing against Norbert Wiener's tenet that information and meaning are synonymous and strictly related to order and probability, Eco advances the fascinating claim that information and meaning are inversely proportionate; that is, the more meaning that is present in a text or message the less information it reveals, and the more information it includes the less meaning it relates. Information is dependent for its value on both originality and improbability. In the sentence "Flowers bloom in the Spring" there is a clear, direct meaning but a minimum of original information. For Eco this is sufficient proof that meaning and information are essentially different, and that certain elements of disorder (the contravention of grammatical rules for example) can actually increase the level of information conveyed by a message. Applying Eco's postulate to Mac Low, we can understand how *Words nd Ends from Ez* is low in meaning yet saturated with information. But the question immediately arises: what precisely comprises this information? It certainly does not add to our understanding of the world, as in Eco's rudimentary example, but it does add to our information about the textual reality of *The Cantos*. The statistical and syntactical generative method results in new information about a latent organization and, as such, it is predominantly self-referential information.

Eco draws attention to a phenomenon extremely relevant to Mac Low: "an originality of organization" that takes the form of a deliberate disorganization which is "its improbability in relation to a precise system of probability" (54). Compared to *The Cantos* themselves, the probability of a human being actually writing *WNEFE* is zero. Indeed, Mac Low's poem could not have been written by a sentient, thinking human being but only generated by an imposed specific (and highly irregular) method of reading. We might consider Mac Low's poem as cultural noise when measured against the probabilities within our own rationally and grammatically governed linguistic culture—however, it is cultural noise solely in relation to the signal sets of its source text, *The Cantos*. "The disorder that aims at communication," as Eco phrases it, "is a disorder only in relation to a previous order," a relation that applies both ways (58). Mac Low violates one set of linguistic probabilities in order to establish a different set: a set based not on rules of grammar, reference, and signification, but on statistical recurrence. This set, moreover, is already latent in *The Cantos*.

Eco abandons the terminology of information theory in the second part of his discussion when turning to the issue of information in poetic language. In this domain the term "information" is given a restricted function to indicate "the wealth of aesthetic meaning contained in a given message"—a use hardly applicable to Mac Low (59). One of the crucial outcomes of *WNEFE* is that it fails to yield much aesthetic gratification and instead exposes a troublesome latent dimension in its source. Through this opening up of a latent order, it is exemplary of the writing-through method first announced by John Cage and to be examined in detail in the next chapter. Like Cage, Mac Low organizes the shattering of meaning and extends comprehension into a type of musical value. The following passage from Cage's introduction to his essay *Anarchy* makes this clear: "My mesostic texts do not make ordinary sense. They make nonsense, which is taught as a serious subject in one of the Tokyo universities. If nonsense is found intolerable, think of my work as music, which is, Arnold Schoenberg used to say, a question of repetition and variation, variation itself being a form of repetition in which some things are changed and others are not" (vi). Both Cage and Mac Low invite their readers to re-experience the old aesthetic pleasure in recurrence, predetermination, and surprise consequences; there are actually fewer opportunities for a reader to complete a word fragment than we will note in Coolidge's poetry in chapter 9. Nevertheless, if not primarily aesthetic in its effects, the book satisfies that condition required by Eco to achieve "poetic meaning" and an aesthetic message: a deviation from linguistic order. And because Mac Low demands his readers focus on a contraventional value (a statistical rule of the letter, not the semantic stability of the word) normative hermeneutic approaches to the poem are a priori doomed to failure. For instance, Mac Low aborts the linguistic convention that capital letters serve to announce a new sentence, a noun, or a proper name; courtesy of the diastic law they instead manifest as incessant, unavoidable disruptions within words and disturbed lexemes.

The methodological centrality of the letter and the embedded letter-chain in the work begs a natural connection to Saussure's obsessive study of paragrammatic pathways.[2] However, Mac Low is neither a linguist on vacation nor a *fou de langage*; it is only Jackson Mac Low as the initiating reader who is required to act as a delirious sleuth, mining deliberately hidden connections. The simple demand made by *WNEFE* might be the impossible demand to precipitate a literal revolution in interpretation and focus on the sublexemic and the grapheme as the complex unit, a demand catastrophic from the conventional sense of language as a double articulation. Certainly, the status and power of the letter in *WNEFE* is unconventional and the outcome paradoxical. Committed to tracking and coding a retrievable proper name, the DCSM engages *The Cantos* as a complex system in maximum lettristic turbulence and effectively corrects the extreme disequilibrium that is *The Cantos*.

We can see how *Words nd Ends from Ez* plays between noise and signal, or more precisely how it promotes noise (understood in Abraham Moles' sense as designating unwanted information) to signal (desired information), blocking a reader's attempts to filter out noise.[3] (Again, this is because the work is for the most part lacking in redundancy.) Mac Low's great achievement is to balance maximum disorder with maximum information in precisely the way Eco describes: "If [the creator] aims at both maximum disorder and maximum information, he will have to sacrifice some of his freedom and introduce a few modules of order into his work, which will help his readers [Eco has 'listeners'] find their way through noise that they will automatically interpret as a signal because they know it has been chosen and, to some extent, organized" (65). As Eco informs, "to measure a quantity of information means nothing more than to measure the levels of order and disorder in the organization of a given message" (49).

Mac Low's radical remodification of *The Cantos* subjects the initial text to just such a double and oppositional profundity—both a dis- and a re-organization. In the terminology of IT, we can say that Mac Low engages *The Cantos* as an initial entropic equiprobability that is filtered via a strategy of reading (the DCSM), thereby creating a selection, therefore an order, and thereby a meaning. Warren Weaver points out that "information relates not so much to what you say, as to what you could say. That is, information is a measure of one's freedom of choice when one selects a message" (quoted in Eco 57). Mac Low selects one of a potential infinity of index names and fixes a single method for reading. This leads us to a claim that the information offered in *WNEFE* focuses on reading methods of potential possibilities and multiple choices. The poem's powerful openness derives from these implications of its methodology; it is a written reading, a radical approach that treats its source text as an entropic system and which exhumes one of an infinity of latent patterns. This leads me to suggest that Jackson Mac Low's great contribution is best situated inside the cultural history of reading and hermeneutics and not in that history of writing that we term "literature."[4]

Let me conclude by returning to the issue of hermeneutic production. To insist on a theoretical practice fixes the poem in its own lacunary silence and material inertia; however, to emphasize that inertia as a sedimentary resistance to absolute knowledge claims precipitates a curious reversal of directions. The poem then becomes the inaugural value of discursive proliferations that, in their totality, constitute the poem's means of self-reproduction. Faced with this chiasmus, the challenge to theory might be to redirect its formations into a critical self-reflection within its own lacunary rupture in an act of appropriative mastery.

# 4

## Transcoherence and Deletion
### The Mesostic Writings of John Cage

*It is a pleasure to witness, so to speak, the action of this hidden principle that forms languages. Sometimes we see it struggling against a difficulty that arrests its path: it seeks a form that is lacking, the materials at its disposal resist.*
—Joseph de Maistre

*A song means filling a jug, and even more so breaking the jug. Breaking it apart. In the language of the Kabbalah we perhaps might call it: Broken Vessels.*
—H. Leivick

I take this short epigraph by H. Leivick that prefaces Harold Bloom's *Kabbalah and Criticism* as my entry into the semiology of John Cage's mesostic (medial-acrostic) writings. My point of reference will be his mesostic treatments (called by Cage the "writing-through" method) of *Finnegans Wake*, a text conceived by Joyce on the wrong side of speech as a subterranean warren of polyglossia, anagrams, portmanteaux, and eponymous theme-words, to which Cage's reductive treatments proffer both homage and a testimonial of descent. Cage's "writing-through" engages an interventional poetics designed to disclose a hidden coherence by eradicating a manifest coherence. In this manner Cage risks both cognitive and formal coherence to advance a variant coherence, which is doubled, sublimated, and paradoxical and what I call a "transcoherence." The central investigation of this chapter pertains to the affinities of Cage's mesostic practice with Saussure's earlier investigations into anagrams, which earned the Swiss linguist his posthumous logophilic reputation. En route I will touch upon a partial genealogy that helps historicize Cage's practice and underscores its complex resonances and affinities.

I feel the meaning that words hide;
they are anagrams, cryptograms,
little boxes, conditioned
to hatch butterflies . . .

H. D. The Walls Do Not Fall, XXXIX

Saussure's research into non-linear textual economies, collected in one hundred and fifteen notebooks between 1906 and 1909, remained unknown until their discovery by Jean Starobinski in the mid-1960s.[1] The research, staggering in its breadth, covers late Roman Saturnian verse, Homer, Virgil, Seneca, Horace, Lucretius, Angelo Politian, and the Vedic Hymns. The search for a latent yet accessible transcoherence was central to the project; the notebooks chronicle an obsessive hunt for a message across a message that is recoverable from the fragments of a theme-name scattered through a text but capable of being reconstituted via a non-linear reading across the textural separation of its parts. Saussure referred to these theme-words variously as "anagrams" and "hypograms" designed to emphasize "a name, a word, making a point of repeating its syllables, and in this way giving it a second, contrived being, added, as it were, to the original word" (Starobinski 18).[2] Saussure later replaced these terms by "paragram," (moving gram), claiming it a more accurate term, thereby altering the topological bias of the text from a surface-depth model to that of a transspatial disseminatory dynamism.[3] Saussure draws attention to a preoccupation in certain Vedic hymns with organizing a text around the syllables of a sacred name (Ms. fr. 3963). The famous *Ṛg-Vêda,* he claims, explicitly declines the sacred name of Agni: agnim, agninâ, agnayê, agnê. Saussure hears the phonemes of a proper name gradually declare themselves transcoherently across a separation brought on by other phonetic elements (Starobinski 15). Yet the centripetal force of paragrams resist containment; they inhabit that position from which language looks at us, a site of elusive and omnipresent alterity; they are what is not seen but nonetheless there, unsettling the coherence of conventional word order by offering an infinity of signifying networks accessed only through nonlinear methods of writing and reading.

In Ms. fr. 3963, Saussure comments: "to write lines incorporating an anagram is necessarily to write lines based on that anagram and dominated by it" (quoted in Starobinski 17). Yet, though assignable to an order of production (either through detection by a reader or deposit by the writer), the paragram does not derive necessarily from a conscious intentionality on the writer's part. Saussure's error at this point lies precisely in not recognizing that paragrams and words-within-words are an inevitable consequence of Western writing's alphabetic, combinatory nature, which ineluctably compromises any monological coherence. By 1908, however, he writes to his friend Leopold Gautier admitting profound perplexity as to the real or phantasmagoric status of the paragram. Through the failure in an obsessive project of venatic reading, Saussure seems to have hit upon finally the vertiginous nature of all textuality, in which the paragram is the transphenomenal aspect that commits writing to unavoidable productional excess. Existing as non-linear threads of flight, paragrams are non-intentional expenditures that pose a constant threat of instability to any coherent textual habitat. Moreover, the logic of the paragram runs counter to Saussure's own notion of the linguistic sign. As Kristeva explains, "in the multivocal totality of the paragrammatic network, the signifier-signifed distinction is diminished and the linguistic sign emerges as a dynamism that proceeds by quantum force" ("Towards a Semiology of Paragrams" 35).

Although Cage's creative interventions in *Finnegans Wake* date back to 1942 (*Empty Words* 133), the mesostic method of "writing-through" did not begin until 1976 when, at Elliott Anderson's instigation, Cage submitted "7 out of 23," the first of his mesostic treatments of Joyce's book, for the planned special issue of *Tri-Quarterly* on *Finnegans Wake* (ibid.). Like the hypograms that Saussure detected, the mesostic method exposes hidden, nonlinear, and translinear relations within a pre-existing work. By both excavating and repeating a theme-name, the mesostic transmutes the source text by way of systematic erasures and repositionings that yield a different text. Cage outlines the rule-constraint governing his method as "first finding a word with *J* that didn't have an *A*, and then a word with *A* that didn't have an *M*, and then an *M* that didn't have an *E*, etc." (*Themes & Variations* 76). Clearly this medial-acrostic structure is governed not by words *per se* but by a finite number of repeated characters coherently organized along a vertical axis with surrounding verbal elements. In this way, "writings-through" reverse the conventional hierarchy in linguistic articulation with lineation determined according to a principle independent of the line. Rather than a letter's placement being governed by a semantic rule (for example, the word *cat* requires the letter *t* to terminate the word), the letter enjoys a strategic control of the construction and distribution of its lexemic neighborhood. Cage's method further mimics the textile model of a constant warp that supplies a fixed system of support for numerous other moving lines, inscribing the shifting domain of "betweens" and "perplications" produced by transits, flights, and selections. Like the late Spanish architect Yago Conde's submission to the competition for the Special Place in Granada, a "guerrilla" conquest exists between and beneath Cage's reading (Conde 254).

Cage himself speaks of a desire "to let words exist" emancipated from the enforced coherence of human intentionality and of his work as an attack on traditional syntax for the explicit purpose of demilitarizing language (*For the Birds* 151). As Cage states, "Syntax, according to Norman [O. Brown] is the arrangement of the army. As we move away from it, we demilitarize language. The demilitarization of language is conducted in many ways: a single language is pulverized; the boundaries between two or more languages are crossed; elements not strictly linguistic (graphic, musical) are introduced; etc." (*M. Writings* x).[4] Brown offers a fitting echo of Hugo Ball's linguistic strategy discussed in chapter 1 and suggests at least one buried continuity from the historical avant-garde to more contemporary work. The attack on coherent syntax is carried out with great force in Cage's writings-through, for the mesostic obeys a skewed, heretical syntactic rule that demands each line appear in a severely vertebral form. Cage abandons flush left, normative linearity in favor of a vertical even "spinal" syntax determined entirely by the formal obligation to disclose a previously imperceptible trans-phenomenon: the decentered and embedded letters that spell out sequentially the name James Joyce. (It is significant that Cage preserves the original page numbers in the left hand margin of the page, thereby introducing the notion of scale and contraction.)

Jumbo

to jAlice

two ways of opening the Mouth i

not stoppEd

water where it Should flow and i know

106      the first book of Jealesies

childsize herOes

howk cotchme eYe

abe to sare stood iCyk

nEuter till brahm taulked him common sex

(Cage *Empty Words* 148)

Such a "verse" form of phrasal lines, generated by a systematic deletion of sections of Joyce's source novel, aptly invokes an architectural analogy. Indeed, Cage's text is the systematically chance-generated ruin of the *Wake*. The canny affinity of this medial acrostic ruin-maker to a central tenet of the eighteenth-century picturesque—namely the purposeful construction of ragged and broken forms—remains unacknowledged among Cage scholars. (For more on the contemporary relevance of the picturesque, see chapter 9.) Designed as a proactive mode of negation, the "writing-through" enters to unsettle and partly destroy the significations it encounters. Compliant to the law of the mesostic and transgressing the different laws of grammar and normative syntax, it is an oxymoronic, if not a paradoxical, construction-destruction, a production realized precisely by a loss. The transcoherent aspect is thus clear: through the destruction of a coherent writing the mesostic paragram constructs a coherent name. This "writing-through" further precipitates the conception of textual cohesion into paradox, for as a systematic method of chance-generation, it produces not only the coherence induced by the mesostic rule, but also a text that—when judged by normative standards of reading and comprehension—is disjunctive and fragmentary at best and utterly incoherent at its extreme. Perhaps the skewed semantics of the quoted passage are worth remarking. Despite the fragmentation and disjunction, the instantly erotic implications of Joyce's own portmanteau method (fusing words in semantic copulation) are not entirely lost in this oddly erotic passage, whose anamorphic narrative becomes insistent via titillating suggestions. Like Alice through a looking-glass, we glimpse a scene of elephantine members ("Jumbo"), oral sex ("two ways of opening the Mouth"), discharge ("water where it Should flow"), and jealousy in which "common sex" replaces common sense.

There are far-reaching ontological implications to this practice, for the mesostic not only organizes and exposes a subterranean, paramorphic signification—heterogeneous to the inhabited grammatical order—but also abolishes all vestige of a locutionary subject behind the text, thereby exposing, via this negative assault, the fundamental alliance between linearity and voice. As such it would seem to be the extreme realization of Eliotian impersonality. However, in its wider ramifications the mesostic establishes the puissance of the invisible or transphenomenal to modify the visible. Likewise, if the poetic line locates, as Kathleen Fraser suggests, "the gesture of [the poet's] longing brought into language," then the paragram marks the emergence of an authorless text, one read into existence (152). In a "writing-through," writing itself loses all monologic ground; an indifferent and impersonal text emerges through systematic chance-generation and its emancipative paragrammatic consequences.

But how does Cage's writing-through *Finnegans Wake* relate to coherent and incontrovertible authorship? In a way it is both correct and incorrect to claim that James Joyce repeatedly embedded his name throughout the pages of *Finnegans Wake*. Joyce never wrote the name "James Joyce" the way it appears in Cage's text; nonetheless Cage's work reveals that name, James Joyce, throughout the *Wake*. Through an interlacing of coherence and incoherence (what I am calling transcoherence), Cage brings to light what is present but unapparent in his source text. In its entirety, the "writing-through" is part of Joyce's book but also the book by Joyce that never was. A fundamental doubleness obtains to this semiology, where every phrasal line functions as the systematic ambience of a single letter and at the same time intertextually engages as an action on another writing constructing in that way "a Whole, which is nonetheless 'two'" (Kristeva "Towards a Semiology of Paragrams" 39).

> *Television kills telephony in brothers' broil.*
> *Our eyes demand their turn. Let them be seen!*
> (Joyce 52)

In so far as Cage's "writing-through" emerges from a reading rather than a locution, Joyce's claim above resonates throughout Cage's mesostic practice; it further bears testimony to Zukofsky's urge in *Bottom on Shakespeare* to trust "the clear physical eye over the erring brain" (167) as well as endorses Heraclitus's claim in his 101a fragment that the eyes are more exact witnesses than the ears. Despite its nomenclature, the "writing-through" is less a contribution to the history of writing than to the cultural and political history of reading—questioning, by implication, the very grounds of coherence upon which interpretive and expository practice rests. Cage abdicates the authorial role to become witness to a text's reorganization and partial-deletion under the mesostic regimen of a system of chance. In this way Cage carnivalizes hermeneutics, repudiating the conventional reasons why we read.[5] A logophilic pursuit and transcription of certain letters replaces normative reading, arriving that way at an incoherently-coherent text. In this teleological transformation of its function, the reader no longer seeks a destination in some interpretative or thematic terminal but instead engages in an optical tracking of the polylogical alterations of a constantly shifting textuality. Like Saussure, Cage reads to liberate those surface and single-letter aspects of a text that pass unnoticed during a conventional reading.

> to "see again,"
> the verb is "see," not "walk on"
> i.e. it coheres all right
>     even if my notes do not cohere.
> Ezra Pound, Canto CXVI:186–87

Cage inherits an optical bias in Western thought that is traceable from Isidore of Seville (c. 560–636) through early insular scribal practice to Joyce himself, whose acrostic interlacements thread *Finnegans Wake* together in both emulation of and homage to the Celtic carpet pages of the Book of Durrow and the Book of Kells. Isidore contested the dominant Aristotelian-Augustinian tenet regarding the status and function of written letters, claiming letters are less the signs *of* sounds than signs *without* sounds. For the early monastic Irish, Latin was an irreducibly *written* phenomenon encountered exclusively with the eye and not the ear. Enjoying a visual autonomy free from conversion into the acoustic realm, language functioned within what Malcolm Parkes terms a "grammar of legibility."[6] There is a further precedent for Cage's method in the *mille quattro cento* shift in sensory bias from the acoustic to the visual, from the phone to the gram recommended by Alberti in his *Della pictura* (1435) and later reaffirmed by Pico della Mirandola. Catherine Ing traces the impact on Tudor lyricists of Thomas More's translation of Mirandola's *Liber de imaginatione* (1501) and the more general influence of Alberti's treatise—both works fix the archetype of sense experience in the visual, implicatively endorsing the primacy of sight over hearing and legitimating such subaltern forms as the anagram, acrostic, the palindrome, and the irreducibly graphic in general (Ing 26–28).

Endorsing this genealogy (wittingly or unwittingly) Cage encourages a severe rethinking of the textual page as a plexus of non-linear subsets. Although the "writing-through" is a fastidious method of detection that logocratic interpretive criteria would judge pointless, heterological, and passive, it nonetheless marks a highly consequential intervention into the sociology of reading, for this shift from interpretive reading to character detection, from negotiating syntagms to pursuing letters, offers, as in Mac Low, an exemplary mode of production capable of inducing "other producers to produce [and putting] an improved apparatus at their disposal," one that turns consumers into producers and readers into collaborators (Benjamin *Reflections* 233).

In an age of incipient miniaturization, it is apt to return to the rumble beneath the word. There is a stubborn, even tautological literalness about that material element we call the letter, one that rubs against Agamben's insistence that language is always "a dead letter" (108). Cage demonstrates how language is frequently a struggle to contain a living letter-chain. When Cage and Brown famously likened grammar to the military line, they pointed to the same carceral effects of the word on the letter that were emphasized early in the twentieth century by the Russian Futurist Velimir Khlebnikov: "You have seen the letters in their words—lined up in a row, humiliated, with cropped hair, and all equally colorless, gray—these are not letters, these are brands!" (63). Tellingly, it is from the spirit of Khlebnikov's observation, not his own critique of grammar, that Cage's "writings-through" find their motivation—if not legislation—as paragrammatic embeds of letters whose non-linear displacements thread and cantilever the source text like so many magnetic nodes or strange attractors.

Because it pursues the letter-chain and not the word, the mesostic "writing-through" is, in principle, a compositional method open to anyone and everybody, requiring no special skills beyond a zero degree of character recognition. It is the democratic gesture in the "writings through" that links mesostic composition to both Lautréamont's poetics of the populace and Brecht's dramaturgical theories. Moreover, the mesostic can be comprehended as a textual application of the architectural principles of Reyner Banham's 1960s "Other Architecture" in which "inhabitants define their own environments by a fluid and playful selection of objects, services, and technologies" (Sadler 38). Banham's architectural position grafts Cage's practice onto the consumerist-inspired thinking of the 1960s, an application presaged in 1934 by Benjamin's call (noted above) for a productive art-consumerism. The urge to restructure reading along an axis of democratically-accessible productivity emerges at the same time as a surge in consumerism and the definition of the latter along the contours of productive choice. This is, of course, the logic governing both the sociology and the architectural space of the supermarket: that second icon (after the automobile) of the immediate post-war age.

Although Saussure and Cage alike pursue a hypogrammatic agenda, hunting non-linear assemblages hidden within and across the line, they differ in their key proclivities. Unlike Cage, Saussure's intention is not to generate a written-reading but to remain entirely within the reader function. Moreover, in the texts Saussure examines, each poet—although obliged to redeploy the phonic elements of the theme-word—is nevertheless free to develop the surrounding text as he wishes. In contrast, the "writing-through" is predominantly a practice of deletion, not expansion, and whereas Saussure traces the repeated chains of syllables and sounds, Cage vigilantly pursues a catena of alphabetic letters. For Gerald Bruns, this micropoetics of the letter inflects an ethical dimension into poetic practice. "Certainly, a crucial link between poetry and ethics lies in allowing words, or particles of words (the sounds of parts of words, and with them the world of things, not to say of others), to live their own lives; it means listening, not tuning things out but letting them take us along" (220). But are "listening" and "sound" really in evidence in the mesostic? Ironically, while Cage the *musi-*

*cian* opts for pursuing the graphic provocation of the silent letter, Saussure the *linguist* traces the acoustic itineraries of paragrams.[7]

The medial acrostic appears to be one variant realization of Cage's famous, if not original, admission: "I have nothing to say and I am saying it and that is poetry." (The sentiment is already present in Paul Valéry's comments on some lines of Baudelaire: "These words work on us [or at least some of us] without telling us very much. They tell us, perhaps, that they have nothing to tell us" [917].) Recall that Cage's texts are transcribed readings or trackings, not compositions *ex nihilo,* and that the mesostic-paragram principle opens up to unlimited combinability a dynamic force applicable to an infinity of nominal, verbal, or phrasal sets, any one of which could function as the organizational axis. (Cage could just as well have read through *Ulysses* for the theme-names of James Joyce, Stephen Dedalus, Molly Bloom, or Harold Bloom for that matter.)

Like Saussure, Cage unwittingly specifies a general condition of finite recombinant writing systems that ensures a text will always be able to offer a transcoherent network of paragrammatic fecundity, whose excess of virtual information will partly impale and partly elude its reader. Because of the omnipresence of paragrams, a text always offers itself not only as a tangible system of semic relations but also as an infinite recombinant potential, thereby attesting to a certain autonomy in language. Cage ultimately demonstrates how infinity can be systemized; in this respect the paragram bears comparison to Cage's ontological disproof of silence in *4'33"*. Much as the latter demonstrates that sound cannot be eliminated, that sound persists as the supplement to silence, so the transcoherence of the paragram reveals how meaning ultimately cannot be foreclosed.

*There is no invention without a commensurate dose of instability.*
—Brian Massumi (85)

The theories of non-equilibrium thermodynamics offered by Ilya Prigogine and Isabelle Stengers dwell at the bifurcation of chemistry and ontology, where a metaphysics of being converts into a physics of becoming.[8] Their research tabulates the vexatious problem of where to place chaos and coherence in the passage of becoming. Is chaos the birth or the breakdown of order? Prigogine's most famous postulate—that the path of self-organizing systems leads from chaos to order (from incoherence to coherence)—might be taken as an overly deterministic and ultimately conservative tenet. My interest here is less in testing the truth of Prigogine's claim than in applying his concept of the dissipative structure as a conceptual tool for approaching Cage's "writings-through" as partly self-organizing structures. Most pertinent is Prigogine's contention that complex stable systems carry within them unstable subsystems that pressure the dominant system into disequilibrium. At a maximal point, the system bifurcates into either a higher complex organization or into chaos. Such bifurcation points (transported and renamed "schizzes" in Deleuze and Guattari's thinking) describe the mesostic method as a dissipative agency. Reading is the outside that seeps into a book-machine's closed system, disturbing its entropic content with negentropic elements: interpretation, analysis, or, in Cage's case, mesostically determined constraint. The result is a new equilibrium created by dissipation. The paragrammatic disposition and mesostic chain introduce a series of bifurcation points and dissipations into the maximum disequilibrium that is the source text. The remnant text provides a higher complex organization as a new state of equilibrium, while the mesostic chain itself functions as the new order within an otherwise chaotic system.

*the possible is one of the provinces of truth*
—Baudelaire (605)

To say that Cage's "writings-through" present an active poetic of the infinite transcribed within the actual is a bold claim to make, so let me conclude by supporting this assertion via a further connection to a contemporary of Saussure's. Edmund Husserl's seminal rethinking of the image as a relation is his great contribution to the philosophical discourse on imagination. Neither a thing nor a percept, an image is an intentional act of consciousness directed to an object beyond consciousness itself. For Husserl, the imagination's central potency is to liberate things from their grounds as facts and grant them an ideal status. Richard Kearney explains this phenomenological intentional act of imagination: "Husserl believes that [the process of imagination] allows us to see beyond the actual mode of existence of a thing to variations of its other possible modes of being.... [T]he phenomenologist refashions the given data of an object ... by freely varying it in his imagination. He or she allows the data to move continuously from the actual appearance of the table to its 'real possibilities'" (24). Husserlian imagination works toward suspending the actual existence of a thing, detaching it from the empirical by subjecting it to free variation in an infinite set of open, ideal possibilities. In a key passage in *Ideas,* Husserl links this infinite free variation to a fictive *poesis:* "[I]t is naturally important to make rich use of fiction for the free transformation of data . . . and we can draw extraordinary profit from what art and particularly poetry have to offer in this regard" (quoted in Kearney 26). In his elaboration however, Husserl makes no mention of the paragram. Yet, despite its counter-eidetic nature—it is, after all, an empirically accessible phenomenon—the paragram's disposition is remarkably akin to the functioning of Husserl's phenomenological imagination. Reading is a modality of consciousness established as an intentional program; it is a reading *of* a text. By opening up alternative contents that transcend the actual material significations, paragrammatic free variation suspends the natural attitude in reading. Like the description of phenomenology as an a priori science that Husserl offers in the second of his *Cartesian Meditations* (1929), paragrammatic readings like Mac Low's DCSM procedures and Cage's "writings-through" operate within the "realms of pure possibility" (28).

By rethinking the paragram not as a latency in general textuality but as a possibility within a strategy of reading that seeks a different coherence than the one normative reading engages, a new historical alignment can be proposed in which Derridean free-play, Husserlian free variation, and Saussurean hypogrammatism reach a confluence on the road to an emergent non-symbolic poetics of the infinite in the actual, a poetics of reading that remains implicit in Cage's mesostic compositions.

Michel Pierssens offers the optimistic view that "[a]s a practice and as a theory, paragrammatism is the dream of a knowledge and of a freedom, of a liberation of the letter through an adherence to its network and journeys: promise of a thrill, certainty of 'glory' for the castaways of the alphabet" (xii). Kristeva, for her part, fixes this adventure of the letter in a grander philosophic theme. Paragrammatic writing, she insists, "is a continuous reflection, a written contestation of the code, of the law and of itself, a way (a complete trajectory) that is zero (which denies itself); it is the contestatory philosophical enterprise become language" ("Towards a Semiology of Paragrams" 40). Yet, insofar as the mesostic is governed by the law of the paragram and its transphenomenal complications, Cage's method (through Pierssens' buoyant promise) "reveals the infinity of meaning, which desire will henceforth pursue" (111). As Saussure did before him, Cage escorts us to the dark side of language that reveals its tunnels of Babel. Transcoherently humans read in this space on an abyssal edge of vertigo and delirium. Here, where reading and desire meet writing, madness erupts in the impossible encounter of infinity by finitude. This remarks at once the temporal law of transcoherent writing and the ontological circumscription placed on the writer. It is the writerly space of Bataille's *impossible.* Coherence requires boundaries, but transcoherence cuts across those boundaries to open up what it simultaneously represses: the unrestricted access to inexhaustible significa-tion. Mallarmé avoided the brink of this madness by retreating into the science of the sign. Saussure, however, stared it in the face: "When a paragram appears, it seems a ray of light. Then, when we see that we can add a second and a third, rather than experience relief from our doubts, we begin to lose that absolute con-fidence we had in the first: because then we begin to wonder whether we could not definitively find all possible words in each text" (quoted in Pierssens 111). We have yet to think through this Saussurean sublime; it remains a mystery whether Cage's nomophilia led him to its experience.

But what would these secular critical claims have meant to Cage? There is a Buddhist belief in *Sarva-dham-sunyatà* relevant to his practice; the phrase trans-lates as "the vanity of all signs." Perhaps the paragram's economy ultimately cor-roborates the truth of that tenet, returning us to the poverty and finitude of the human inside the infinity of language. And if the issue, finally, is not to make the paragram some minimum poetic aspiration but to emphasize its omnipres-ence as a virtual, disruptive, and transcoherent force in the written, then Italo Calvino best articulates this call of the moving gram to human endeavor: "Only the ability to be read by a given individual proves that which is written shares in the power of writing, a power based on something that goes beyond the indi-vidual. The universe will express itself as long as somebody will be able to say, 'I read, therefore it writes'" (139).

# A Chapter of Accidents

## Disfiguration and the Marbled Page in Laurence Sterne's
## *The Life and Opinions of Tristram Shandy, Gentleman*

> [O]thers on the contrary, tucked up to their very chins, with whips across
> their mouths, scouring and scampering it away like so many party-colouring
> devils astride a mortgage.
> —Laurence Sterne, *The Life and Opinions of Tristram Shandy, Gentleman*

> *ut magis legere libeat in marmoribus quam in codicibus*
> —St. Bernard

This chapter digresses from contemporary matters in order to delineate the odd
trajectory of a single wordless leaf in Laurence Sterne's *The Life and Opinions
of Tristram Shandy, Gentleman;* I conduct this exploration according to Jarry's
'pataphysical rule of the anomaly, which governs *exceptions* and is the subject
of chapter 10.[1] At the same time this chapter exemplifies the accidental felicities
that obtain in that minor species of miscognition Dick Higgins and I named
"creative misunderstanding." The textual-scholarly battles as to precisely what
constitutes a paratext (those various aspects within the cover of a book that
frame the text proper) form the broad background for this odd configuration.
Jerome McGann, a scholar adamantly committed to socializing the study of literary texts, stresses the need to focus on those material aspects previously dis
regarded as peripheral or irrelevant. Among these, he cites "typefaces, bindings,
book prices, page format" (McGann 13). Unlike Genette's investigations into the
paratextual in his book *Seuils,* McGann addresses the non-linguistic elements
enclosing or juxtaposing texts-as-such and, while acknowledging the usefulness of Genette's itemized set of paratexts (prefaces, dedications, notebooks, ad-
vertisements, footnotes, etc.), additionally insists that by restricting itself to the
linguistic aspects of a format Genette's methodology problematically ignores

those extra-linguistic phenomena McGann himself considers crucial to textual understanding. As McGann states, "[t]he text/paratext distinction as formulated in *Seuils* will not, by Genette's own admission, explore such matters as ink, typeface, paper, and various other phenomena which are crucial to the understanding of textuality. They fall outside his concerns because such textual features are not linguistic" (13).

Rather than extending the debate between two distinguished textual scholars, let me ask how and when does the non-linguistic periphery become linguistic and by that interrogation turn to *Tristram Shandy*. In the middle of volume III of the first edition, Sterne abruptly defamiliarizes the reading experience by simultaneously interrupting both the narrative flow and the book's bibliographical conventions with a decorative marbled leaf. The leaf is marbled on both recto and verso but with two distinctly different patterns of marbling; it is hand-inserted into the normal collation as a sequential leaf that contains page 169 on the recto and 170 on the verso. How are we to interpret this? Karen Schiff offers a convincing figurative reading of the leaf's significance. "In the context of the narrative," she observes, "it is obvious that this image represents Walter Shandy's ejaculation, a subject that also starts off the novel in volume I. The colors of the original marbled page can all be found in the body, and white and yellow pigments are splattered in the top layer. And Sterne would prefer a reading practice that mimics the unpredictability of sexual experience" (9).[2] I will return to Schiff's claim later; suffice it to say at this point that in an unprecedented gesture within the history of the novel, Sterne deterritorializes a decorative endpaper, endowing it with both metaphoric significance and mimic power. In this manner McGann's non-linguistic periphery suddenly becomes a contraventionally repositioned paratextual element essential to the narrative of the most heterological and anomalous of eighteenth-century novels.

It might be useful to look at the historical rise of marbling. Marbled paper's characteristic polychrome random patterns are obtained through a process of floating different colored inks and dyes on a gelatinous substance that is then scattered into random chromatic patterns. (In more recent developments the ink and dyes are stroked with a comb.) After the liquid is marbled in a container, the blank sheet of paper is dipped into it. Imported into Europe from Turkey in the seventeenth century, the practice became widespread by the middle of the eighteenth century; its mass-production soon influenced the style of textiles, furnishings, and wallpapers as well as endpapers. It was soon applied to the leather covers of books to create a marbled effect upon the leather (known as "bark," "marbled," or "tree" calf). The fact that marbling, though a process of

mass-production, produced popular, unique artifacts with an accidental, aleatoric, one-of-a-kind design is of crucial cultural importance; whereas the history of printing develops through moveable type to the stereotypic reproduction of identical texts, marbling registers as a radical interruption by stochastic
singularity. Certainly, the marbled page in Sterne's novel inflects "a forcework"
(to adopt a term of Krzysztof Ziarek's) into the narrative sequence; it is a *poeitic*
rather than poetic unsettling of the accepted modality of the readerly-narrative
relation. Yet how do readers engage a marbled page or panel?

Long before the age of Sterne, the optical lure of marble and its seductive
power to lead readers away from textuality drew significant early comment. In
a letter to William St. Thierry, Saint Bernard notes "it is more diverting to read
in the marble than in the texts before you" *(ut magis legere libeat in marmoribus
quam in codicibus)* (quoted in Camille 1992, 62). For his part, the Abbé Suger
delighted in the fact that "[on] all sides there appears so rich and so amazing a
variety of forms that it is more delightful *to read the marbles* than the manuscripts" (quoted in Didi-Huberman fn. 143, 244). In Barbara Stafford's somewhat
fanciful interpretation, the phenomenon of marbling was symptomatic of a sen-
sual opposition to neoclassical dictates of order and proportion and aided in ex-
ternalizing the hidden, irrational forces within the Enlightenment (200). Indeed,
in a move that supports Schiff's erotic reading of the page, Stafford boldly links
the counter-aesthetics of marbling to the "liquid psyche" (204) of the libertine:
"To stray, rove, ramble was a symbol of revolt because it inevitably led one from
the straight road of collective duty, or right line of direction, into secret com-
partments where mistake, blunder, and sin reigned" (201). Theoretically speaking, the paratextual impact of marbled endpapers would vary according to the
content and nature of individual texts. Along the criterion of Stafford's interpretation, a first edition of de Sade's *Philosophy in the Bedroom,* for example, with
its call to libertine deviance and singularity, would find its content symbolically
evoked by marbled endpaper. However my copy of the 1784 edition of Dr. Johnson's *Dictionary,* sporting both its original marbled endpapers and marbled calf
boards, offers itself as a fundamentally ironic artifact precisely through its paratextual implications, for in this case the marbling, in its idiosyncrasy and mutation, undermines Johnson's heroic attempt to counter the analogous "marbling"
of lexical change in a living language by the fixity of definition. Johnson supplements his own definition of marbling—"To variegate, or vein like marble"—
with a quotation from Robert Boyle: "Very well sleeked *marble* paper did not
cast any of its distinct colours upon the wall with an equal diffusion."[3] This sup-
plementation, with its haunting transposition of that static marbled page into

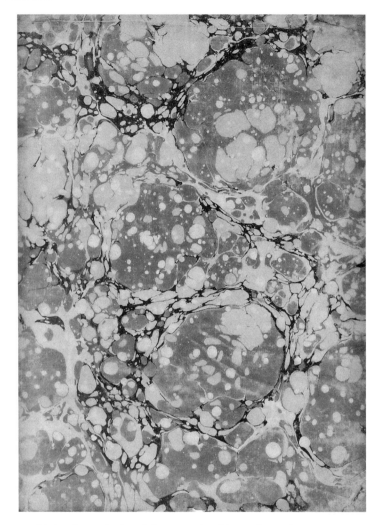

Fig. 1. Marbled endpaper (reduced) from Joseph Addison *The Works*. Printed by J. Basker-ville for J. and R. Tonson, Birmingham, 1761. The original is in polychrome (Source: the collection of Steve McCaffery and Karen Mac Cormack).

the mural fluctuations of *cinema lumière*, certainly undermines Johnson's near-tautologous definition, but imagine the social consequence of depositing a piece of marbled paper à la Sterne in the place of the definition.

At this point I will return to Schiff to substantiate and at the same time de-velop her sexual interpretation of the marbled page. An excursus into the Quattro-cento extends the semiosis of marble beyond the parameters established by both

Schiff and Stafford. In his remarkable study of dissemblance and figuration in the paintings of Fra Angelico and his contemporaries, Georges Didi-Huberman examines the persistent phenomenon of *marmi finti,* or painted marble, in Quattrocento paintings.[4] His study develops from a surprising observation made in the corridor of the Convent of San Marco in Florence of painted "blotches" that seemingly defy all subject and figural categorizations. The author describes his book "as a microhistory. . . into the way the mystery of the Incarnation has given form and originality to the Christian world of images" (4). The Incarnation is a perplexing mystery at the heart of Christian meditation, a mystery of the spirit as Aquinas pointed out attainable only by passing through and beyond the corporeal (*Compendium theologiae* 201). Dissemblance, dissimulation, or the visual conversion of a figure constitute the basic tenets of a long theological traditional (traceable to Dionysius the Areopagite) for the figuration of the divine. Marble and its representation, long before its simulation on paper, constituted a key element in the dogma and exegesis of that penetration of the sensible by the intelligible known as the Incarnation. As well as the central mystery of Christianity, incarnation is also the basic event precipitating the strange itinerary of Sterne's plot: of a life told (announced) from the moment of conception, not birth. Indeed, the entire formula of *Tristram Shandy* is suspended in the ontological paradox of an incarnation, in a narrative staging of presence before representation, of a life before birth, announced via an explosive counter-narrative moment in the text that connects to both a medieval semiotics of marbling and a heretical genealogy of semen (a spermal theme, I might add, that reoccurs in chapter 6).[5]

Exegesis suggests a series of directions, associations, and digressions away from a central narrative—in other words it marbles a text. While offering something that approximates a parodic reversal of such exegesis, Sterne nonetheless preserves its major dynamic as a removal of intellectual concentration through paratextual digressions away from the central *historia* of the novel. By incorporating a marbled leaf into the body of the text Sterne adopts a mode of fictive representation heavily saturated with a theological code; to a medieval reader, the marbled surface would be received as anything but a decorative, paratextual displacement. A veritable poetics of exegesis developed in the Middle Ages devoted to following "the path of the uncanniness of form—figures that are not valued for what they represent, but for what they show visually, beyond their aspect, as indexes of mystery" (Didi-Huberman 7). With this in mind, we move closer to Walter Shandy's ejaculation as a dissembled figuration in a marbled page.

Didi-Huberman builds a compelling argument for the centrality of fictive marble in a visual poetics and dogma of the Incarnation, linking it to the "patch" or "blotch" of paint mentioned earlier and often found in Fra Angelico's work. The "patch," a term Didi-Huberman takes from Proust, designates the "way of naming those zones, those moments in the painting where the invisible vacillates and spills into the visual. It is a way of naming the 'cursed part' of paintings, the indexical, nondescriptive, and dissemblant part" (Didi-Huberman 9). In a similar manner Sterne's marbled "patch" registers as a moment of paratextual implosion when both the peripheral and external move into the textual field of the narrative; the patch thereby becomes "the pictorial place for a contemplation that no longer [needs] visible objects to occur, but only visual and coloured interiority"(ibid. 9–10). A further affinity suggests itself: in Fra Angelico's "Holy Conversation," subtitled "Madonna of the Shadows," there is a physical separation of the historical from the patchwork. Beneath a narrative space that occupies the painting's upper compartment are four smaller panels of *marmi finti* that seem to form a decorative yet incongruous exergue. Like endpapers, indexes, endnotes, or afterwards, they are fixed physically outside of the work's figural regimen. Although most commentators overlook the panels, Didi-Huberman connects them to a tradition of "blotchist" painting that imitates the abstract, variegated, accidental lines in Italian marble, and links the formlessness of that stone to episodes in the life of the Virgin Mary: her marriage, celestial coronation, the massacre of the innocents, and the Annunciation (33). Examining a corpus of such paintings, Didi-Huberman remarks upon the singularity of the formal setting of this pictorial marble in terms that describe precisely the movement of the marbled page in Sterne's narrative, inserted into and interrupting the narrative thread in a critical position: "These multicolored zones, odd in their formless audacity, generally participate in the *locus* or ground—but they have the peculiarity of being in some way *projected* forward in the painting, often in the central part, into the foreground. They thus exist *between the background and the foreground*. They are like a 'ground' set right in front of us as if moving forward" (33–34).

In effect, painted or fictive marble comprises a meta-materiality that deploys one material (paint) to create a representation of a different, formless, material (marble). Going beyond this iconic function, the *marmi finti* are designed to convert the viewer's gaze and introduce through the negation of orthodox figuration the mystery of precisely that which cannot be figured within a figure. It is on this paradoxical basis that Didi-Huberman terms these representations of marble "patches of negative theology" (56); in other words a chromatic apophasis irrupts. It is precisely in this manner that Sterne's marbled leaf both supplements and overturns the common notion of textual representation and marks a negative narrative moment in narratology itself and, being neither narrative, decoration, nor illustration proper, registers a perplexity inside its own ontic status. It is the coincidence of an accomplished, albeit negative, figuration of the highest of Christian mysteries with "the most humble affirmation of the material means the painter has at his disposal: his colored vestiges" that is remarkable in the paradox of Fra Angelico (Didi-Huberman 56). Indeed it is the culminating paradox of the completion of mimesis in its very repudiation that makes this patch practice a triumph in dialectical dissemblance: the double valorization of the mystery beyond meaning and representation, and the pure visuality of material disfiguration.

The identification of stone as the figure of Christ was a persistent theme throughout the Middle Ages. In his *Summa de exemplis et similitudinibus rerum,* and with a fecund demonstration of what Saint Jerome calls *tropologia libera,* Giovanni di San Gimignano devoted forty chapters to the significance of stones.[6] All stones are figures of divine love; marble is a figure for beauty, goodness, and prudence; Mary is chalcedony and her virginity asterite, and Christ is chrysolite. Analyzing Fra Angelico's Prado "Annunciation," Didi-Huberman draws attention to the dialectic placement of color to create an astonishing effect:

> [I]n the entire central zone, the place occupied by the angel, the marble is composed of blue and yellow nuances, two colors we can call *heavenly,* inasmuch as they are the colors also used in the star-studded ceiling and, at left, in the "real" sky Angelico painted, an ultramarine sky traversed by a great ray of yellow light. But strangely—significantly—the "heavenly" marble is nuanced on the right, just below the Virgin, with hematite, incarnate, the same color that forms the Virgin's bosom and robe nearby, and the incarnate of her cheek. It is as if, at this moment, the marble itself *was being incarnated,* just as the Virgin in the red mantle is being covered with a heavenly, ultramarine cloak. There is something like a double movement, an encounter—the covering of the flesh with heavenly glory: a movement in the image of the very movement of divine Incarnation. (69)

The significance of the relative disfiguration and amorphousness that constitutes the *marmi finti* in paintings of the Annunciation becomes apparent. Painted marble functions as a seminal figure in its most literal sense: a figure of insemination, its colored formlessness containing a dynamic of virtual form.[7] Substituting the Greek word *seme* here for Logos not only establishes a connection between the divine Incarnation and Tristram's more common, maculate version, but also folds the locutionary into the sexual, thus folding word into seed.[8]

In a magisterial fusion of geology and Genesis, Albertus Magnus offers a theory of the formation of stones that parallels the birth of Adam and further enriches the reading of Sterne's marbled page. Stones originate, he avers, "in a divine virtue of the place *(loca generant lapides)* such that, beginning with the material mixing of water and earth, the clay comes to dry, to 'agglutinate,' and that is how it becomes a stone" (quoted in Didi-Huberman 74). Recalling the actual production process of marbling paper, we realize that it too involves agglutination, an insemination of liquids into liquid in a receptacle. Both medieval exegesis and Sterne's radical intervention into the common rules of narrative reach confluence in this complex moment of marble. The evidence, of course, is not available to determine whether Sterne's radical *détourne* was intentional, a creative misunderstanding, or an accidental coincidence, and because of this I'll decline the cul-de-sac of speculation. The evidence is sufficient, however, to stake the claim that via this striking parallelism of conception, annunciation, and marble, Sterne's novel "accidentally" opens up the broad theme of the mystery of the Incarnation and folds historical evidence into a contemporary reading of Sterne's novel sufficient to both enrich and complicate the registration. By inserting a polychrome marbled leaf, Sterne not only represents the formless figuration of Walter Shandy's *jouissance* but also inflects the Pseudo-Dionysian representation of the Incarnation as *marmi finti*, as an amorphous annunciation without speech, thereby evoking through both a negative mimesis and an alien semiosis that ontic space in which stochastics collide with abstraction.[9]

This paradoxical space awaits rediscovery in our own *ricorso* to the great tsunamis of modernity: the drip paintings of Jackson Pollock, the shotgun art of Niki de Sainte-Phalle, the poured paintings of William Anastasi, and, perhaps most of all, to one of modernity's lesser-known works. For the marbled route back through Mr. Shandy's bedroom to Fra Angelico's holy space takes us via a faulty landscape to those liquids love is made of. Duchamp's small private piece of 1946, *Paysage fautif* (Faulty Landscape), is an abstract work that bears a remarkable resemblance to *marmi finti*. Indeed, it too, like Sterne's page, is of direct pertinence to the history of incarnational disfiguration. Measuring eight-and-a-quarter by six-and-a-half inches, the piece comprises Duchamp's own seminal ejaculation onto a patch of Astralon backed with satin. In a 1953 interview with the Janis family, Duchamp speaks of a parallel rendition in the figuration of *The Large Glass*: "'The splashing of liquid,' for example, could be readily compared to 'semen … etc.,' he confessed, 'liquids, you know, that love is made of'" (quoted in Francis Naumann 50). Duchamp's seminal piece not only inaugurates the numerous neo-Dadaist sperm works of the 1960s but also completes a medieval tradition of disfiguration, where the work is completed by destroying it, thus returning the figure to the actual thing.

Mina Loy's short poem "Brancusi's Bird" brings Didi Huberman's theory of disfiguration to a complete inversion. In this famous poem, Loy extols the paired down curvature of Brancusi's sculpture as the quintessence of Cubist, Futurist, and Vorticist aesthetics; its signification as bare essence is built over several lines. The poem ends with the following passage that fittingly mimics this chapter's historical wandering:

> This gong
> of polished hyperaesthesia
> shrills with brass
> as the aggressive light
> strikes
> its significance
> The immaculate conception
> of the inaudible bird
> occurs
> in gorgeous reticence (19)

In effect Loy inverts the entire choreography of the Incarnation. Here the sound of a brass gong replaces the transmission of Logos while at the same time the inseminating Holy Paraclete itself receives the insemination in the same "gorgeous reticence" as does the Virgin in Fra Angelico's paintings.[10]

## Postscript

Karen Schiff cogently argues that Sterne's larger design in *Tristram Shandy* involves nothing less than a new and deliberately unsystematic method of reading. I include here a transcript of one original and erroneous paragraph from an earlier draft of this chapter. The error arose when I consulted my copy of a tenth edition of *Tristram Shandy* (6 volumes, 1775) and not the first. In the copy

I checked, the marbled leaf is accidentally inserted in the wrong volume. I add here verbatim the original passage before its alteration in the light of reading Schiff's article:

> In Chapter VII of the novel, Sterne suddenly defamiliarizes the reading experience by simultaneously interrupting both the narrative flow and the book's bibliographical normativity with a decorative marbled page. The leaf is marbled on both recto and verso but with two distinctly different patterns of marbling and is inserted between the sequential, integral leaves containing pages 22 and 23 respectively; its own pagination—21 recto–22 verso—repeats the pagination of the earlier leaf. How are we to interpret this? The random patterns of the marbling offer an apt metaphor *sans mots* to describe the irregular and errant mind of Uncle Toby (the novel's central character).

Through a 'pataphysical felicity, this erroneous reading occasioned by the accidental placement of the marbled leaf is not entirely incorrect; indeed the plausibility of my reading can be supported by ancillary material. Saussure, for instance, forcibly enunciates the formlessness of primary mentation that begs comparison to marble: "Psychologically our thought—apart from its expression in words—is only a shapeless and indistinct mass. . . . Without language, thought is a vague, unchartered nebula" (111–12). Lyotard similarly elaborates upon the protean, atmospheric nature of thinking: "Thoughts are not the fruits of the earth. They are not registered by areas, except out of human commodity. Thoughts are clouds. The periphery of thoughts is as immeasurable as the fractal lines of Benoit Mandelbrot. . . . Thoughts never stop changing their location one with the other. When you feel like you have penetrated far into their intimacy in analyzing either their so-called structure of genealogy or even post-structure, it is actually too late or too soon" (5). Indeed, my accident in plausible, though incorrect, interpretation stands as a minor example of the type of creative misunderstanding of which the greatest must surely be that brought to my attention by Gregory Ulmer and which first appeared in my book *North of Intention*. In August 1610 Galileo sent Kepler a short note containing the cryptogram:

SMAISMRMILMEPOETALEUMIBUNENUGTTAURIAS

Ulmer outlines the uncanny misunderstanding by which a false decoding arrives by accident at a staggering truth:

Recognizing it as an anagram Kepler translated it into five Latin words—
*'salvue umbistineum germinatum martia proles'* (Greetings, burning twins
descendents of Mars)—which he understood to mean that Galileo had
observed that Mars has two moons. Galileo, however, actually meant the
message to read, *'altissimum planetam tergiminum observavi'* (I have dis-
covered that the highest of the planets [Saturn] has two moons). The interest in the paragrammatic mistranslation is that the sense intended is
referentially wrong (with his primitive telescope Galileo mistook the rings
of Saturn for moons), while the interpreted sense is referentially correct.
Mars does have two moons, although they were not observed until 1877.
(151–52)

From sperm to paper to stone and unformed thinking back to sperm as art, from
Fra Angelico through Sterne to Duchamp, Loy and Kepler: that is a Shandean
sprogue to be sure.

# 6

## From Muse to Mousepad
### Informatics and the Avant-Garde

*Technology has put art to the rout.*
—David Lehman

The institutional origin of the avant-garde is well known; its formative impetus being none other than Napoleon III who in 1863 set up the *Salon des Refusées* as a deliberate countermove to the jury tampering of the then director-general of the Imperial Museums of Paris. The *Salon* exhibited Manet's new painting *Déjeuner sur l'herbe* to a scandalized audience, Impressionism was born, and with it the European avant-garde. But Western poetry's origin occurs much earlier in a quasi-theological scenario of purloined voice. In his *Theogony* the shepherd-poet Hesiod finds himself possessed by capricious female vocalities. The Muses address him: "'Shepherds dwelling in the fields, base cowards, mere bellies; we know how to say many false things that resemble real things; and we know also, whenever we are willing, how to say true things.' Thus spoke the daughters of great Zeus, they whose words are exactly fitted, and they gave me a scepter, a wondrous branch of luxuriant laurel, having plucked it; and they breathed into me divine song so that I may celebrate the things that will be and the things that have been" (quoted in Calame 208). Hesiod's etiological myth of his own poetics of empowerment differs markedly from the prevalent *doxa* that links poetic voice to subjectivity. In its archaic formulation, poetry is not strictly human and accordingly disturbs any attempt to identify voice with human subjectivity. The poet is dispossessed by a whimsical power that disturbs not only vocal integrity but also the certainty of truth. (This origin is also profoundly ironic when we bear in mind that the meaning of *Hesiod* translates literally as "who utters voice.")

The majority of contemporary mainstream poetry has lost touch with this ancient (and persistent) radical asymmetry that constitutes poetic voice. But does the twenty-first century usher in at least an analogous return, a reconnection to a primal duplicity between human agency and a prosthetic technology similar to that connecting Hesiod to the Muses? Jed Rasula's erudite examination of the voice-over in current mass media and technologies suggests an affirmative answer to this question, and this chapter addresses two proclivities—avant-garde if you like—that corroborate Rasula's claim.[1]

In the closing section of "East Coker," Eliot advanced a crisis in poetics that still pertains to all post-millennial agendas. In the midway of his life, situated between two wars in a struggle to use words to forge new beginnings, but each of which is destined to be different kinds of failure, Eliot reflects on the pathos of a temporal irony: at the moment the poet has finally taken control of his words she can only express an obsolete content. The consequence is a debilitating itinerary. That crisis, a personal one of spirit in Eliot but also synecdochal of his generation, is being answered today by a paradigm shift from a primogenitary deployment of words to a creative/uncreative redeployment of existing information. "Post Language," "Flarf," and "Uncreative Writing" commonly name the ongoing struggle for a twenty-first-century vanguard poetics that rather than confront the institution of art embraces (or critically engages) the age of informatics. Both Flarf and the uncreative writing of Kenneth Goldsmith openly celebrate a poetics reactive to data overload. As Craig Dworkin accurately asserts, "the recycling impulse behind much conceptual writing suits a literary ecology of alarming over-production" (*Against Expression* xlii-xliii). If one formulates "informatics" as the "informational sublime," then both Flarf's and Goldsmith's practices emerge as two local poetics of resistance to the data-times-speed equation of informatics. Understood as the quantum manifestation and velocity of information and its access, informatics is the direct outcome of technological supercession that allows the vast transportation of information in virtual space; it is a hyperspatial archive whose growth and accessibility is currently uncontrolled. Into this info-context enters the poetics of Flarf (also known as "Google-sculpting" and "search-engine collage"). The gods of Hesiod fled when the Internet was born; "home" is now the interface, which has become a control booth and reception point for hyperspatial and disembodied acoustic, semantic, and visual sensibilia. (We will note anticipations of this new home in chapter 8's discussion of the Situationist strategy of the *dérive* and the spontaneous aspirations of New Babylon.) As projective verse and proprioception developed against the backdrop of cybernetics and quantum theory, so Flarf figures against (or better within) the ambience and interfacial abundance of informatics. There is a common thread between these two poetics: the search and inscription of information; yet the data is reconfigured, albeit within two different fields: info-textual in the case of Flarf and proprioceptive physiotextual in Olson's case. As a corollary to the above scission, there is a broad shift from seriality to interaction. (Seriality itself was a response to the modernist embrace of fugue structures in poetry: the initial plan of Pound's *The Cantos,* Bunting's *Briggflats,* and Zukofsky's scheme for *A* alike.)

Flarf was born as a joke, a light-hearted and occasional counter-aesthetic sortie onto the Internet when poet Gary Sullivan, in a neo-Dadaist flourish, entered "Mm-hmm," a deliberately bad poem, in a poetry contest sponsored by Poetry.com.

> Yeah, mm-hmm, it's true
> big birds make
> big doo! I got fire inside
> my "huppa"-chimp(TM)
> gonna be agreessive, greasy aw yeah god
> wanna DOOT! DOOT!
> Pfffffffffffffffffffffft! hey!
> oooh yeah baby gonna shake & bake then take
> AWWWWWL your monee, honee (tee hee)
> uggah duggah buggah biggah buggah muggah
> hey! hey! you stoopid Mick! get
> off the paddy field and git
> me some chocolate Quik
> put a Q-tip in it and stir it up sick
> pocka-mocka-chocka-locka-DING DONG
> fuck! shit! piss! oh it's so sad that
> syndrome what's it called tourette's
> make me HAI-EE! shout out loud
> Cuz I love thee. Thank you God, for listening![2]

Sullivan offers his own multiple definitions of Flarf in a manner and style evocative and perhaps parodic of Breton's definition of surrealism in the 1924 "Manifesto of Surrealism."

> Flarf: A quality of intentional or unintentional "flarfiness." A kind of corrosive, cute, or cloying, awfulness. Wrong. Un-P.C. Out of control. "Not okay."

Flarf (2): The work of a community of poets dedicated to exploration of "flarfiness." Heavy usage of Google search results in the creation of poems, plays, etc., though not exclusively Google-based. Community in the sense that one example leads to another's reply—is, in some part, contingent upon community interaction of this sort. Poems created, revised, changed by others, incorporated, plagiarized, etc., in semi-public.

Flarf (3) (verb): To bring out the inherent awfulness, etc., of some pre-existing text.

Flarfy: To be wrong, awkward, stumbling, semi-coherent, fucked-up, un-P.C. To take unexpected turns; to be jarring. Doing what one is "not supposed to do." [quoted in Hoy]

We can supplement this with a description of the "movement's" aesthetics offered by Flarfist Michael McGee in the online Flarf Files: "deliberate shapelessness of content, form, spelling, and thought in general, with liberal borrowing from internet chat-room drivel and spam scripts, often with the intention of achieving a studied blend of the offensive, the sentimental, and the infantile." If Hesiod presents a veritable poetic of hijacking, Flarf offers one of imperial dictate, thoroughly bad taste, and interception. The primary poetic method of choice is to enter egregious search topics into that new "shabby" equipment of informatics—the search engine—to generate odd data for subsequent cutting and grafting. Additionally Flarf harvests from other profanely invoked Internet detritus such as spam scripts. It's a moot point whether this method marks a quantum development of modernist collage technique; yet, in spirit at least, it effectively catabolizes, if not directly inverts, Wallace Stevens' famous assertion in "Adagia" that "[t]he poet makes silk dresses out of worms" (157). Under the governing paradigms of desecration, negativity, bad taste, *détournement*, and parasitism, it's now Web worms that the poet drops into boutique Microsoft silk dresses.

It should be pointed out that Flarf is less egregious than typical of many contemporary Anglophone trends in poetry. Canadian poet Rob Read's *O Spam, Poams* recycles junk e-mails into poetic entities, like the following taken from his poem "> Subject: hello:"

soberanis resureccion
suhoski hidden schlotzhauer

neel campney tokarz klinger
Easterbrook nern pharr
marichalar schoeninger
rumly florens
better milner (36)

The lineage of Kurt Schwitters' *merz* constructions and collages comes readily
to mind, as does Russian Futurist zaum, but oh how distant is Read's work from
Ball's inner alchemy of the word. (Read subsequently expanded this work into a
free service, sending out spam poems to all people who request them.) Another
example is the British poet-fictioneer Joseph Walton, who is making his own
madcap excursions into Internet vocabularies to harvest rap epics and Flarf-
like poems. True, no doubt, to the spirit of Pessoa, Walton also writes under a
plethora of pseudonyms including Jow Lindsay, Francis Crot, Helen Bridwell,
Marianne Munk, Kyle Storm Beste-Chetwynde, and Karen Eliot. His Sad Press
is an online conceptual project in itself, hilarious in its faux facts and fake ex-
istences. Here is one stanza from his poem "Praxis Bogarter" written as Karen
Eliot:

yeh & the cards
rammed water voters
past the hearts of treex taught
the formation of shadows
cast in the backs of chavs
who w/ breath melted w/ enchanted
worms & chests melted w/ earth . in ropes
melted w/ poured roots & glue . enchained is
in glass castles like classroom wall pasta gases,
so.[3]

A good example of Flarf is Michael McGee's *My Angie Dickinson,* the title of
which alludes, of course, to Susan Howe's *My Emily Dickinson.* By playing off the
felicitous conjuncture of surnames—one a contemporary actress and film star,
the other a canonic figure of nineteenth-century American poetry—McGee attempts to update the putative shock-value of Dickinson's poetry on her own contemporary readers. McGee's originality, I believe, lies in his intertextual method
of composition; by keying into a Google search the name "Angie Dickinson" as
well as incorporating words and syntactic fragments from Emily Dickinson's

own poems, McGee is able to generate by "intuitive searches" and subsequent "fine stitching together" poems like the following:

> Violet virgin mary voodoo
> mother is Isis—and there—
> eerie Precision
> of the eyes—Violet!—
> elegant avian "neck"—
> the well-machined
> two daughters of Gun-
> toting, bank robbing, Siamese twins—
> such Matchless entertainment
> in a "wife-beater"—shirt—(21)

Preserving Emily Dickinson's idiosyncratic use of dashes and emotive indicators ("Violet!"), McGee produces a poem of smooth illogicality. In its general tenor and style, his "Violet Virgin," like Sullivan's "MM-hmm," would not be out of place in the *Dada Almanach*. However, its dialogic aspiration and intertextual effects (nothing less than an updating of Emily Dickinson from the pious reader domain to the wild pranks of cyberpoetry) lends a singularity to the venture, and the text successfully demonstrates Flarf's subversive as well as ludic potential.

   Dan Hoy is surely correct in judging Flarf to be indicative of a "retro-Futurist proclivity relying on the virtual realm as a method of navigating reality." Rather than Marinetti's "words in freedom" Flarf embraces the "data for grabs" ethos and the attendant potential to generate surprising constellations; Flarf is the intuitive samplings of a plunderpoetics, a delirious cornucopia of poetic potency made possible by Google's search engine. The result is a recycling of the feces of the world data bank and the sewage spam of our neo-liberal, digital "McWorld Culture."[4] To Flarfists like Tony Tost and Kasey Silem Mohammad the Internet offers a vast dissipative structure susceptible to facture by feeding, with Flarfists operating as tactical remoras attached to the body of a great info-Leviathan afloat in hyperspace. Flarf's ludic potential is obvious, but it tarnishes its contemporaneity when it invokes not only Futurism's uncompromising alliance with the new technology, but also the Dadaist's anarchic anti-aesthetic embrace of chance throw-away, word assemblies, and Duchamp's aesthetic of indifference. The shock value of its political incorrectness and the desired repulsion that Flarf seeks in both image and juxtaposition makes little or no significant advance on the tactile violation of textual data evident in Burroughs' cut-up method, which is itself an echo of the "reading-across" methods used by eighteenth-century-avatar Caleb Whitfoord first proposed and demonstrated in *The New Foundling Hospital for Wit*.[5] Moreover, Flarf poems—composed by means of a harsh juxtapositional technique and the surprising phrasal constellations created by this technique, and delivered by the Internet equivalent of Hesiodic inspiration—bear a striking formal similarity to the disjunctive texts of non-Flarfist Bruce Andrews and other contemporary Language poets. That said, the Flarf method highlights the general volatility of Web-housed data when available to imaginative, maverick *détournement* and effectively underwrites one common paradox of informatics and technology: that its functional design remains incommensurate to its applications and uses.

One is left wondering, however, whether search-engine collage is in tacit collusion with the late-capitalist infrastructure of information technology and registers more as a symptom than a critique of informatics. Neither the poems nor the poetics of Flarf reflect the rise of informatics as an American reaction to Sputnik's surveillance capabilities and the Cold War ethos in general. Flarf, as previously mentioned, emerged exclusively within a socio-economic and ahistoric aesthetic discourse as a communal attempt to write deliberately bad poems and, not surprisingly, apologists for Flarf assume a decidedly apolitical position. Mohammad claims its desiderata to be "a blend of the offensive, the sentimental and the infantile" urging Flarf to be "as shameless as television" (quoted in Hoy). Gary Sullivan describes its language as drawing on "the naïve, the sentimental, the 'fucked-up,' the unschooled, the ignorant, the misogynist, the right-wing, homophobic, racist, fundamentalist Christian" (194). With such omnivorous selection, it's difficult to see how Flarf's criteria can be readily assimilated into any notion of a critical avant-garde. Eschewing the politicized aesthetics of *détournement*, Flarf settles for an unquestioning dependency on, and uncritical acceptance of, "corporate tools and algorithms" (Hoy's terms) to actualize poems that seek a complacent positioning within a decidedly counter-literary discourse and whose aspiration is not only to a "cloying awfulness" but also to the identical non-viscerality evident on television and more insidiously in video-action games. It's a moot point as to whether the utilization of corporate data engines as neutral writerly prostheses demonstrates a false consciousness around the politico-economic foundations of search engines. Certainly Utopian-Flarfists such as Tony Tost abnegate any possible critical stance as this vatic passage woefully attests: "the act of Google-sculpting is not only a unique process [. . .] that is unique to the new medium, but: the act of Google-sculpting will likely become well known at least in the poetry world, and then will become a possible map or model for the writing process in general, and will therefore cause unforeseen changes in the writing process/ poetic psyche/ imagination etc." (quoted in Hoy).

In their collaborative work *Apostrophe*, Bill Kennedy and Darren Wershler-Henry offer a more interesting deployment of techno-informatics, a work available in conventional book format and also in an online Web version. The text is the outcome of a genuine cyborg cooperation utilizing Kennedy's specially designed software (the Apostrophe Engine), which is capable of infiltrating the Google search engine to retrieve online clauses beginning with the words "You are." The potential scale of the project is worth comment, for all online writers are capable of inadvertently contributing to the poem. Additionally, in a democratic gesture, Wershler-Henry and Kennedy have made the software freely available for download and use. The authors explain the workings of this software upon the poem's expanding online version:

> When a reader/writer clicks on a line of the digital version of the poem, it is submitted to a search engine, which returns a list of phrases. The apostrophe engine then spawns virtual robots that work their way through the list, scraping the pages for phrases beginning with "you are" and ending in a period. The robots stop after collecting a set number of phrases or working through a limited number of pages, whichever happens first. The apostrophe engine records and spruces up the phrases that the robots have collected, stripping away most HTML tags and other anomalies, then compiles the results and presents them as a new poem, with the original line as its title . . . and each new line as another hyperlink. At any given time the online version of the poem is potentially as large as the Web itself. (288)

*Apostrophe* marks a clear advance on Flarf belonging to that genealogy of programmed autopoetic mechanisms that began in 1983 with William Chamberlain and Thomas Etter's RACTER program (short for *raconteur*) and its first text, *The Policeman's Beard is half constructed*. It is also composed in that spirit of human-mechanic alliance that Donna Haraway sees as a positive inflexion of the technological substratum of informatics: the liberating potential of the cyborg as a new post-human bardic synthesis of human, machine, and data. The ontological implications brought up by *Apostrophe* are complex. Barthes' prophetic scriptor who moves freely through a plethora of textual regurgitations remains human if not authorial, but for the most part *Apostrophe* is produced out of the miasma of data by the virtual robotic. The end product, however, salvages a profoundly human and contemporary content. Through its 289 pages, *Apostrophe's* robot interceptions and recyclings constantly refract a sexual, socioeconomic world embedded in, yet recoverable from, the neutral permissiveness of Web data:

> you are dead a philosophical meditation my fourth brief conversation with the 2 mg regimen of Klonopin clonazepam prescribed me by my GP Iran/Iran so far away or, A Flock of Seegullibles . you are not feeling all that great but, . you are a pre-sentient mass of cells, this country will protect you and your rights to the nth degree . your are frying on Quality X . you are planning on spamming, don't bother . you are excited . you are asking—you know this window opened up where, for the first time, really in 40 years or so, the country was paying attention to the moral issue of what we should do about people who live in poverty . you are busy . you are a black chef, don't you say to the troops "Hey, you know what, you knuckleheads? If a tape comes up of one of you beating the dogshit out of the black guy, Im going to be kind of pissed" . you are right about that . (132–33)

*Light dies before the uncreating word.*
—Alexander Pope, *The Dunciad*

Kenneth Goldsmith's self-styled conceptual and uncreative writing maintains a more problematic relationship to informatics—rather than redirecting data to creative ends by means of virtual robots (Kennedy's revamped muses), Goldsmith adopts the techno-mechanic persona of a word processor, a cyborg identity radically different from Stellarc's, behind which he produces a writing *ex utile*. (Goldsmith undoubtedly would have been readily accommodated in Pope's satire.) His sustained project bears comparison to the earlier age of cybernetics of which Goldsmith inflects the sepulchral side; indeed, his work can be readily admitted into Adorno's category of "pseudo-activity." Where Olson's investigations into proprioception lead him to an interest in the sub-ontological transmission of data via tissue, glands, and organs, Goldsmith explores the hyperspatial and material management of information switching. Craig Dworkin explains Goldsmith's conceptual writing as a "writing in which the idea cannot be separated from the writing itself in which the instance of writing is inextricably intertwined with [ . . . ] the material practice of *écriture*." In other words, while intransigently non-utilitarian, Goldsmith's conceptual works do not involve a dematerialization of the art object; quite the opposite, they all inhere as material organizations in space, the worked-through consequence of the idea, the material realization of the concept. This introduces a perversely Kantian inflexion, for if Lyotard is correct in claiming masochism to be the propelling force of the Kantian sublime, derived from a conflict between the "conceptual" and the "presentational" (77), then Goldsmith's conceptual endeavors represent a resurgence of the logic of Kantian "reflective" taste—that capacity of a "conception" to be "realized" in a satisfying or corresponding manner.[6] Goldsmith has called himself "a collector of language"[7] with the self-proclaimed commitment to be utterly uncreative by the age of 40.[8] So far his accomplishments increasingly confirm this goal of his. Goldsmith's trajectory is becoming clear: from conceptual projects haunting the margins of literature to current ones that purportedly evacuate entirely any morsel of the literary. The earlier projects, such works as *Fidget* and *No. 111 2.7.93–10.20.96,* have an undeniable aesthetic attraction akin to some works of Oulipo. Indeed, *No. 111* can incorporate in its entirety a short story by D. H. Lawrence ("The Rocking Horse Winner") precisely because that story obeys Goldsmith's constraint of phonemic termination, ending as it does with the sound *er* in "winner."

Arguably *Fidget* marks the culmination of the New York School and its cross-cultural syntheses. Updating John Gay's *Trivia, or the Art of Walking the Streets of London,* Goldsmith's itinerary perversely celebrates a single locale: Manhattan present in its referential absence, an imploded metropolis of body parts and movements. The work attempts to document Goldsmith's every movement for thirteen hours. Recorded on Bloomsday (June 16) 1997 on a small tape recorder and later transcribed and edited, it itemizes a choreography of physical movements with their proprioceptive consequences as well as one instance of auto-eroticism (Goldsmith masturbates), thereby offering a paratactic continuum of minimal physical movements. Fundamentally an oral text documenting the passage of actions into words and words into book, *Fidget* stands as the polar opposite of surrealist automatic writing, recovering a single body's dissipative motions in brief sentences whose cumulative effect Marjorie Perloff likens, in her afterward, to the claustrophobic prose of the later Beckett (90).[9] Here is a short sample:

> Body turns one hundred eighty degrees. Pushes on top.
> Thumbs press. Fingers push. Press. Body shakes. Thumb
> pushes. Mouth opens. Lips lick. Hands lift. Plunge. Emerge.
> Immerse. Elbow out. (*Fidget* 47)

In addition to reading *Fidget* against the ghostly backdrop of *Ulysses* and Beckett, we need to read it against the background of a relatively unknown, unpublished non-literary endeavor: the obsessively detailed diary of the Rev. Robert Shields of Dayton, Ohio. Shields died in October 2007 at the age of 89, leaving behind him a personal diary of his final 25 years that methodically chronicles his life in five-minute segments of hilarious bathos. The diary comprises thirty-seven million words written on paper and currently occupies ninety-one boxes. Shields described his work as "uninhibited" and "spontaneous." Here are four typical entries:

> Aug. 13: 8.40 A.M. I filled the humidifier basin mounted over the Futura baseboard heater.
> 8.45 A.M. I shaved twice with the Gillette Sensor blade (and) shaved my neck behind both ears, and crossways of my cheeks too.
> July 25, 1993. 7.00 A.M. I cleaned out the tub and scraped my feet with my fingernails to remove layers of dead skin.
> 7.05 A.M. Passed a large, firm stool, and a pint of urine. Used 5 sheets of paper.[10]

So why is Shield's diary less worthy of critical engagement as conceptual writing than *Fidget*? Significantly Shield's diary is structured around the constant iteration of the first person pronoun. (In this respect it is closer to the spirit of O'Hara's personism than to *Fidget*.) It is precisely because Goldsmith's book avoids such an egological axis that it illuminates the ontological (or 'pataphysical) paradox that an obsessive preoccupation with the details of a "self" actually leads to that self's disappearance. Ruben Gallo perceptively notes that the protagonist of *Fidget* never gets dressed and remains a nude "hero" throughout the impersonal recitation of his own body parts and ephemeral motions (50–51). However, by eschewing the first-person pronoun and by collapsing the listed bodily motions onto the temporally sequential plane of language, with a claustrophobic specificity, Goldsmith effectively renders *Fidget* both a naked text and a profoundly decentered one. Where Proust succeeds magnificently in eliminating a narrative subject, replacing it with the flows and collisions of objects and sensations (a truly counter-Kantian achievement), Goldsmith offers a subject completely atomized. An impression emerges from the catalog of plural and separate movements of a morcellated corpse, a parade of body parts that Derek Beaulieu likens to a crime scene (Beaulieu 61).

As a document of traces, a record of past movements, *Fidget* is not without its ambiguities. The incessant minimal recording, together with the absence of any pronoun to indicate a site of human utterance, not only suggest, like *Apostrophe*, a ghost-like presence, but render many passages susceptible to cleaving between the constative and the imperative forms. "Grasp. Reach. Grab. Hold. Pull. Hold. Grab. Push. Itch. Push" (62) is a passage that could be taken as a score for some Fluxus performance.

But need we read *Fidget* as a collapse in lyric centeredness, a contortion of autobiography, or as an exercise in auto-analysis as Gallo does? Read as an epic text of tracking and self-surveillance, *Fidget* inflects a more sinister theme (persuasively outlined by both Foucault and Anthony Giddens), namely the implosion of an ideological state apparatus onto the level of a mundane, non-rhetorical, anti-lyrical self. To my mind, however, *Fidget's* greatest triumph in negativity lies in its inability to complete itself; its ultimate "achievement" then is to end up as a compromise formation, as demonstrated by the fact that boredom from the project instigated an unbearable ennui in the writer himself. The curious subtext of Goldsmith's narrative can be constructed from the numerous paratexts and related interviews and articles that discursively frame (and contaminate by elucidation) all his projects. The anecdote of him buying a bottle of Jack Daniel's bourbon to ease the monotony of his *Fidget* project is now near legendary. Progressively intoxicated, Goldsmith starts to slur his speech, blurring words to such a degree that they become impossible to transcribe in the sober surroundings of his Manhattan scriptorium. He decides to end the book at hour 22:00 by retranscribing the opening chapter backwards:

> etarapes regniferof dna bmuht thgiR. flac thgir sehctarcs dnah thgiR .ydob dniheb tsiF (84).

In a veritable boustrophedonic flourish, Jack Daniel's emerges as the successful hacker into Goldsmith's project of self-surveillance; rather than the tape recorder it is booze, that never-failing prosthetic antidote to ennui, which finally and deliciously subverts the project.

## Profound Boredom or: *The New York Times* in an Age of Mechanical Transcription

*The habit of newsprint . . . are the limits of literacy.*
— Charles Olson

I will address Goldsmith's *Day* as a gesture toward a limit text at the threshold of the ideology of poetics. The rhetoric of the interrogations embedded in his project articulate a ricochet of eschatologies: the end of Language writing, the demise of poetry, the exhaustion of literature, and the separation of concept from creativity. *Day* quite literally offers itself as a document of thantopraxis, a death writing installed among a constellation of negative categories: not-now, unoriginal, uncreative, "a poetry of living death" (Riding Jackson), non-nutritional. Goldsmith has been keen to distinguish his practice from the potential literature of Oulipo, seeing in their work an end product of "blandly conservative [. . .] fiction" (Bök "Unacknowledged Legislation" 189). His more recent work additionally throws the category *literature* into contingency. Whereas *Fidget* stages the tedious and meticulous accumulation of data, *Day* presents a radical instance of information management. Replacing *techne* with mechanics, the mammoth project of *Day* implicates a poetic of the "uncanny replica" while at the same time throwing down the gauntlet to the potential literature of procedural constraint. It does this by taking on two of the most difficult constraints of all: to be "uncreative" and "unengaging."

A conceptual document of truly Sumo proportions, *Day* occupies the entirety of an 866-page large octavo book and records a single act: the transcription of all the words and numbers found in the *New York Times* edition for Friday, September 1, 2000; it can be succinctly summarized, as Joshua Schuster suggests, as "one long quote" (103). *Day* also falls under the law of the reprint, which is typically a mundane occurrence; in this case it becomes an egregious event. Thought otherwise, *Day* is dictation spectacularly disembodied and confined within the choreography of drudgery. And if Nancy is correct to speak of poetry as "the praxis of the eternal return of the same," then *Day* catabolizes such a praxis, debasing it in its very institution (5). Accurately reflecting the current status of labor in advanced (and now reducing) economic zones of the global scene, *Day* enacts the activity of laborious transcription as information portage, thereby implementing a "poetic" of forwarding, quantitative reiterations, and data replication. The work offers itself as the very emblem of a pure transference offered minimally (in its magnitude) without distraction or controversion; in so doing Goldsmith proffers a profoundly secularized *anamnesis* as well as an elitism available to everyone. The project conveniently fits into modernism's embrace of the quotidian and mundane, be it Duchamp's urinal or Williams' red wheelbarrow. There is something reminiscent also of Rilke's *Dinggedichte* ("thing poems") and Spicer's dream of facturing poems out of real objects. However, *Day*'s mythopoetic mentor is of course the uncreative repetition of Echo, the nymph in love with Narcissus. Paradoxically purged of the poetic that it never had, *Day* instantly evokes Cage's enigmatic definition of poetry recorded in his *Lecture on Nothing*: "I have nothing to say and I am saying it and that is poetry." It also ranks as an egregious instance of Pound's quip that poetry is the "news that stays news," it also stands as a laborious refutation of the adage that today's news wraps tomorrow's fish and chips. Goldsmith believes *Day* to be unreadable owing to the boredom largely induced by the shift in format. As McLuhan long ago pointed out newspapers offer a mosaic, cubist format of modular detachable sections and page continuation cues that not only allow for, but actually promote, skimming. A reader moves perhaps from the front-page banner headlines to the Sports and Weather sections, carefully avoiding the mountains of statistics in the stock market reports, casually perusing photographs and ads along the way. The supreme paradox of *Day* is to preserve the unit of the book by shattering the ephemeral performativity of the newspaper. In a subtle sense, *Day* exposes the nakedness of its initial concept; yet at the same time, by actualizing the concept (making it "real" by not making it "new"), Goldsmith exacerbates the info-commodity he is apparently attacking, thereby contributing to commodity culture a quizzical, because familiar, instance: a book born from a newspaper, destined to be marketed and sold for $20 (a price far larger than a newspaper) to a readership disinclined from the outset to read it. The "reader" is, of course, a function assumed by the singularity of the one who is reading—but who will read *Day*? Admitted, there is a tangibly rhythmic quality in places— the incessant deluge of statistics in the stock market reports for instance and the repetition of prices in the columns of ads, as well as the occasional, hilarious juxtaposition—but such aesthetic morsels are few and far between. For the most part, any attempt to read the work involves entering that condition the character "I" feels on his surprising return to life in Edward Dorn's great epic of the *Gunslinger*: it's like "trying to read a newspaper/from nothing but the ink poured into your eyes" (159). *Day* is a practically useless text; it offers none of the instantaneous information of the newspaper and thrusts any aesthetically concerned "conceptual" reader into judging without criteria—a veritable Lyotardian "paganism."[11]

As well as shifting its information, *Day* raises the newspaper from its status as a categorized object to the level of an "uncreation" and splendidly so, regurgitating the *New York Times* as a trace inscription and a supplement that is radically removed from the category of instant news and thereby from the categories of value and workability. Where *Fidget* offers a nude protagonist, *Day* offers a text stripped of all the familiar multimedia features of the newspaper's voco-visual arrangement; it presents a raw, naked format of unmitigating uniformity without the relief of typographic variation. In Goldsmith's denuded non-creativity, it is only the concept that is clothed in the spurious "ornament" of its own realization. As a propaedeutic to boredom and as a glaring example of uncreative, nutritionless writing, *Day's* obvious value lies in its effective social exposé of human habit and expectation, for it demonstrates that we *don't* read a newspaper—rather we read *in* it.[12] But does it offer anything more than a belated defamilarization, an alienation effect carried out upon the category of the quotidian? If literature "is the act of writing that specifically addresses those who should not read," as Rancière avers, then *Day* is a curious literature of reversal offering to a literate constituency an unreadable tome (Rancière 15).[13]

Goldsmith's concern in *Day* is not with aesthetic defamiliarization but with obdurate exemplarity, as demonstrated by carrying out a totally useless labor, with the attendant consequence of transcribing an immense and theoretically unreadable tome whose value is admitted triumphantly to be zero. In fact, to actually read *Day* seems beside the point (as Goldsmith himself admits). And if "thing" is that which is not open to interpretation, as Pessoa claims, then Goldsmith's *Day* is certainly not a thing. Indeed, in its unreadablity, the work proposes itself for cognitive encounter *at a distance.* In other words *Day* should be taken in much the same light as Duchamp's readymades, as provocations to a line of interrogative thinking such as: What precisely is it? Why produce this in the first place? What happens to the information in its recontextualization? Why is reading *Day* a different experience from reading The *New York Times*? The questions raised by *Day* cannot be answered on an aesthetic level (there is no operative, recuperative aesthetic but rather an anaesthetic—the boredom factor). Rather the answers are to be sought on the social and factually tangible level. This ineluctable trajectory to speculation on the reader's part has interesting consequences. If Celan and Jabès envisioned the exile and orphaning of poetry, Goldsmith solicits its absolute death. His projects carry a universal admonition of *poesis* and literature in general. In Goldsmith's "poetic," the writer is precisely the one who doesn't write (if writing is to be considered an original inscription). As such it argues against Mallarmé's magisterial formulation of dance as "a poem set free of any scribe's apparatus" (109). Uncreative writing is profoundly gravitational, stultifying any dance of the intellect at the same time it repositions the creative principle *inside* the concept. (In this sense Goldsmith's paratexts—his many printed comments and interviews—are best considered as "leaks" from an uncreative core into exegesis that sully the purity of his projects.)

In the current *nomos* of art, with its governing anarchic, nominalist aesthetics in which "art" is anything that is called "art," Goldsmith's uncreative project is a testament to probity. Goldsmith can never be charged with fraudulence precisely because Goldsmith never claims *Day* to be original literature. His abnegation of any recognizable aesthetic situates him in the shadow of a catena of august precedents starting with Rimbaud's own rejection of poetry as a poetic act and repeated by Breton, Eluard, and Laura Riding Jackson. Goldsmith also seems to respond to Nietzsche's call for an artistic Socrates (the philosopher who claimed his wisdom was based on the fact that he knew nothing). This epistemological paradox surely situates in Goldsmith's posture of conceptual, mindless transcriptionism, or put more bluntly, *Day* seems to offer the quintessential antidote to poets and poetry alike. The implications of *Day,* however, do not escape the Platonic postulate of the *nature* of poetry. Poems do not transmit discursive thought *(dianoia)* but actually petition it. As Badiou puts it, "The poem is . . . . an offering, a lawless proposition" (Badiou 17). By contrast *dianoia* is the act of intellectual vection towards concatenation, that is to say a move to an intelligible matheme.[14] Moreover if *Day* (over and beyond Goldsmith's intention) actually insinuates a poetry without poetry, then it situates within a felicitous parallel to Derrida's own mature (later) thematizing of a messianic religion without religion.

*Day*'s method instantly evokes comparison to that of the fictional Pierre Menard's "rewriting" of Cervantes' *Don Quixote.* There is, however, a critically contingent difference. Whereas Borges' character unwittingly and paradoxically writes an identical text that is a different text precisely because the historical context of the writing is different, Goldsmith transcribes his source text within a commonly shared historical ethos. It is similarly tempting to compare *Day* with Duchamp's readymades, but anything beyond a superficial comparison will elicit three significant differences. First, Goldsmith, unlike Duchamp, adds the category "work" to "art," thus combining the appropriative act of the readymade with the drudgery of transcription. Secondly, whereas Duchamp chooses his *tout faits* from the commodity world of hardware stores, plumbing shops, and restaurant suppliers, Goldsmith chooses mediated data: less the readymade than the already read. Thirdly, while Duchamp deracinates his readymade, radically recontextualizing its manifestation, he never strips it of its use-value; its instrumentality is nascently retained. (It's possible, of course, to read *Day,* but the act of reading would not yield the news *per se* as would the source text on its day of publication; in other words its use value as instant and relevant information is temporally denied.) If Goldsmith introduces the category of labor back into the avant-garde work of art, it is a paradoxical maneuver within a conceptual project. Indeed, Goldsmith in part pulls off an effective atavism, resuscitating the humble activity of the medieval scribe in the cause of the archive and in so doing foregrounds an ambivalent history of volatile origins in reappearance.[15] This mobilization of the past for avant-garde ends in the age of informatics is itself an echo of Khlebnikov's own Orphic glance to the past, his discovery, in Jan van der Eng's words, "of forgotten but never completely lost archive resources of construing, which leads to unexpected significations of the language structure."[16] But this Orphic dimension asserts itself in a different manner, in a way phrased most eloquently by Blanchot: "How can I recover it, how can I turn around and look at what exists *before,* if all my power consists of making it into what exists *after?*" (327). The fundamental difference between Goldsmith's transcriptions and Duchamp's recontextualization lies in this predicament at the heart of Orphic recuperation.

## Unoriginal originality

Cocteau poses a paradoxical predicament crucial to Goldsmith's uncreative writing: "An original artist *cannot* copy. So he only has to copy to be original" (32). To the features of uncreative writing, boredom, and zero nutrition should be added that of unoriginality, for there are antecedents to almost everything Goldsmith has produced so far. *Fidget's* ghostly, intertextual dependence on Joyce's *Ulysses* is transparently obvious. Goldsmith's work was composed on Bloomsday, both texts record one man's movement through a city on the identical day, and both contain masturbatory episodes. *Fidget's* method also finds a precedent in Andy Warhol's own uncreative practice in his novel *a: A Novel,* a verbatim transcription of the group conversations and comments from a tape-recorded evening. *Soliloquy,* Goldsmith's 2001 transcription of every word he spoke over the course of a week, begs comparison with David Antin's shorter and more cognitively appealing "talk poems." As a vast copying, *Day* calls to mind not only Duchamp's readymades, Warhol's appropriative art and a legacy of canonic fictional copyists (Borges' Pierre Menard, Melville's Bartelby, and Flaubert's Bouvard and Pecuchet) but also Barthes' *scriptor* reduced to a servile absurdity. Goldsmith, of course, extols his own *intentional* unoriginality and admits to numerous precedents (especially the work of Andy Warhol). I wish to present some of the unacknowledged precedents in certain modernist texts and earlier precedents. The poetics of eavesdropping (Goldsmith's chosen method in *No. 111*) can be traced back through Marianne Moore to Apollinaire's café poems such as "Les Fenêtres" and "Lundi rue Christine," both of which originated in snatches of overheard conversation. Goldsmith's canny *détournement* of marketing strategies and paradigms into the discourse of literature derives from Marinetti's packaging of Italian Futurism, which stood in stark contrast to Kahnweiler's high art shuffling of Braque and Picasso. Goldsmith's 2005 work *Weather* (a transcription of an entire year's one–minute hourly weather bulletins from the New York radio stations 1010 WINS) has its august precursor in the concluding section of Tobias Smollett's 1778 *Travels Through France and Italy,* which fastidiously offers a daily register of the weather in Nice over a year.[17] But Goldsmith's precedents do not end there. His attempt to facture an unnamable object is in the same spirit as Joyce's *Finnegans Wake,* his proud claim to be "a collector of language" conjures up the great antecedent specter of Walter Benjamin, and even Hegel noted art's intimate connection to uncreativity.[18] Goldsmith's works, it would appear, are literature's "write-overs," and "eavesdroppings," the contorted echoes of former texts.

That said, Goldsmith's work is as successful in its own way as that of Duchamp, effectively constructing an institutional oxymoron by which a vast project of uncreativity is generating a plethora of critical and nutritional exegeses (including the bulk of this chapter). A text conceived as a self-regulating system is one that would draw in external sustenance at the same time as it expels elements of itself. This is an ecological and thermodynamic way of phrasing the relationship of *Day*'s material obduracy to the critical attention it is attracting. Goldsmith's oeuvre establishes an effective double bind: to write about it is to write about nothing of worth, a writing degree zero in which the relation between physical expenditure and aesthetic merit is fundamentally undermined. Like Duchamp, Goldsmith situates the issue of art outside the formal aspects of the artwork itself; it's in this sense that he can be called a "conceptual" writer. Also like Duchamp, the ethical inflection of the work is oriented to the reader as a call for *responsible* reception. (Goldsmith himself maintains that "conceptual writing is more interested in a *thinkership* rather than a readership" ["A Week of Blogs" 138]). It proves unproductive to evaluate Goldsmith's work in a strictly literary dimension, precisely because Goldsmith's conceptualized "labor" has more pertinence in the production and discourse of twentieth and twenty-first-century art. Critical engagement must focus not *on* but *around* his work. Does Goldsmith sense this as a limitation on his oeuvre, that its ultimate fate is to be tied down by a "useful" and normative critical discourse of legitimation? If he does, perhaps his crowning project will be to sabotage this paradox by an act of unsurpassable, uncreative disappearance, a project so successful that it will attract no critical attention, thus passing by the institution of the avant-garde completely and generating a posthumous tomb to the unknown creator.

So where does Goldsmith's originality lie? In an e-mail exchange with A. S. Bessa (published as the prefatory material to his book *6799*), Goldsmith makes clear his material ambivalence toward the book as an inherited, traditional, and ideological format now situated in an age of alternative linguistic transportation, both actual and virtual. Indeed, perhaps Goldsmith's truly vanguard contribution to the ongoing discourse of the avant-garde is his Ubuweb project, for the ideology of this project can be traced to a paradigm switch in pluralistic practice from formal innovation on the level of the object to innovation in distribution. (Like Kennedy's and Wershler-Henry's *Apostrophe*, all of Goldsmith's works are available online at various websites.)

More than eight decades ago Cocteau claimed progress is no longer available to poetry, that only its mode of distribution can be progressive: a claim that is proving increasingly prophetic.[19] "[T]he new avant-garde" states Gene Youngblood more recently, "is all about creating autonomous social worlds that people can live in. Art is central to that but the art is not what's avant-garde. What's avant-garde is metadesign, the creation of context" (13). The web in its variant offerings of the open book and of the hard copy archive affords such a context. So perhaps trans-architect Marcos Novak is correct in conceiving the Internet and its attendant new media as the belated realization of Constant's *New Babylon (to be considered in chapter 8)*: a vast ludic space open to delirious psycho-textual-geography and flaneuristic *dérives* through an entanglement of photo-linguistic data that make possible a liquid architecture in cyberspace.[20] In addition the Internet finally renders operative the Mallarméan dream of all existence ending in a book, for what is the Internet if not an open and continuously expanding book available for paragrammatic engagements, festive appropriation, and imaginative reconfigurations?

Christian Bök claims Goldsmith to be "our James Joyce of the 21st century," a judgment that on the surface might seem as trivial as it is irresponsible.[21] (One might equally claim Goldsmith to be the Roy Lichtenstein of the tenth century, the *Bestia Trionfans* calling Wisdom from its cave, or the absolute Racine of conceptual writing.) Bök's claim, however, is defensible and remains beguiling. For if Lyotard is correct in asserting Joyce's greatest achievement to be that of rendering the unpresentable presentable inside the signifier (80) then this fact is pertinent to Goldsmith's work when we install the latter within the "sublime" (unrepresentable) and untotalizable condition of informatics. So perhaps today's

Apollo needs a tenth muse, "Data," not to possess a poet's head but to serve as custodian of materially and hyperspatially embodied information to finally conflagrate the history of the archive so it can emerge as the phoenix of information transport—a veritable messianic anabasis. The projection of language to the threshold of nothingness was the sovereign challenge laid down by both Mallarmé and Beckett. Mallarmé's infinite suggestive verbal web and Beckett's worsening words are the affiliate instruments writers have inherited to either utilize or ignore. Is uncreativity the nothing of creativity or its inverted potentiality? Is it the potentiality to reframe the "uncreative" within the conceptual and thus vivify useless production? However, if Goldsmith in his crusade against value addresses the sedimentary condition of hypertrophic information—the heaps of unproductive obsolete, unyielding facts, and statistics that characterize the eschatolic side of information culture—then his uncreative writing is best explained through Baudrillard's critical engagement with Saussure's paragrams. Informatics is itself symptomatic of more encompassing contemporary technocapitalist formations, a vast disemboguing of commodities and language into irreducible and inescapable sedimentation. Baudrillard elucidates the sepulchral side of this "affluent utopia" when considered in the broader context of production: "Just as every commodity, that is to say, everything produced under the sign of the law of value and equivalence, is an *irreducible residue* that comes to bar social relations, so every word, every term and every phoneme produced and not symbolically destroyed accumulates like the repressed, weighs down on us with all the abstraction of dead language" (202). It would seem that *Day* along with Goldsmith's other uncreative writing is preeminently a symbolic rather than conceptual action, a ritual cancellation of meaning and the *poetic* extermination of value along the lines of archaic composition that Saussure investigated (unsuccessfully) in his *Cahiers d'anagrammes*.[22]

# 7

# Parapoetics and the Architectural Leap

*Limits are what any of us are inside of.*
—Charles Olson *Collected Prose,* 170

*I have divided this chapter into three uneven sections. The first offers a "soft" manifesto-like exposition of parapoetics; the second discusses a related matter: the problematics of the frame; the final section comprises a partial mapping of and a few suggestions toward areas of potential parapoetic investigation. Judged on the normative criteria for academic writing it is premature, partial at best, and thoroughly inconclusive. Seen as an attempt to realize a parapoetics intervention, it will be judged to be an utterly abortive attempt—and quite correctly so. However, as the speculative and tentative tenor of the first part indicates, the third part is a probe into uncertainties and unknowns. An in-depth discussion of the important architectural contributions by the Situationists is notably absent; that discussion, however, can be found in chapter 8, which is devoted to the radical labyrinths of Constant and Arakawa and Gins.*

## I. Parapoetics

The death of God, the end of Man, the end of theory, the death of the subject, the death of art courtesy of Hegel, the death of man courtesy of Foucault, the death of Marxism courtesy of North American English departments, the end of narrative courtesy of my friend with a smile like those horses in Picasso's "Guernica": having survived a tedious necklace of such mortifications and eschatologies I'll not add to the list the death of the poem (first announced in North American academic circles in the 1970s when poetry was misunderstood as being entirely lyrical expression). But I will pose for provocation the following question: where does poetics go when poetry is no longer considered important? We have already encountered in chapter 6 Kenneth Goldsmith's turn to uncreative writing in response to the sensed exhaustion of literature and crisis point within all accretional paradigms. (Why write another good poem, let alone "make it new" like a belated modernist?) This is hardly a novel cultural dilemma. In his 1969 Alexander Lectures, Walter Jackson Bate tracks this "burden of the past" between 1660 and 1830. Crisis is a notion frequently complicit with endings; I sense no crisis in poetics but do note complacency in matters of potentiality and scale. Accordingly I want to consider a shift into a purposefully fuzzy and still virtual discipline I will call parapoetics. Conceived along the lines of David Carroll's notion of the paraesthetic, the term denotes a critical responsibility to approach poetry through its relation to extra-poetic domains and discourses. To borrow Carroll's own description, parapoetics is figured as "something like [a poetics] turned against itself . . . a faulty, irregular, disordered, improper [poetics]—one not content to remain within the area defined by the [poetic]" (Carroll xiv). (Affinities to those aspects of picturesque theory that I deal with in chapter 9 may be noted in Carroll's quoted passage.)

Celan believed that naming occurs in the depth of language; yet to accord to naming a definitional power is to arrest being as a living process of becoming. Dr. Johnson warns that to "circumscribe poetry by definition will only show the narrowness of the definer" (331), a sentiment endorsed by Friedrich Schlegel in his oxymoronic definition of romantic poetry as that poetry which exceeds definition. Similarly, I want to avoid a specific predetermination of what constitutes parapoetics and leave it suspended as an anomalous or non-determined concept, thereby allowing critical desire to put mastery at risk. Abandoning the pursuit of theoretical dogmatism, it will require that a negative capability be applied within the pernicious doublet Foucault concatenates as power-knowledge.

The *Concise Oxford Dictionary* offers numerous meanings for the prefix *para*: "1 beside. 2 beyond. 3 a modification. 4 a diametrically opposite relation. 5 a form of protection or warding off." The larger OED adds further variations to these seemingly contradictory senses that strike me as particularly attractive to poetic practice. In composition it has the same senses, with such cognate adverbial ones as "to one side, aside, amiss, faulty, irregular, disordered, improper, wrong" that also express subsidiary relation, alteration, perversion, simulation, etc. What is appealing in *para* is its evasion of the janiformity of a *post,* whose consequences Derrida points out involve "a surrender to the historicist urge."[1] Among other things, *para* provokes a shift from temporal to spatial conceptualization and positioning. Moreover the lateral adjacency of "beside" offers a multiplicity of satellite invocations: the friend, neighbor, relative, lover, guide, witness, and judge. *Beside* also is between, interstitial, and intervalic, as well as extra and outside. Accordingly this chapter will be concerned with more the situation of parapoetics than its ontology; in other words I will focus on where it is and can be rather than on what it is. Although I leave parapoetics purposefully undefined, it is important to inscribe and activate its forces. Redirecting Derrida's call to architecture, I write, "Let us never forget there is a poetics of poetics" and that poetics is beside poetics (Derrida "Point de Folie" 326). Heuristic rather than foundational, parapoetic desire does not seek to adumbrate upon the specificity of a discipline but rather to probe the fungibility and centrifuge always latent within the ontologically or intellectually discrete. As such, it takes its place within the anti-Kantian lineage that denies the specificity of art; it also offers a countermove within the current new "anxiety" of specialization rather than influence. Operating as a probe into uncertainties and as a force of disruption among stability, parapoetics aims to transform a total unity into multiplicity.

Foucault and Blanchot both encourage the "thinking of the outside" as a critical practice of transgression, one that refuses the stability of alterity while at the same time avoiding the incorporating move to totality. Parapoetics demands that singular disciplines or practices remove themselves in order to achieve a self-comprehension that avoids a transcendental installation of the theoretical attitude, and submit to a voluntary disability. Assuming the burden of this kind of thinking, parapoetics works against promulgating any discursive formation as a complete and closed system and instead seeks to go beyond the discretion of Deleuze's "fabulation of a discipline to come." Free from a fixed definition, it's also emancipated from a predetermined destination and able to install itself within the dialectical tensions and determinants of any number of target fields. Rather than serving as the critical mode of poetics, a species of self-policing and of external probing, parapoetics signals a shift in critical desire away from the poem as such toward other disciplines and discourses. Working between the seams and cracks consequent to the inevitable play between discourses, upon and without the hyphenated space of power-knowledge, parapoetics adopts more a contaminatory than a combative stance, marbling the smooth and certain propositional plane of discourse and ideas. It does not support disciplinary cross-dressing and is not to be deposited in other disciplines as some governing metatheory. Deracinated and detached from poetics proper, and maintaining its distance from any discourse that seeks to master or explain, it can be likened to a hesitation within a caesura. With explorations beyond affinities and analogies, parapoetics will situate interstitially, the way punctuation falls *between* meaning. Circumscribed within the broad thematics of disciplines and movings, parapoetics focuses on the interval where contamination, uncertainty, and misprision precipitate discovery, unforeseen collaboration, and contestation. As regards specific dynamics, in parapoetic logic an entrance is the continuation of an exit by other means. Accordingly parapoetics will always be both considerably more and a little less than poetics proper. And, who knows, perhaps poetics after the postmodern is a parapoetics inside it.

## II. The Frame-Up

> *All movements have direction. But why just one direction and not several?*
> *Movements can produce breakouts and new connections.*
> —Yago Conde, *Architecture of the Indeterminacy,* 251

Ronald Aronson encourages us to think of theory as a tool, not a framework (227), and much of Derrida's *The Truth in Painting* explores the philosophical intricacies of working and engaging the frame. As we saw in chapter 2's discussion of the "postmodern," frames both individuate and recontextualize; their ultimate power is cartographic. We see the acute stakes of framing in our current geopolitical and sexual climates: on one hand the melting of national boundaries and proactive deframings under the pressure of economic ideologies in Europe and North America (NAFTA and the EU), and on the other a Balkanization of Europe and Africa from political and ethnic pressures to maximize restricted territorial coding. The struggle toward legal ratification of same-sex marriage is a debate fought out in a judicial theater that hinges on the right to install a frame within an existing frame.

Framing, of course, is the prime culprit whereby *objects as such* are transformed into objects *of* theory, thereby guaranteeing a pacification of the chosen object field and the impossibility of the latter to modify the theoretic domain. For this reason theoretical endeavor remains antipathetic to empiricism whose method runs counter to such framing, an implication that Gerald Bruns specifies when asserting that "What we take poetry to be cannot be exhausted by examples, because examples are always in excess of our experience and understanding" (5). Despite theory-frames being designed to ensure a unilateral flow of power sufficient to preserve the integrity of its method, the logic of the frame moves against settled internal preservation. Frames are caught up in a contradictory logic insomuch as external elements and forces constantly threaten the boundaries they set out to demarcate. Rather than preservers of integrity, frames are conduits facilitating a promiscuous transit of forces from inside out and from outside in; they organize a contradictory yet mutual relation of an exterior to an interior, which, like Foucauldian thresholds, constructs an untenable divide between incompatible forces struggling for dominance. Frames are ineluctably mobile, vibratory, and true to an insect rhythm we will engage more fully in the final chapter; they efface entrances as well as offer entrances through effacements. French architect Bernard Cache supports this claim, arguing that "the structure of the modern frame offers a certain amount of play. . . . The rigid parts of the frame still retain a certain geometry, but their articulation is mobile and their equilibrium results from the play of tensions that run through the system as a whole" (108–9). Derrida only pragmatizes this observation in his suggestion to "work the frame" as both boundary and conduit. Deleuze and Guattari emphasize the omniprobability of the frame to reverse its function and deframe the internal in a way that it forges a relationship to the external that opens the internal up to the outside (cf. Deleuze and Guattari *What is Philosophy?* 187).

The topological quirkiness of the frame bears comparison to the nature of dissipative structures, defined and investigated in the field of nonlinear thermodynamics by Ilya Prigogine and Isabelle Stengers. As Fernández-Galiano explains dissipative structures are "forms of supermolecular organization requiring the continuous dissipation of energy and matter through the increase of small random fluctuations"(114). The theory of dissipative structures is emerging as a formative notion in numerous disciplines, provoking Fernández-Galiano to consider it "the new scientific paradigm of the age" (ibid.). Both buildings and the city can be conceived as open thermodynamic systems dependent for their existence on nutritional elements and energy flows. A city and a cell are homomorphic systems insofar as both exist in and depend upon an outside world; both must remain constantly open in order to draw sustenance from flows of energy and matter toward it. As Prigogine and Stengers observe, "[T]he city and the cell quickly die when separated from their mediums, for they are part of the worlds that nourish them and constitute a sort of local and unique incarnation of the flows that never cease to transform" (quoted in Fernández-Galiano 79). Likewise, both cell and city require the constant dissipation of energy—be it in the form of waste produce or the movement of populous—in a constant spreading beyond frames and boundaries. In sharp contrast to the practice of comparative poetics outlined by Earl Miner, parapoetics does not work to constitute and defend the discrete frame of the poem as such, but rather explores how the frame can be challenged to open up a porous, transactional poetics without borders.

## III. The Architectural Leap

*The language revising its own architectures is the cloud palace and drift of*
*your desire.*
—Robert Duncan

Stein's call in the "Rooms" section of *Tender Buttons* to "act as if there is no use
in a center" is cannily prophetic of contemporary cultural desires; in current poetics (as evinced in many of these chapters) the ideas of rupture, seepage, and
commingling seem more attractive than the ones of discretion and continuity.
Derrida leaves "what is writing" an open question; the same is required of poetics. Feeling that contemporary poetics has reached an impasse in *exclusively* poetic territories, I wish to propose a leap or "becoming" toward both urban texture and architectural theory as initial parapoetic domains. An exclusive focus
on the poem-as-such severely curtails the potential critical range of poetics. For
poetics to maintain a vital critical function a radical readjustment of its trajectories seems required; Arakawa and Madeline Gins refer to this as the "poetic
leap." The purpose of this leap isn't simply to obtain knowledge or display it in a
different discipline, nor to plunder a terrain for concepts and ideas useful to one's
own practice. The leap involves *the knowledge of how and when to delay knowing,* and how to be active in a state of suspended certainty. To recycle yet again
Arthur Koestler's inspirational adage, "[t]he prerequisite of originality is forgetting, at the proper moment, what we know." Through the leap, one is no longer
beside but elsewhere. In the spirit of Bataille's oxymoronic formulation (that to
love poetry one must hate poetry), the initial poetic leap will be a turn against
its traditional object field and detach poetics from poematics. Disciplines too,
like structures and language, are simultaneously closed and open; they contain
a restless heterogeneity within a constricting frame of the homogeneous. To insist on the specificity of both the poetic and the architectural is to seriously limit
both research and the critico-creative enterprise inside, between, and across the
two. Perhaps the new paradigm should be escape, a poetics of leaving rather than
of becoming. Beyond a critical engagement with the heterogeneity within the so-
called homogeneous lies an urgent need to shift not the mode but the target of
poetics' transitivity.

Aaron Betsky has emerged as the popular theorist of that decentralizing condition and dissolution known as sprawl. Sprawl shatters the tense logic of the
frame. Not only is sprawl an architectural and urban presupposition, it's the
very condition of modernity. Pollution is sprawl, contemporary knowledge is

sprawl; sprawl is the authentic landscape of the contemporary but enters painting as early as Turner; it is the welcoming de facto fate not the cursed share of architecture. As Betsky insists, "The issue is not how to stop sprawl but how to use
its composition, its nodes and its leaky spaces to create a kind of architecture."[2]
As a blotchist or formless spreading out from strategic nodes—malls, airports,
etc.—sprawl constitutes both the unplanned deterritorialization of physical structures and modernity's urban given; it registers the contemporary city's picturesque inclination to a heterology and centrifuge whose resonant inclination is
to deframe. Betsky's name for this formless dystopia is exurbia, "where human
forms meld into the remains of nature and where order becomes so thin that we
recognize its most basic components." For Betsky urban sprawl may even provide a redemptive dimension that takes us "away from the high-rise tendencies of
the city [and putting] us back on earth where we confront the realities of ground
and weather." While declining the temptation to dangle such redemptive carrots
I would insist, however, that in maintaining parapoetics as a deliberately non-
determined concept, I advocate a certain conceptual and creative sprawl.

Why the leap into architecture? From "stanza" to the "prison-house of language" architecture has played a dominant role within the very formulation of
the linguistic. Architectural metaphors haunt writing to a degree sufficient to
cause us to question a merely benign metaphoric presence. One of Heidegger's
lasting insights is into how both language and architecture ground us in the
world. In architecture, as in language, man dwells (poetically or not) whether in
unimpeded mobility or confinement: "We appear to ourselves only through an
experience of spacing which is already marked by architecture" (Derrida *Chora*
*L* 324). Not only Gins and Arakawa, as we have seen, but also Heidegger and
Derrida suggest that prior to becoming social subjects we are all architectural
bodies.[3] However, to Derrida's grammatological conception of architecture as
"a writing of space, a mode of spacing which makes a place for events" (ibid.),
a qualification needs to be annexed: architecture too is the materialized conception of dwelling, and that dwelling is fundamentally a relation of ontology
to spaces; in that sense it serves to return being to its problems by way of *oikos*
rather than *poeisis*. Moreover, if Bachelard is correct when claiming that all inhabited space bears the essence of the notion of home, then the link between
reading and dwelling appears to be far from a strained analogy.

Imbedded deep in Judeo-Christian cultural memory, the myth of Babel implicates the two distinct phenomena of architecture and human speech, from
which has developed an enduring complicity. The metaphoric saturation of architectural terms in other discourses (including both philosophy and literature)

is well known: the prison house of language, deconstruction, the poem's fabric, foundation, etc. Indeed for Derrida the architectural metaphor of ground marks the very core of philosophy (*Chora L* 105). But beyond a haunting metaphoric presence, architecture has consistently offered writing a constructive model and, though perhaps not yet sister arts, architecture's intimate relation to the literary is historically tangible, even down to its grammatological contours.[4] Architecture provides the formal model for Saint Teresa's *Interior Castle,* Jeremy Taylor's *Rules and Exercises for Holy Dying* (figured in the preface as a tour through the rooms of a charnel house), George Herbert's *The Temple,* and Christopher Harvey's *The Synagogue.* The arguments of Donne's magnificent sermon "Death's Duel" are built around the three prime architectural supports of foundation, buttress, and contignation: "[t]he foundations suffer them not to sink, the buttresses suffer them not to swerve, and the contignations and knitting suffers them not to cleave" (Donne 165). In his 1850 advertisement to *The Prelude,* Wordsworth recalls his conception in 1814 of the relation of his two earlier poems—*The Excursion* and *The Recluse*—in architectural terms that recall Herbert: "[T]he two works have that relation to each other . . . as the Antechapel has to the body of a Gothic Church" (IV, 4). Even his minor pieces when collected and "properly arranged, will be found by the attentive reader to have such connection with the main work as may give them claim to be likened to the little cells, oratories and sepulchral recesses, ordinarily included in those edifices" (ibid.). More recently, Ronald Johnson's long poem *ARK* adopts as its formal model "a kind of *naif* architecture on the lines of the Facteur Cheval's Ideal Palace, Simon Rodia's Watts Towers, or Ramond Isidore's mosaic house in the shade of Chartres" (Johnson 56). The final and one-hundredth book of *ARK* is Johnson's earlier poem, *Radi  os,* a selected textual deletion of *Paradise Lost* (discussed in chapter 2), which Johnson envisaged and "conceived as a kind of Dymaxion Dome over the whole" (*ARK* 50, 56). Mark Scroggins elaborates on *ARK's* architectonic features: "[Johnson] calls his poem a 'model for a monument.' And its three major divisions reflect this spatial metaphor: 33 sections of 'Foundations,' 3 of 'Spires,' and 33 of 'Ramparts.' *ARK,* in turn, was to have been a 'dome' over the whole, a crowning and covering shell like that over Monticello, the U.S. Capitol, or the Roman Pantheon. The poem, then, is conceived of as in some sense a literal object, a literal architecture" (295). In his *De vulgari eloquentia* II. 9,9 Dante offers a distinction between *stanza* (literally "room") and *canzone* that illustrates the presidential status of architectural thinking: "[W]e must observe that this word [*stanza*] has been invented solely with respect to the art [of the *canzone*]; namely, in order that in which the whole art of the canzone is contained should be called stanza, that is a *room* able to hold, or a receptacle for the whole art" (98). The interrogative crux structuring the entirety of Augustine's *Confessions* (a book that frequently addresses the infinite as a locus) is a strictly *spatial* problem articulated as an architectural issue of impossible housing: I call on you, Lord, to you the Infinite to come and inhabit me, I who am but finite. Mark Danielewski takes up this topological impossibility in his 2000 debut novel *House of Leaves* where the house on Ash Tree Lane is bigger on the inside than it is on the outside.

For its part, the materiality of language has provided an abundance of architectural possibilities. The dramatic and decorative possibilities of the letter shape as an interior space functions as the basic premise of the medieval "inhabited" initial. Later, Johann David Steingruber brings about a more complex fusion of function and the fantastic in his 1773 *Architectural Alphabet.* The thirty-three plates of this work comprise a formidable achievement and present patently feasible functional designs. Steingruber's quintessentially Baroque wit is retained as a trace element in Steven Holl's investigation into the intimate congruence of certain letterforms and architectural design in relation to context and urban syntax.[5]

Offering an attractive alternative to Bloom's formulation, Viktor Shklovsky argues for a deflection rather than an anxiety of influence. Put simply, the theory advances that artistic or disciplinary influence is transmitted not in an immediate and direct line within the same discipline, but in an entirely different domain. The transmission of artistic and cultural influence travels like the knight's move in chess, not from fathers to sons but from uncles and aunts to nieces and nephews (cf. Conde 195). Rather than literary continuity via canon and hierarchy, why not a deflectional move to string theory, philosophy, biophysics, or architecture? (It's the trail of the transmission out of its current site that's important.) A recent example is Language writing's influence on musicology as seen in Brian Ferneyhough's embrace of disjunction in his New Complexionism. If we approach the virtual interrelations between poetics and architecture through a Shklovskian model, we may adopt an architectural configuration and rethink the concept of a poetic movement and poetic practice in general as the construction of a project in relation to a chosen program, itself relating to an actual preexisting site. Additionally, the programmatic ideology of architecture facilitates rethinking that socio-ontological problematic complex named "community" through the architectural notion of "site." Site as living and active locus and topos has a fecund, aristocratic history stretching far back beyond Charles Olson and William Carlos Williams through the *genius locus* to Aristotle's claim that "place is something, but it also has a certain power" (*Physics*

4.1.2086, quoted in Didi-Huberman 18). Bernard Cache's Deleuzean-informed architecture allows poetics to abandon the otiose binary of form and content and take up the innovative triplet of frame, vector, and inflection. Cache's complex theorizing on the status of the image warrants careful scrutiny and perhaps, additionally, a bold application in *poesis*. Similarly, it might be asked: how would catachresis find an architectural realization, or equally, how could an axonometric method find a poetic one?

Perhaps then we can learn more about the discourse of the poem by examining it from architecture's alterior positions and through a purposeful displacement of poetics toward architecture. The dialogue between these two practices occurs as much within as between each other, and the integrity of both should be risked. Parapoetic strategy seeks out not only what is confluential but also conflictual in architecture and poetics, as well as what each is displacing and becoming. Contemporary architecture shows a cartographic caution around establishing boundaries and domains. Indeed, it is beginning to understand that discrete disciplinary issues cannot all be raised in architecture itself (involving, among other things, the broader philosophic issues of ontology, presence, history, topos, memory, and mimesis); there are additionally the related wider socio-political issues of urbanism, the city, and context, and perhaps most paramount, a relation to human bodies, as well as the broader matters of coordination, material, scale, and the broad relations of interiority and exteriority.

Bernard Tschumi is not alone in stressing that the paramount purpose of architecture is conceptual. Tschumi compares it to Lacanian psychoanalysis, whose goal is not curative; rather the patient's recovery occurs as a felicitous indirect effect: "To make buildings that work and make people happy is not to [*sic*] goal of architecture but, of course, a welcome side effect" (267 n. 6). I currently concur, however, with Robin Evans in seeing architecture as the construction of the preconditions that govern the way bodies occupy and negotiate space— a credo not far removed from Yago Conde's claim that "[t]he habitual exclusion of the body and its experiences of [*sic* from?] any discourse on the logic of form would be instances of the lack of any intertextual impulse" (197).[6] Architecture is a form of action centering on users, and the key question of architectural form is a question of architecture's relation to the scale and matter of human freedom.

However, having said that I have to admit that the question of what "is" architecture has become much more difficult to answer in recent times. Traditionally, architects are subject to comparable constraints as a Poet Laureate. Forced into a species of contextual bricolage as a compromise formation, their profitable work is commissioned construction within predetermined spaces and for the most part within fixed, urban, and spatial exigencies. Owing to the governing economy of commission and competition, the vast majority of architectural projects remain conceptual. With the rise of paper and information architecture in the 1960s and subsequently virtual architecture, the practice found itself suddenly liberated from the binding functionalist mandates and free to investigate numerous theoretical issues. As a consequence, contemporary architectural theorizing emerges not as a self-certain or consensual discourse but as a vibrant metamorphic terrain of dispute. In Solà-Morales's estimate, "[a]t the present time, [architectural] criticism resembles hand-to-hand combat: a contest between information seeking public recognition and the power of collective sanction vested in those supposedly able to bestow it" (138). Philosophy's impact on recent architectural thinking has been consequential, precipitating both attempts at application and actual collaborations.[7] As early as 1970 Robin Evans envisioned his *anarchitecture* to function as the tectonic of non-control (Evans 11–33), and in 1973 architectural historian Manfredo Tafuri proclaimed "from now on form is not sought outside of chaos; it is sought within it" (96).[8] Much contemporary architecture seems to challenge its seemingly inescapable parousial condition by attempts to destabilize presence and orientation (as we will see in the next chapter in the case of Constant and Arakawa and Gins). Solà-Morales contrasts effectively the traditional locus of stability, durability, and memory with the contemporary Deleuzian locus of event:

> The places of present-day architecture cannot repeat the permanences produced by the force of the Vitruvian *firmitas*. The effects of duration, stability, and defiance of time's passing are now irrelevant. The idea of place as the cultivation and maintenance of the essential and the profound, of a genius loci, is no longer credible. . . . From a thousand different sites the production of place continues to be possible. Not as the revelation of something existing in permanence, but as the production of an event. (103–4)

Sentiments echoed in Cache's tenet that "if the expression 'genius loci' [*sic*] has a meaning, it lies in the capacity of this 'genius' to be smart enough to allow for the transformation or transit from one identity to another" (15). The recent works and proposals of Peter Eisenman, Koop Himmelblau, Nigel Coates, and Bernard Tschumi appear extremely provocative in this area. Architecture's traditional investment in functionality include as its central desiderata safety, stability, permanence, control, anesthesia, consumption, and comfort. All are called into question as requisite elements not only in the Situationist architecture and Arakawa and Gins' *Reversible Destiny* sites (discussed in chapter 8) but in the diverse works of Archigram, Daniel Libeskind, the late John Hejduk, and Zaha Hadid.[9] Indeed, early in 2001, the radical procedural architects Gins and Arakawa abandoned architecture for their newly formed practice of *Bioscleaveconfigurature*. As well as a common belief that there can be a positive quality to disequilibrium and contradictions, it is the trenchant, uncompromising repudiation of architectural modernism's functional ethic and its attendant emphasis on problem solving over problem production that unites these architectural thinkers.

Even though German Romanticism is known to have avoided the linguistic in the simple complicity sought between architecture and music, and despite Victor Hugo's famous warning that "the book will kill the edifice"—a prediction at the heart of this problematic relation between poetics and architectural theory— current architectural thinking, via Derrida's impetus, is being redirected to the architectonic possibilities of language, textuality, and writing.[10] Peter Eisenman's advocacy of discursive rather than figurative architecture is preeminent in this regard. Such architecture would open the mirrored possibility of how writing can be inscribed in architecture and equally architecture in writing, the virtuality of a diagrammatic model for writing readily lending itself to a parapoetic scrutiny.[11] Eisenman himself believes (perhaps over ambitiously) that such a writing-as-diagram is possible and will provide "a means of potentially overreaching the question of origin (speech) as well as the metaphysics of presence" (*Diagram Diaries* 213). Eisenman stresses the diagram's deconstructive potential as the following vertiginous and typical sentence suggests: "The diagram helps to displace presence by inserting a not-presence as a written trace—a sign of the not-presence of the column—into the physical column. This trace is something that cannot be explained either through function or meaning" (ibid.). However, the axonometric nature of the diagram offers a more parapoetic potential. The chief feature of axonometric diagrams is parallel projection, which effectively collapses the governing dualism of vertical and horizontal planes, freeing up the possibility of thrusting the observer into decentralized disequilibrium.[12] Axonometric presentation maximizes presentational possibilities, showing more sides than it is ever possible to view—axonometry was the aspiration of Gertrude Stein in her cubist style-lives. For Eisenman, "The diagram is a tactic within a critical strategy—it attempts to situate a theoretical object within a physical object [and is capable of producing] spatial characteristics that both blur iconic forms and produce interstitial spatial possibilities" (*Diagram Diaries* 202, 206). There are clear intimations that poetics is already exploring at least the effects of axonometry. The disjunctive poetics that emerged in the late 1970s produced texts by Bruce Andrews whose immediate effects are decenteredness and read-erly disequilibrium. Ron Silliman's "new sentence," through its paratactic em-phasis and rule of non-integrating sentences, constructs precisely those inter-stitial spatial possibilities that Eisenman speaks of.[13] The white hiatus between letters, words, and sentences—what Silliman calls the twenty-seventh letter of the alphabet, marking the virtual space of non-integration—makes reader inter-vention possible on the level of semantic construction and connotative tracking. A similar quality of axonometric distortion occurs in much of Clark Coolidge's poetry and in the systematic-chance-generated texts of John Cage and Jackson Mac Low (as discussed in chapters 3, 4, and 9). In his 2000 book *Alien Tatters,* Coolidge retains the sentence as the minimal unit of composition, with gram-mar and syntax functioning in a superficially normative way.

> Monkey come down from that roof with my mother's
> dowery. These baleful scenes can be made to explain. It was
> just that dare of a day. Expediency Beranger they called for.
> A collided ice to the vitamin point.

> Mondo Pianissimo of the bulky Colorado. This is not as
> silly as might be turned to in times of expectancy, clearing
> right out. Pencil-thin silhouette just down the barrel from
> all aim. The cow made smaller by the light (41).

Although the two most characteristic features of the new sentence—parataxis and non-integration—stylistically dominate in the passage, catachresis and gram-matical transgressions help attain an intense quality of disequilibrium. Consid-ered axonometrically, not as a text but an architectonic, we can say that the gram-mar and syntax function as the vertical and horizontal elements in an "angled" axonometric structure through which "diagonal" elements (in the form of cata-chresis and undecidability) provide informational and semiological distortions.[14]

Eisenman is additionally attracted to text and trace as ways of denying ar-chitecture both originality and expression. He seeks a radical incorporation of alterity in which a work is defined in terms of another author, a process that involves "a search for the signs of absence within the necessary presence of archi-tecture" (Eisenman and Derrida 132). This incorporation of otherness in same-ness is precisely the method of Ronald Johnson's *Radi os* and John Cage's vari-ous "writings-through" already scrutinized in chapters 2 and 4. Both treat a source text using methods of written readings through which the latent text is exhumed and the source texts partly deleted. Johnson's source is *Paradise Lost* and Cage's include *Finnegans Wake, Walden,* and Thoreau's *Notebooks.* To give another example: in *A Humument,* a text excavated from W. H. Mallock's forgotten 1892 novel *A Human Document,* British artist Tom Phillips paints over vast areas of the pages, creating efficacious rivulets of text that open up a latent content. Each page of Mallock's novel offers Phillips a reservoir of paragrammatic possibilities and a tactical opportunity for local improvisations within constraint. The exhumed text releases a difference in sameness, the result being a stunning intermedia work: part text, part pictorial transformation in pen, ink, and acrylic gouache. But beyond its visual impact, *A Humument* raises the following proprietary question: exactly whose words are these? The Victorian Mallock's certainly, and reproduced in the exact same place on each line as he planned. Yet they serve to deliver a new text, a text out of a text; they present Phillips' text as the text by Mallock that Mallock never wrote.

Parapoetics might also address how applicable to poetics are the three deconstructive questions that Eisenman sees evoked by the diagrammatic: 1. Can the metaphysics of presence be opened up or displaced? Is there another way to think of presence other than through fullness? 2. Is there a way to rethink the relationship between the sign and the signified as other than an unmotivated relationship? 3. Is there a way to rethink the subject as other than a subject who is urged by a desire to have architecture communicate a sense of place and ground? (Eisenman *Diagram Diaries* 212).

Let me digress briefly on a parallel but variant history of reception, specifically the deconstructive and the folding turn in architecture and literature. Marc Wigley claims that architecture (circa the mid-1980s) was "the last discourse to invoke the name of Derrida" ("The Translation of Architecture" 6). Without doubt the strategic introduction of instability into stable structures and relations remains deconstruction's major theoretical contribution to architecture. Jeffrey Kipnis clearly states the architectural demands of deconstruction: "The architect must find methods to simultaneously embody more complex organizations of multiple and contradictory meanings while at the same time meeting the responsibility to shelter, function and stand" (quoted in Eisenman and Derrida 138). By 1993, however, interest in deconstructive architecture had significantly waned, and attention shifted to the architectural implications of Deleuze's concept of the fold. Greg Lynn suggests that folding offers an alternative and preferable fluid and connective logic when compared to the deconstructionist impasse of conflict and contradiction. Where deconstruction inspired an architecture of brutal diagonals, plication encouraged curvilinear, folded, and heterogeneous forms. "If there is a single effect," Lynn notes, "produced in architecture by folding, it will be the ability to integrate unrelated elements within a new continuous mixture" (8). Deleuzean curvilinear logic facilitates dissipative structures with porous movements of external forces into interior domains (and vice versa) and the concomitant inclusion of non-colliding discontinuities. This proclivity to generative theory is generally absent in the literary field where deconstruction and plication (despite Rodolphe Gasché's warning that general textuality is irreducible to the properties of specific literary texts) have largely fostered a critical apparatus to be laminated over texts for interpretative purposes and has had a comparatively weak impact on the production of primary texts. This linked but uneven development is not to be lamented but rather noted for opening the possibility of cross-disciplinary intercourse.

Shifting focus from predominantly theoretical matters, I want now to suggest that the most fruitful target for parapoetic attention is the city. Wittgenstein, a practicing architect himself, compares language to "an ancient city: a maze of little streets and squares, of old and new houses" (8e) while Sherwood Anderson writes of a post-melancholic, neglected city of words rebuilt and recast by Gertrude Stein:

> There is a city of English and American words and it has been a neglected city. Strong broad shouldered words, that should be marching across open fields under the blue sky, are clerking in little dusty dry goods stores, young virgin words are being allowed to consort with whores, learned words have been put to the digger's trade. Only yesterday I saw a word that once called a whole nation to arms serving in the mean capacity of advertising laundry soap.
>
> For me the work of Gertrude Stein consists in a rebuilding, an entire new recasting of life, in the city of words. (7–8)

Architectural theories and debate, however, provide more complex notions of the city than Wittgenstein's and Anderson's simple metaphoric renditions; civic theories might modify literary encounters with the city. Architecture tells us how it frames light in space and expresses its commitment to creating photic and thermal as well as human circulation. Architecture also tells us that the interior of its products marks its living history; in this way architecture emerges as a form of action. Buildings and their complex articulations onto, and relations to, towns and cities are characterized like language by defeasibility and lability; they assume and evolve through numerous functions independent of both architectural form and original purpose. This feature specifies the paragrammatic force of dwelling, the occupied house or building thereby serving as a dissipative structure.

This specification, however, does not eliminate a certain perdurability of form. Reflecting on the Palazzo della Ragione in Padua, Aldo Rossi notes how "one is struck by the multiplicity of functions that a building of this type can contain over time and how these functions are entirely independent of the form. At the same time, it is precisely the form that impresses us, we live it and experience it, and in turn it structures the city" (29). Rossi's pragmatic observation allows us to return to Wittgenstein's description of language in a non-metaphorical way. There is no city just as there isn't a language, only linguistic utterances and architectural usage and events. The growing displacement of structural and general linguistics by pragmatics is symptomatic of a shift in interest from form to usage and language conceived as both a changing dwelling and a lived experience. In the light of this shift, Barthes' highly competent semiological readings of the city appear less relevant to living than to Lebbeus Woods' call to "build our buildings and then discover how to live and work in them" (80).[15]

British architect Nigel Coates, founder of NATO (Narrative Architecture Today, a.k.a. "Nigel and the Others") emerged from the Thatcherian design-boom of the 1980s with an ebullient theory of city architecture that combines filmic handling of space with collage and surprise. There is something flaneuristic about Coates' methodological approach to city architecture: "It's about getting under the skin of the city, about going with the flow, seeing where it takes you, and then responding in appropriate ways. A healthy city, or a city you want to be in, is always changing; it's an organism, not a machine running on fixed lines. This sense of a city being alive informs both our response to the city as architects, and the individual buildings we design" (quoted in Glancey 14). Notwithstanding this laudable declaration of commitment, Coates' projects so far (apart from the proposed redesign of the sleazy environs of King's Cross) do not reflect a particularly positive response to the prevalent social predicament of poverty, the need for shelter, low-income domiciles, etc. According to Glancey, Coates approaches the city "as a vibrant organism rather than a grid of geometric lines. It's about living, about meeting people, about accidental encounters, changes, risk-taking, sex" (ibid.). Such sentiments would not be out of place in any number of Situationist texts on unitary urbanism.[16] However, that critical awareness of governing ideological or economic forces so apparent to Constant and Jorn is notably absent in Coates' notion of the organic, vital city and his neo-liberal soft planning. The myopic range of Coates' vision becomes apparent when measured

against the ominous backdrop of co-optation and global economic controls outlined succinctly by Richard Rogers:

> Despite all our new wealth—material and intellectual—most of the world's
> inhabitants are denied the opportunity to lead decent lives. The swollen
> stomachs and shriveled faces of Third World children, the cold and squalor
> that our pensioners have to endure, the increasing number of people who
> live lives in boxes and doorways stand as an indictment of a society which
> has the capacity to eradicate poverty but prefers to turn its back. And be-
> yond the exploitation and injustice which is so central a feature of our civi-
> lization looms the prospect of ecological disaster. . . . The predicament in
> which we find ourselves has a direct bearing on our appreciation of archi-
> tecture. For in architecture, as in other areas, an exciting surge of crea-
> tivity, discovery and invention has been frustrated by the same selfish in-
> terests that now sustain global poverty and threaten the environment. . . .
> The despoliation of our built environment is only a small part of a broader
> pattern—a pattern in which new advances in ideas and technology are
> harnessed not to public values but to private interests" (7–9).

We must remain alert to architecture's ominous expansion in the hyperrealism
of the neo-liberal dream; we must stay vigilant against the colonizing force in
which architecture is mobilized by a hyphenated telos of planning-for-profit. It
is an alarming fact that this link of architecture and building to property, ownership, and profit is not a recent discovery. In early medieval times we find Hilde-
bert of Lavardin placing architecture in the category of "*ultra privatum pecuniae
modum fortunae*," that is to say "mercenary" things and financial gain (quoted
in Lefaivre 200).

   "Cities are in reality great camps of the living and the dead where many elements remain like signals, symbols, cautions. When the holiday is over, what remains of the architecture is scarred, and the sand consumes the street again"
(Rossi 10). Here Rossi's meditation on temporality and decay, marked as it is by
the philosopher's distance and transmitted from the transcendental position of
the theoretical attitude, seems most akin to Gibbon's musing on the ruins of the
Roman capitol that sparked in him the idea to write the *History of the Decline
and Fall of the Roman Empire*.[17] Yet elsewhere, Rossi realizes that cities are first
and foremost a composite of artifacts, and to ignore (as urban studies do) "those
aspects of reality that are most individual, particular, irregular, and also most
interesting" leads to useless, artificial theories (21). Late in the first century C.E.,

Juvenal emerged as the critical conscience of Rome, thus inaugurating a legacy of poetic scrutinization of the city as the dysfunctional hospice of incurables. John Gay, Samuel Johnson, the Shelley of *Peter Bell the Third,* Baudelaire, Aragon, and Eliot: all were fascinated and repelled by the inoperability of the metropolis. From Dioce to Wagadu, the dream of civic construction haunts Pound's *Cantos* as a thematic balance to the lure of fragments and floating signifiers.[18]

Despite the digital information highway and the extended community brought about by electronic intercourse, Georg Simmel's 1903 reflections on the metropolis and mental life seem more pertinent than ever. What distinguishes the metropolitan inhabitant is a blasé attitude to life caused by the collision of internal stimuli with a constant extra-sensory bombardment. Partly a product of and partly a defense against metropolitan overload, the blasé subject struggles for an autonomy and circulation homologous to the flow of currency and commodities.[19] The fascinating power of the city can be specified in an economic, ideological irony: that the people who use the city are simultaneously and for the most part unconsciously used by it. Tafuri isolates and elaborates the capitalist nature of the Western city: "Objectively, structured like a machine for the extraction of surplus value, in its own conditioning mechanisms the city reproduces the reality" of the modes of production (81). The soft city, transparent city, the wired city, the digital city: whichever you choose, cities still need to be experienced as sites of consumption and production. Yet to resuscitate Le Corbusier's vision of architecture as the supreme mediator between realism and utopia seems as arrogant as it is ill advised.

In conclusion let me suggest that you receive these rambling thoughts and observations as a caveat against the fruit of that marriage of practical reason and the Kantian faculties we baptized some time ago as specialization. The current ideology governing graduate studies does not encourage attacks on thetic dogmatism. Rather it supports the trenchant ideology of the frame. Doubtless an argument can be made that specialization safeguards the heterogeneity of discourses from domination by a single master narrative. However, the adverse consequences of the frame and the frame's governing contradictory logic have already been outlined. Aaron Betsky calls for an anchoring inside the amorphous vertigo of sprawl by means of slow space. Decelerate the speed of today and make the world stand still.[20] Against this moot tactic of survival I would suggest a *becoming* through agencies of difference toward a spiral poetics, a clinamen architecture, a poetics of folding so as to construct free spaces that can only function as ephemeral interstices.

Hölderlin insists that the highest poetry is that in which the non-poetic element also becomes poetic.[21] I wonder if the call in this claim to added negativity is pertinent to research. Let's attempt to problematize our specialist knowledge by placing it in a broader cartography; map antithetical and intersecting zones as a preliminary to nomadic practices; deframe and rethink research along spatial not chronological lines akin to Jed Rasula's notion of accidental research in which conceptual agility replaces a focused detailism. Experience at least the "internal drifts" of disciplines and even contemplate the possibility of random access research. According to Marcos Novak, "Our understanding of territory is undergoing rapid and fundamental changes: with the scope of pragmatic experience both space and community are rapidly becoming non-local." Random access is emerging as the most powerful virtual tool in epistemological capital. Novak believes it's becoming "a way of life characterized by precise and instantaneous affiliation. . . . [D]isembodied proximity implies the extension of random access to progressively larger parts of our experience." I would extend the applicability of Novak's claim to the disciplines of knowledge. Novak further suggests that "[t]he virtual and cyber worlds form a continuum. . . . There is something of what we call cyberspace in virtuality and something of what we call virtual reality in cyberspace. . . . Cyberspace is always the 'exterior' of virtual reality, because it always reserves the additional space of possibility, in contrast to actuality. Possibility is the fundamental characteristic of everything that is 'other,' since possibility always contains the unknown" (ibid.). Derrida's essay on Tschumi's *Point de Folie* introduces the term *maintenant* as a temporal indicator that marks the time, the only time, when both endings and beginnings occur in the protracted space of a becoming.

That said, as I'm ending, the poet in me thinks I should add a coda: "The poem may well be dead, but as the architect said one is never finished with the poem."

## "To Lose One's Way" (For Snails and Nomads)
The Radical Labyrinths of Constant and Arakawa and Gins

*The city is the realization of the ancient dream of humanity, the labyrinth.*
—Walter Benjamin, *Arcades Project*

Hermann Kern concludes *Through the Labyrinth,* his magisterial study and exhaustive cataloguing of that eponymous architectural form, with a short chapter on the labyrinth "revival." Since 1982, Kern contends, "a renewed interest in labyrinths has swept the globe" (311). Although his catalogue is daunting, neither the contributions of Constant nor of Arakawa and Gins are given consideration. This chapter attempts to contextualize Constant's *New Babylon* (Nieuw Babylon) project as well as the labyrinth elements in Arakawa and Gins' truly post-ontological procedural architecture. In congruent and dissimilar ways, these contemporary projects modify, but in some aspects also perpetuate, this five thousand-year-old architectural obsession.

In its classic (i.e. Cretan) sense, the labyrinth is a walled unicursal path designed to direct the pattern of movement to a central point. The perimeter of the structure has a single opening that serves as dual entry and exit points; the path consists of seven circuits, the form of which suggests a vital anthropological connection to breathing. As Kern points out, "[t]he path does not move in a straight line but rather in the rhythm of systole and diastole. Hence, much like a chest expanding to inhale" (24). The origin of the seven-circuit labyrinth is shrouded in mythology and mystery. Kern speculates that it has a Neolithic source, emerging from celestial observation rituals or initiation rites; in both possibilities Kern notes an intimate relation to dance. It is also strongly possible, according to Kern, that the labyrinth developed from cave cults in which winding, natural caverns symbolized the bowels of the earth or the uterus of the Earth Mother. The path, marked as an inner, then outward circuitry with a central point to be reached and then departed from, affords obvious comparison to the path through life to death to rebirth. Indeed, in the Christian appropriation of the labyrinth, it is Christ who replaces Theseus as the protagonist in an Easter ritual of rebirth. The medieval contribution to the history of this design is the *"computus"* labyrinth used as "a symbol of the astronomical determination of the date of Easter" (Batschelet Massini, quoted in Kern 110). It is also worth noting the morphological affinities between the classical labyrinth and early Greek writing practice. Ancient Greek poetry was written in boustrophedon, with lines alternating direction from left to right and right to left, in imitation of the turn of the ox in plowing. All writing in early Greece took the form of *scriptio continua*, a practice of undifferentiated writing without capitalization or word breaks.[1] Both phenomena occasion a cancellation of space (respectively, the empty retinal movement back across a page and the meaningful differentiation between verbal units) and together bear a remarkable affinity to the unicursal labyrinth design; it might be said that the labyrinth precipitates a "baroque" embellishment upon an architectural boustrophedon.

As intimated above, the labyrinth is incapable of avoiding a centrifugal pull into allegorical and metaphorical contaminants: the labyrinth of life, of love, of existence. As well "[i]t suffices for a short time to follow the trace, the repeated course of words, in order to perceive, in a sort of vision, the labyrinthine constitution of being" (Bataille *Inner Experience* 83–84). This passage, taken from Bataille's short essay "Le Labyrinthe" and so insistent on the profound link of the labyrinth to writing, should not be dismissed as a merely figurative application of an architectural term. Indeed, in the case of Bataille, as Denis Hollier argues, the question that insists itself is precisely this: What precedence should be given to the labyrinth of words? Is such textuality the ur-space that the classical labyrinth subsequently concretises in architectural space? Hollier describes this textual condition: "[The] labyrinth is basically the space where oppositions disintegrate and grow complicated, where diacritical couples are unbalanced and perverted, etc., where the system on which linguistic function is based disintegrates, but somehow disintegrates by itself, having jammed its own works" (58). An inoperative, autodestructional writing is called for and inscribed in constant errancy through an undecidable space. As Hollier states, "[N]either the category of subjectivity nor the category of objectivity can exist in this space, which, having made them unsound, nevertheless has no replacement to offer. . . . In this sense one is never either inside or outside the labyrinth" (58).

## I. The story so far . . .

The labyrinth myth is famous. Once upon a time a sea god, Poseidon, sent a white bull to the court of King Minos at Knossos for ritual slaughter, but Minos does not kill the animal. In revenge Poseidon engenders in Pasiphae (Minos's queen) an uncontrollable lust for the bull; a monstrous hybrid results from her sexual gratification: half-man, half-beast. The ever-ingenious Minos hires the architect Daedalus to construct a private space in which to house the savage beast, known as the Minotaur, who cruel Minos feeds with captured victims. But death gives way to a love story: the captured Theseus, fully expecting to become the Minotaur's snack, discovers to his felicitous surprise that Ariadne, one of the king's daughters, has fallen in love with him. Ariadne supplies Theseus with a thread of gold by which he can retrace his course through the winding structure; brave Theseus enters the labyrinth, slays the Minotaur, retraces his steps back along the thread, sets the palace on fire, and escapes with Ariadne to Naxos where in typical male fashion he deserts her. The rest is architecture and speculation.

Conjecturally a choreography, allegory, architecture, and celestial computer, the labyrinth is a complex anomalous notion, misunderstood and misapplied in its multifarious resonances.[2] The prototypical classic, Minoan, or Cretan labyrinth (from which all early labyrinths derive) functions equally as a kennel, the prototype of our contemporary zoo, and an architectural death trap. Both a home and a feeding tract, it is a wrapped model that includes a labyrinth inside a labyrinth: the Daedalian construct *per se* plus the curvilinear anfractuosities called the Minotaur's intestines. And the demonic rite of passage demands the move through one into the other. (I will return to this intertwining theme of architecture and death later in this chapter.)[3] Occupants of the classic labyrinth cannot map it; interior movement is entirely local, provisional, and motivated by the binding purpose of arriving at a central destination; as such, labyrinths initiate serpentines not trajectories. As an occupied site, or situation, a labyrinth might best be considered as a continuously cursive movement constructed on the rhetorical model of an extended periphrasis, and as Pierre Rosenstiehl astutely discerns, "It is the traveler and his myopia who makes the labyrinth, not the architect and his perspectives" (quoted in Damisch 31). In other words a labyrinth is only a labyrinth to unwitting users. How convenient it would be then for the dweller not to think and react emotionally, for without thought and feeling, the body of the person would be processed mechanically into and out of the structure.[4]

There is a popular terminological confusion between maze and labyrinth, the former not emerging until the late Renaissance. The maze and the labyrinth are topological variants involving two vastly different logics of passage; in the latter, ambulation occurs along and around the convolution of a single path; the architectural subject is never actually lost in a labyrinth. Linear, deterministic, and with zero requirements of choice from its perambulator, Eco likens this topology to a skein which upon unwinding, "one obtains a continuous line. In this kind of labyrinth the Ariadne thread is useless, since one *cannot* get lost: the labyrinth itself is the Ariadne thread" (80). The maze, or *Irrweg*, gains in complexity, presenting choices among alternative routes, of which some are deliberate dead-ends.[5]

Architect Bernard Tschumi appropriates two figures from Bataille to construct his own architectural binary: he opposes the labyrinth, which is understood as intransigently non-conceptual and a pure, immediate ontological experience, to the pyramid, which is comprehended as "a dematerialization of architecture in its ontological form" (Tschumi 43). Together the pyramid and the labyrinth articulate the ruling paradox of architecture: the impossibility to conceptualize and experience space at the same time. Tschumi likens the labyrinth to "the dark corners of experience . . . where all sensations, all feelings are enhanced, but where no overview is present to provide a clue about how to get out. Occasional consciousness is of little help, for perception in the Labyrinth presupposes immediacy" (42). A labyrinth of this kind offers, first and foremost, a disorientation of architectural time; the required itinerary is one of local decisions and indeterminate windings and returns in which erroneous decisions and unproductive movements are impossible. One cannot get lost in a labyrinth, nor even make a mistake, so in this respect Tschumi's claim that "there may be no way out of a labyrinth" is architecturally incorrect (43). One can and does, however, experience an illusion of being lost in the windowless, unicursal edifice.[6] Indeed, the classical labyrinth is prototypical of what Germano Celant calls "deprived space," a space in which "'participants' can only find themselves as the subject, aware only of their own fantasies and pulsations, able only to react to the low-density signals of their own bodies" (quoted in Tschumi 43).

## II. Background: The Refusal of Architectural Functionalism

Before proceeding to a more detailed discussion of the labyrinth in both Situationist and Arakawa and Gins' procedural architecture, a brief historical background is necessary to explain the grounds for a shared common *telos*: the uncompromising repudiation of the planetary malfeasance named functionalism.[7] The date 1933 is marked in the history of Western architecture by the ratification of the Athens Charter, which outlined and endorsed the nature of "the future city." This charter thereby encoded the Corbusian style and principles of the modern "functionalist" city predicated on the twin linked paradigms of utility and efficiency. As Rayner Banham elucidates:

the persuasive generality which gave this Charter its air of universal applicability concealed a very narrow conception of both architecture and town planning and committed the CIAM *(Congrès Internationaux d'Architecture Moderne)* unequivocally to: (a) a rigid functional zoning of city plans, with green belts between the areas reserved to the different functions and (b) a single type of urban housing, expressed in the words of the Charter as "high, widely-spaced apartment blocks wherever the necessity of housing high densities of population exists." (quoted in Sadler 22)

The anesthetic safety of suburban housing and apartment blocks, so stifling to spontaneity and freedom, brutally actualized an architecture of alienation and constraint, in turn bolstering the contamination of the claustrophobic tranquility of bourgeois life. It is the settled, juxtaposed immobility of this officially sanctioned "A"rchitecture that Constant and Gins and Arakawa confront with a vehemence and determination unmatched in force.

The justifiable diatribes against pacifying functionality in architecture, however, do not originate with Constant. Prior to *New Babylon*, in the 1920s, Czech cubist architecture launched a direct attack on stability, one that aspired to a disorder built into permanence. Robert Harbison's colorful description effectively conveys the psychological and emotional impact of this architecture:

In its exciting moments hardly an inch of the fabric holds still. We have entered a world, like some fairground prank with mirrors, without a truly flat surface anywhere. So the entrance of Josef Chochol's flats on Neklanova in Prague with its appended prismatic porch induces something akin to paranoia. For us there can be no rest or relaxation but a kind of mental circling like that of a bird looking unsuccessfully for a perch. Finally of course this design raises the doubt brought on by any building which tries to enshrine a moment of crisis: will one's identity continue susceptible under its methodical attack, or will one begin to find its terrible uncertainty diverting? (Sadler 172–73)

The affinities to, and inspirations upon, Situationist unitary urbanism are found in numerous architectural projects from the mid-1950s on. Aldo van Eyck calls for cities of "labyrinthine clarity" that offer individual users and dwellers "a relative freedom of choice in the use and discovery of its spaces and places"; such clarity is the desideratum in his 1955 design for the Amsterdam Children's Home, which seeks to facilitate playful interaction and chance encounters among its child residents (Sadler 30). Contrasting yet sympathetic to *New Babylon* is

Rayner Banham's proposal for a "City as Scrambled Egg" approach to urban core planning—an approach Sadler estimates to be a liberal appropriation of Situationist unitary urbanism stripped of its politics. As Sadler explains, "[t]he core of Banham's Scrambled Egg City would be a labyrinth negotiated by pedestrians in ways that confound the logic of rationalist planning" (30). Banham launched this plan and others in his 1955 "Other Architecture" as "an alternative to rationalist orderliness" with a governing proposition "that inhabitants define their own environments by a fluid and playful selection of objects, services, and technologies, rather than submit to a monumental architecture imposed by the architect"; this approach clearly confesses to its Situationist affinities (Sadler 38).

A broad pessimism about the positive function of the architect in capitalist society characterized the radical architecture of the late 1950s and early 1960s. Michel Colle bemoaned the "cadaverous rigidity" of Corbusian architecture, with its "[a]rchitectural rigor mortis brought on less by its choice of materials, than the intransigent and uncompromising rationalism that spawned its angular regulative grids which culminate in the concept of the functional machine for living in" (quoted in Sadler 7). *Potlatch* (the magazine of the Situationist International, subsequently referred to as SI) called the machinic aesthetic of Corbusian rationalism both a "scab" and a "neo-cubist crust" (quoted in Sadler 10). The Situationists located the flaw of functionalism in a fatal choice of priorities: that of collective over individual interests; in response both the SI and the British Independent Group (IG) turned to a non-Cartesian "cluster model" of the city that provided a mega-structural model for emphasizing and preserving individual habitation. In its somber reassessment of rational functionalism, the SI pitted an expressionist will (seen as inherent in Bauhaus) against the technocratic rationalism of its later practitioners. Asger Jorn, in his debate with Swiss sculptor Max Bill, accuses him of converting Bauhaus from artistic inspiration to a dead doctrine without inspiration. The SI further detected a causal link between planned functionalism and alienation; in response they offered an extreme antidote in the form of disequilibrium and dysfunction.

The Situationists capitalized on the then recent sociological studies of Henri Lefebvre (*Critique of Everyday Life* 1946) and Pierre-Henri Chaubart de Lauwe (*Paris and the Parisian Agglomeration* 1952) that cogently exposed the non-unitary nature of cities as fragile yet dynamic micro-sociologies, locating authenticated life at a hypo-spectacular level beneath the dense lamination of images and commodities spawned by official urban capitalism. (By contrast, the avant-gardist IG voiced a more conciliatory relation to image and mass consumerism.) The SI advanced theories for participatory, spontaneous urbanism in lives not prearranged by transportation, work hours, and techno-functional facilities that fostered habit, convenience, passivity, and consequent ontological alienation. This anti-technological proclivity arose from a conviction that technological spin-offs in the domestic arena and the workplace are servo-mechanical and totalitarian in their mass organizational effects. Specular urbanism amounts to nothingness and drew acrimonious comments from Raoul Vaneigem who compared it "to the advertising propagated around Coca-Cola—pure spectacular ideology" (quoted in Sadler 16). For Vaneigem both information and urbanism function to "organize silence," and in liberal democracies and totalitarian regimes alike the urban ideal portrayed is nothing but "the projection in space of a social hierarchy without conflict" (quoted in Sadler 16, 18).

Constant and Guy Debord supplied a terse theoretical model for such "ideal" urbanism: *unitary urbanism,* defined by them as "The Theory of the combined use of arts and techniques for the integral construction of a milieu in dynamic relation with experiments in behavior" (quoted in Knabb 45). No boundaries are acknowledged in such a construction; the separation of life into private and public domains and work and leisure spheres will be abolished. Conceived as a complex and protean activity, unitary urbanism was deliberately designed to intervene in the workings of everyday life; it aimed at establishing a harmony between human living and human needs that opens up new possibilities "that will in turn transform those needs" (quoted in Wigley 132). Debord, for instance, proposed a radical alternative to the Athens Charter's functional zoning plans that would link traffic flows to the key function of housing, work, and recreation by simply rethinking the function of the automobile as an adjunct not to work but to pleasure. In contrast to the CIAM, which argued for the home as the shelter of the family and the nucleus of town planning, unitary urbanists insisted on the necessary transformation of architecture "to accord with the whole development of society, criticizing . . . condemned forms of social relationships in the first rank of which is the family" (Sadler 27).

Where Arakawa and Gins offer an "architectural body" (as we will shortly see), the Situationists propose a "psychogeographical body," redolent with Mallarméan impersonality whose daily mandate is the practice of *dérive,* which is defined by the SI as a "mode of experimental behavior linked to the conditions of urban society: a technique of transient passage through varied ambiences" (quoted in Knabb 45). Vincent Kaufmann describes this practice as a "walking purged of autobiographical representation . . . requiring the enunciatory and ambulatory disappearance of the walker" (Kaufmann 61). This latter condition is worth comparing to Kenneth Goldsmith's *Fidget* project described and discussed in chapter 6, but it's more apposite to the concerns of this present chapter to lay down the fact that it is precisely this repudiation of any flâneuristic self-consciousness and the embrace of spontaneous and non-habitual movement that connects the *dérive* to labyrinthine circuitry. Debord remarks on the intimate connection between the *dérive* and architectural labyrinthine construction: "Within architecture itself, the task for *dériving* tends to promote all sorts of new forms of labyrinths made possible by modern techniques of construction" (53). Returning to the classic model of the labyrinth, one might say the *dérive* provides the Ariadne thread that is itself the labyrinth. The radical break with the classical model lies however in the variant desires of the labyrinth dweller. The unicursal structure of the classical model guarantees upon entering a sure return; by contrast the *dérive,* whose soft architectural form is determined entirely by human desire, consecrates and celebrates irreversibility.

Kaufmann notes "the frequency of the figure of the labyrinth from which the Situationists have no intention of exiting, a kind of ultimate refuge from the society of the spectacle" (62). In their planned psychogeographic alteration of Les Halles (the famous Paris market complex), the SI proposed replacing the central pavilions of the market with a series of Situationist architectural complexes, erected in the vicinity of perpetually changing labyrinths. There is a link by strategy here that graphs labyrinthine complexity onto fundamental instability and morphological change. In this way, the labyrinth is refashioned as an evanescent and constantly mutating site that fulfills Bataille's own revisionist labyrinthine desire to always lose one's way.

## III. Constant and *New Babylon*

*New Babylon* expanded from Constant's 1957 design for a permanent gypsy camp at Alba in Italy; the name "New Babylon" was first used in 1960 at Guy Debord's suggestion (illus. Wigley *Constant's New Babylon* 80-81). Its origins and initial development, however, lay in a specific cartographical disruption enacted during the years of 1957 and 1959. As part of their psychogeographic explorations Debord and Asger Jorn produced several cut-up tourist maps of Paris. These maps discarded whole areas and reassembled only an axis of "psychogeographical" intensities that offered a would-be traveler drifting itineraries of desire. Psychogeographic maps such as "The Naked City" and "Psychogeographic Guide" (illus. Wigley *Constant's New Babylon* 19) are conscious reactions to the Cartesian grid and return cartography to disorientation and multiple lines of flight, thereby extending the practice beyond a mapping of physical terrains to that of intimate states of consciousness and feeling.[8] Constant's *New Babylon* was envisioned to be the architectural realization of such a map as an inhabitable city.

Like Arakawa, Constant came to architecture through painting, and *New Babylon* would be inconceivable without his prior involvement with the visual arts through the COBRA group during the late 1940s and 1950s.[9] Founded in 1948 by three young artists—Asger Jorn in Copenhagen, Constant (then Constant Nieuwenhuys) in Amsterdam, and Christian Dotremont in Brussels—COBRA embraced and developed an imaginative practice whose anti-aesthetic, anti-theoretical paradigms of spontaneity, decomposition, desire, and the complete psychological emancipation of the individual set them apart from mainstream Surrealism.[10] The ontology and praxis of childhood provided one of their major retroactive sources of inspiration. COBRA's brute anti-formalism, its unconditional vitalist embrace of spontaneity, and its energetic immediacy all establish their model in the panoply of expressions, graphic and acoustic license, and the general play of children. Breton and Bataille before him had caught upon the paradoxical quality of children's art: that its playfulness, innocence, and spontaneity engendered subversion and restlessness. As Bataille noted in his reflections on *l'informe*, children indulge in formal distortion rather than formal construction. If Constant listened and heard the call of brute desire emerging from the child and consecrated the latter as a countercultural hero-model during his COBRA years, then he left the group with the anticipation of even greater potential for the child as a mobilizing architectural figure. The model was already nascent in Peter Bruegel the Elder's 1560 painting *Children's Games* (now in the Kunsthistorisches Museum, Vienna), but there were at least two ready precedents that proved influential on the designs and vision of *New Babylon*, namely Aldo Van Eyck's sixty playgrounds in Amsterdam designed between 1947 and 1955, and Peter and Alison Smithson's 1952 plan for the Golden Lane Housing Project in London. The latter of these developed out of a close analysis of the movement patterns of children playing and took the form of a spreading network that approximated a maze rather than a labyrinth, in which solid organization disappears in favor of free mobility.

Constant's short essay from late 1959, "A Different City for a Different Life," offers a succinct description of *New Babylon* (there referred to as "the city of the future"):[11]

The city of the future must be conceived of as a continuous construction on pillars, or else as an extended system of different constructions, in which

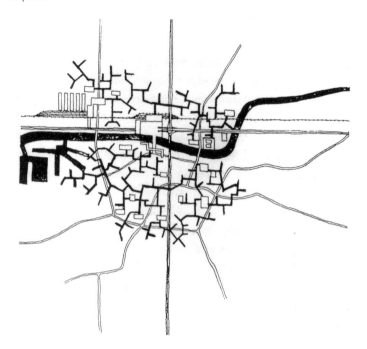

Fig. 2. Golden Lane Housing Project by Alison and Peter Smithson, 1952 (Source: de Zegher and Wigley *The Activist Drawing*).

> premises for living, pleasure, etc., are suspended as well as those designed
> for production and distribution, leaving the ground free for circulation
> and public meetings. The use of ultra-light and insulating materials, now
> being tried experimentally, will allow for light construction and broadly
> based supports. In this way it will be possible to build a multilayered city:
> underground, ground level, stories, terraces, of an expanse that may vary
> from a neighborhood to a metropolis. (111)

In their collaborative *Mémoires,* Debord and Jorn refer to the image of a "floating city," an image realized in Constant's megastructure, which was envisioned
as suspended 16 meters above the ground and representing "a sort of extension
of the Earth's surface, a new skin that covers the Earth and multiplies its living space" (quoted in Sadler 129–30). The design took the form of a paratactic,
cluster configuration of loosely interlocking sectors suspended above the terrain in which were housed a number of movable partitions, the effects of which
Constant summarizes as "a quite chaotic arrangement of small and bigger spaces

that are constantly mounted and dismounted by means of standardized mobile construction elements, like walls, floors and staircases" (quoted in Sadler 132). Unlike Arakawa and Gins' ubiquitous site in a locally circumscribed area, *New Babylon* was planned to literally leech over cities and countries. Cartographic schemes for *New Babylon* were drawn up for several European cities: Amsterdam, Rotterdam, Antwerp, Paris, The Hague, Cologne, Barcelona, and a vast plan for the Ruhrgebeit.[12]

The *dérive* supplies the link between Situationist architecture and agency. Indeed, *New Babylon* remains prototypical of architectural *dérive*, its most important feature being the vast and unconditional participatory potential of its occupants. Constant referred to *New Babylon* as "a creative game with an imaginary environment" (quoted in Sadler 123) and as late as 1964 admitted the plan was "nothing but a suggestion" (quoted in Wigley *Constant's New Babylon* 67). New Babylonians are presented with a multiplicity of control options: temperature, lighting, humidity, atmosphere, and walls, with the shape of the architectural space open to alteration at a mere push of a button. Constant's project demands a broad architectural shift from worker to player, from *homo faber* to *homo ludens*, and under the temporal rubric of ephemerality, *New Babylon* replaces controlled function with spontaneity among a plethora of individual creative options. (It comes as no surprise that it is the modern airport, predicated on transient passage rather than sedentary "dwelling," that offered Constant the vision of his future city.) There is an intimate equation of mobility to creative freedom in this provisional, boundaryless anti-architecture *à pilotis*.[13] The Situationist architect will be a new Daedalus of constructed situations whose architectural aspirations manifest as the endless diversionary traces of both visible and invisible labyrinths in a soft architecture of the *dérive*.[14] Situations will provide the germinal forces for architectural and environmental reconstruction, and discrete artistic practice (sculptures, paintings, and poems) will be replaced by imaginative practices of everyday life.

Within this condition of structural impermanence and change, the labyrinth figured importantly as an architectural agent of disorientation, a psycho-somatic quality Constant valued as an instrument for lateral thinking and experience.[15] In March 1955 the SI announced the first "do-it-yourself labyrinth" in the form of a New York Building, "that showed the first signs of the applicability of the *dérive* to apartment interiors: 'The rooms in the helicoidal house will be like slices of cake. They can be made larger or smaller at will by shifting partitions. . . . This system makes it possible to transform three four-room apartments into a single apartment with twelve or more rooms in six hours'" (quoted in Kaufmann 63).

In the light of such designs the uncanny apposition of the commodity's logic of built-in obsolescence and the SI's impermanent architectures might prove to be a permanent and irreconcilable irony.

In *New Babylon*, structure and metamorphosis are designed to have a direct impact on bodies (I will soon note this too in relation to Arakawa and Gins' *Reversible Destiny* sites). "*New Babylon*," wrote Constant, "is one immeasurable labyrinth. Every space is temporary, nothing is recognizable, everything is discovery, everything changes, nothing can serve as a landmark. Thus psychologically a space is created which is many times larger than the actual space" (quoted in Sadler 143). (We will note a similar imperative to variety among the theorists of the picturesque discussed in the next chapter.) The labyrinth and the city became one. Constant's salient contribution to the history of the labyrinth lies in his fundamental repudiation of the static classical model while retaining its archaic force. In his Yellow Sector, Constant installed two labyrinth houses expressly designed to "take up and develop the ancient forces of architectural confusion" ("Description of the Yellow Sector" Wigley 122, illus. 88–89).

*New Babylon* is to be a dynamic labyrinth, a collective assemblage (and disassemblage) designed to serve the whims of a society dedicated to play in which explosive creativity—spontaneous and instinctual—are upheld as the paramount *desiderata*. Constant finds attractive not only the polymorphic provisionalities of the dynamic labyrinth but also its power of inducing efficacious disorientations. The new Babylonian "takes an active stance vis-à-vis his surroundings: he seeks to intervene, to change things, he travels extensively and wherever he goes he leaves traces of his ludic activities. Space for him is a toy for exploration, adventure, and play" (Constant "The Principles of Disorientation," quoted in Wigley *Constant's New Babylon* 225). By envisioning a "Zone of Play" containing "'labyrinth houses' consisting of a large number of rooms of irregular form, stairs at angles, lost corners, open spaces, culs-de-sac," there is the constant possibility to realize *dérive* (quoted in Vidler 213).[16]

As late as 1974, Constant, reflecting on the problematic nature of such a highly processual "construction," frankly admits to an ideological, political, and economic impasse: "A dynamic labyrinth cannot be designed, it cannot originate in the mind of a single individual. It arises in the first instance as a non-stop process that can be initiated and maintained by the simultaneous activity of a great many individuals. And this implies a social freedom and, concomitantly, a massive creative potential, that are inconceivable in the utilitarian society" ("The Principle of Disorientation," quoted in Wigley *Constant's New Babylon* 225). The situational and collective nature of the dynamic labyrinth presupposes play and creative leisure as the governing ideological paradigm and lifestyle. In light of this, Constant is aware of the compromise formation that any limited laboratory form of experimental space will offer: "The essential precondition for a dynamic labyrinth, namely the simultaneous creative activity of a large number of individuals, resulting in a collectively generated situation, cannot, of course, be realized in the context of an experimental space. The experimental space is no more than an (imperfect) object of study" (ibid.). Despite his unqualified commitment to spontaneity and emancipation, Constant, like Arakawa and Gins, elevates the heuristic to an architectural imperative. This agenda becomes clear in his exhilarating 1962–63 hybrid *Labyratorium (Labyratoire),* which was designed to incorporate the playful meanderings and disorientations of labyrinthine space within the scientific and hermeneutic experiments of a laboratory condition (illus. McDonough 99). The design and technology that make up the *Labyratorium*—complete with atmospheric obstacles and transformations in temperature as well as visual space (by means of sliding mirrors)—precipitate a gamut of sensory defamiliarization and novel experiences induced through impediments. Thus, it would be misleading to paint an image of *New Babylon* as a constant creative mutation. Constant's Rotterdam labyrinth (1966) contained "rooms that exposed their occupants to sounds, colors, and smells" as well as rooms that compressed occupants into cramped, small areas in which they had to crawl their way through (Sadler 149). And at least one aspect of the project backfired: Constant's plan of wiring the labyrinth with a telephonic update of the Ariadne thread so that the occupants could phone out with their reactions actually helped keep their behavior conditioned and rational.

Constant's designs have some surprising morphological evocations and premonitions. The L-shaped labyrinths (found in some *Reversible Destiny* designs) are evident in the Orient Sector, the 1959 plan of the Yellow Sector. They are also visible in the lesser known *Architectural Maquette* of 1958, which structurally anticipates Arakawa and Gins' *Antimortality Fractal Zipper City* whose contours similarly all derive from abutting twin L-shaped labyrinths (see *Reversible Destiny* 252–53). A colored sketch from 1968 shows a mobile labyrinth of open, intersecting cubic spaces forming a multilevel construction connected by ladders; these features instantly evoke a Piranesi open plan, with the *carceri* deprived of their solidity but not of their spatial illogic.[17] The chain of evocations does not end here. Constant peoples his labyrinth with cyclists riding up the ladders, suspended monocycles, and a more complex wheeled vehicle (an intentional allusion to both Marcel Duchamp and Jarry's Père Ubu in this staffage is not inconceivable). Freely drawn circles undercut the angularity of the structure with

Fig. 3. *Architectural Maquette* by Constant, 1958 (Source: *October* 79).

hints of dynamic cyclic action (see de Zegher *The Activist Drawing* 116). But perhaps the most surprising morphological evocation is that of the simple wooden,
multilevel fishing platforms found around Stanleyville in the Belgian Congo and
in Vieste, Italy (see Rudofsky 107–8). The startling apposition may be chance (I
will argue a more plausible influence of a different image in Rudofsky's book on
Arakawa and Gins in part IV of this chapter), but it is worth noting the func-

tional return of the labyrinth and the link of dynamic labyrinthine form to cultural conditions vastly different from the urban complexities of Paris and other large European cities. Piranesi's spatial illogicalities and the consequent architectural dangers are picked up once more in a 1969 color crayon drawing of a "labyrinthine space" but in this instance they become synthesized with the flat modularity of modernist space (see de Zegher 117).

Omar Calabrese claims the labyrinth to be a "profoundly baroque" figure that most frequently draws critical and creative attention "during 'baroque' periods" (131–32). Thus with its perpetual motion, dynamic change, and consequent labyrinthine, architectural insecurity, it is not fanciful to claim that *New Babylon* approximates Baroque atmospherics. At the same time *New Babylon* elicits a different consideration through various Deleuzian topics. Deleuze's impact on contemporary architectural thought is considerable and notably through a single publication: *The Fold*. Evidence of this narrow importation of Deleuze's concept of plication can be gathered from the contents page of *Folding in Architecture*, edited by Greg Lynn and published in 1993: "Architectural Curvilinearity" (Greg Lynn), "Folding in Time" (Peter Eisenman), "Unfolding Architecture" (Chuck Hoberman), "Out of the Fold" (John Rachman), and "The Material Fold" (Claire Robinson). Notwithstanding the architectural usefulness of folding, there are two more of Deleuze's concepts that seem strikingly apposite to Constant's project. One agenda of *The Fold* is to rehabilitate the Baroque as a transhistoric phenomenon of folding; indeed, Deleuze's book is redolent with architectural suggestions (pre-eminently the Baroque or Leibnizian monad conceived as a two-story windowless building). Early in the book Deleuze introduces the *objectile*, a technological concept newly formulated by a former student of Deleuze: the French architect, Bernard Cache. "The *objectile* refers to our current state of things, *where fluctuation of the norm replaces the permanence of a law;* where the object assumes a place in a continuum by variation . . . . The new status of the object no longer refers its condition to a spatial mould—in other words, to a relation of form-matter—but to *a temporal modulation that implies as much the beginnings of a continuous variation of matter as a continuous development of form*" (Deleuze *The Fold* 19, my emphases). This describes *New Babylon in nuce*, where form, solidity, and consistency give way to "temporal modulation" and continuous, unpredictable variation of architectural matter. Moreover, if we theorize the inhabitants of such *objectile* architecture as *subjectiles*, if we in other words theorize the dweller as a free agent of *objectility*, we approximate the entire *desiderata* of Constant's project. Cache's *objectile* immediately conjures up Deleuze's similar notion of *becoming*. For Deleuze, becoming is a profoundly ahistoric move to "create something new" (*Negotiations* 171). "Becomings," he informs, "belong to geography, they are orientations, directions, entries and exits. . . . There is no terminus from which you set out, none which you arrive at or which you ought to arrive at. [Becomings] are acts which can only be contained in a life and expressed in a style. Styles are not constructions, any more than they are modes of life" (*A Thousand Plateaus* 2–3). Given this Deleuzean inflection, "becoming" accurately describes both the structure and occupation of *New Babylon* as dynamic labyrinth.

Is Deleuzean architecture in a state of constant becoming? Mark Wigley specifies the presiding paradox in *New Babylon*. How can one present a multimedia megastructure that is ever changing, subject to the wills and creative intervention of its users, from within? And in this instance what is it to be within? "Since the basic principle of *New Babylon* was constant change, any one representation of it or any one medium of representation, was clearly suspect" (Wigley "Paper, Scissors, Blur" 33). Thomas McDonough similarly ruminates on the irresolvable paradox that was *New Babylon*: "The basis of this utopian city lay, after all, in the conviction that the need of a truly free society would be so complex, so changeable, that any attempt by a single architect to anticipate them would lead to inevitably repressive results" (97). Let's recall here Tschumi's comments on the dark spaces of experience, where sensory enhancement collides with the absence, the impossible presence, of an overview. The unavoidable architectural aporia locates in the utter triumph of provisionality in a constantly changing labyrinth whose architects (constructively and destructively) are the new Babylonians themselves. The sociological consequence of this paradoxical anti-architecture is clear: an increase of unprecedented enormity in the powers by which inhabitants determine their own architectural surrounds and vectors. Constant himself was aware of the paradoxical nature of his project: "the structures are anything but permanent. It is effectively a matter of a microstructure in continuous transformation, in which the time factor—the fourth dimension—plays a considerable role" (quoted in McDonough 97).[18] We still remain, however, in a version of deprived space, albeit one significantly transposed from the individual to the collective level.

Marc Wigley concludes that "Constant dedicated himself to drawing a mirage" ("Paper, Scissors, Blur" 52); it is difficult to rescue *New Babylon* from the detritus and misprisions of historical contingency. Constant too was aware of the impossibility of *New Babylon* in the economic climate of the 1960s. His entire project, and the SI movement as a whole, was predicated on the validity of a general theory of leisure conceived in a state of post-capitalist abundance. Both mistakenly assumed a future characterized by the total automation of production, collective ownership of land, and a potential lifestyle of unbounded leisure. In the nascent neo-liberal stages of the twenty-first century we are closer to actualizing the former but moving further and further from the latter. Moreover, the celebration of ephemerality and change carried a more ominous burden of its own kinetics of impermanence: a Heraclitan urbanism whose potential to violence is the omnipresent norm. The Situationist Ivan Chtcheglov (pseudonym of Gilles Ivain) warned against the "explosion, dissolution, dissociation, disintegration" that threatens the continual drifter (quoted in Sadler 145). Given its embrace of anarchic freedom, *New Babylon* remains a constantly uncertain, unhomely locale, where the "space of desire is finally understood as a place of conflict" (Wigley *Constant's New Babylon* 69). Constant himself had already noted this sinister return of the Minotaur to the labyrinth. He admitted that, "*New Babylon* is an uncertain universe where the 'normal' man is at the mercy of every possible destructive force, every kind of aggression. . . . The image of a free man who does not have to struggle for his existence is without historical basis . . . man's aggressivity does not disappear with the satisfaction of his immediate material needs" (quoted in Wigley *Constant's New Babylon* 69). "To really appreciate architecture," Bernard Tschumi comments, "you may even have to commit murder" (100).[19]

We might be justified then in writing off *New Babylon* as an inevitably failed utopia; yet some of its prophecies may in fact have been realized. Constant's vision waxed and waned under the conceptual guidance and apothegmic challenge of the belief voiced by Walter Benjamin that the labyrinth ranks as the ancient dream of humanity and that the city is its realization. But perhaps the actualization transcends the civic dimension and takes an immaterial, hyperspatial form. Both prophetic and reflective, *New Babylon* finds its realization in the technologically inspired mobile cities of Archigram and, as Marcos Novak insists, in the electronic circuitries of the web.[20] The fifth point in Constant and Debord's 1958 "Amsterdam Declaration" defined unitary urbanism as "the complex, ongoing activity which consciously recreates man's environment *according to the most advanced conceptions in every domain*" (quoted in Wigley *Constant's New Babylon* 87, emphasis added). Constant readily embraced contemporary technology; the computer was central to *New Babylon* and, in spirit at least, his visionary project augured the realm of virtual and cyber-architectonics.

Catherine de Zegher endorses this prophetic, labyrinthine, technological dimension of *New Babylon*: "Prefiguring the current debate about architecture in the often placeless age of electronics, Constant seems to have conceived of an urban model that literally envisaged the World Wide Web. In the network of sectors in *New Babylon*, one configures his or her own space and can wander in an unobstructed way from site to site, without limits" (10).

In his "Theory of the Dérive," Debord seized on the fecund analogy of ocean and city, likening the "psychogeographical relief [of cities to] constant currents, fixed point and vortexes which strongly discourage entry into or from certain zones" (quoted in Knabb 50). This link of city to ocean served as a formative analogy in *New Babylon* and is currently intransigently installed as the governing metaphor of the World Wide Web (itself a metaphor). The *dérive* returns in the activity of "surfing," set against the more protentive act of "navigating." Moreover, it resuscitates the ancestral phenotype of the new Babylonian in the Baudelairean flâneur, with streets, crowds, cafés, and peregrination updated to a solitary, seated manual connection to a world of websites, search engines, interfaces, and links. It is beyond dispute that the web and Internet have successfully incorporated many of the features of *New Babylon* and have realized certain of Constant's aspirations: de-centeredness, user control, multiple choice and variations, and sensory euphoria. We have traced the impact of the web and informatics on contemporary trends in poetry; in chapter 6 we discussed how the Internet gave rise to Google sculpting (Flarf) and a poetics of information management (Goldsmith). But hold back on euphoria, for questions linger beneath superficial comparisons. What, for instance, is the fate of collective lived experience, so central to *New Babylon*, in an age of digital immaterialism? The triumph of machinic interactivity is indisputable when considering the fate of intersubjective communication. As media theorist Lev Manovich elucidates, when surfing the net a human user addresses a machine, with communication "centered on the physical channel and the very act of connection between addresser and addressee" (206). Web sites, computer games, and virtual worlds are governed by a specific temporal dynamic that Manovich describes as "constant, repetitive oscillation between an illusion and its suspense" (205). Historically speaking, the emergence of the World Wide Web was not born with post-industrial capitalism but rather as a consequence of it. In our contemporary global, techno-political condition under neo-liberalism it is sobering to reflect on the fact that *New Babylon* drew criticism from the SI for its attempt to integrate mass living into a totally technological environment, thus constituting an extension, not rejection, of capitalist ideology.

## IV. The Labyrinth in Procedural Architecture: Arakawa and Gins' *Reversible Destiny*

*A map of the world without utopia on it is not worth looking at, because it excludes the only country where mankind is constantly landing.*
—Oscar Wilde

Any discussion of Arakawa and Gins' position in the history of the labyrinth must take into account the labyrinth's function within their wider, revolutionary project *Reversible Destiny*, whose own urgent context seems accurately formulated in the following statement by British architect Neil Spiller.[21] "'The architectural subject' is changing (by 'subject' both the body and practice is meant). Traditional notions of architectural enclosure are unable to respond to the growing range and virtuosity of the body and this is an escalating problem. Architectural theory has been slow, if not frighteningly inert, in understanding and facilitating the metamorphosis of its own subject, both spatially and biologically" (104). At the outset I must admit that I find one aspect of Gins and Arakawa's self-historicizing problematic. The subtitle of their book *Architecture Sites of Reversible Destiny* is "Architectural Experiments after Auschwitz-Hiroshima." To grammatically link two vastly discrete events, both horrendous and genocidal but so contextually different, strikes me as ethically—because historically—irresponsible. It is a ghastly irony that Heidegger commits the almost identical conflation in his notoriously minimal break with taciturnity around the matter of the Nazi extermination of the Jews (and others) in his 1949 second Bremen Lecture: "Agriculture is now a mechanized food industry, in essence the same as the manufacture of corpses in the gas chambers and extermination camps, the same as the blockade and starvation of the countryside, the same as the production of the hydrogen bombs" (quoted in Lang 16). Leaving aside whatever these comments reveal about Heidegger, their substance should warn against grasping at essences and reveal the danger of analogy and the irresponsibility of false copulas. I will need to touch on the historic trauma named "Auschwitz" toward the end of this chapter when I consider *Reversible Destiny* (with its slogan "We have decided not to die") against certain bio-political assertions of Giorgio Agamben; these will provide the bridge into this book's final two chapters, which examine the strange affiliations of the event named "Auschwitz," arguably history's most atrocious anomaly. Ironically, it is a Situationist who introduces and briefly alludes to these two event-atrocities (Auschwitz and Hiroshima) in relation to urban planning. Writing in 1961, Raoul Vaneighem notes with bitter sarcasm that "[i]f the Nazis had known contemporary urbanists, they would have transformed concentration camps into low-income housing"; later in the same article he writes, "to destroy one's adversary with H-bombs is to condemn oneself to die in more protracted suffering" (Vaneighem 123, 126).

A different, more practical problem I face is my limited exposure to *Reversible Destiny* sites. Rather than explore the multilevel labyrinth or the *Site of Reversible Destiny—Yoro Park* in Japan (see Arakawa and Gins *Reversible Destiny* 194–213), my knowledge of their work is restricted to computer-generated images and texts in books and magazines, as well as personal discussions with Ms. Gins on the odd occasion. Strictly speaking, at this point of time, we should discriminate between two "Reversible Destinies": the texts, images and models, i.e. the sum of its representations, and the growing number of realized constructions. We must additionally and constantly stay alert to the fact that *Reversible Destiny* is *not* a paper or computer architecture but intended for construction, habitation, and an ethical program for living. Unlike Constant, Arakawa and Gins have brought some of their visionary architecture to reality, and as more *Reversible Destiny* sites are built and utilized, more pragmatic answers will be forthcoming to the questions their project raises. These answers will be supplied by the users, the dwellers, the "Reversed Destinarians" of reversible destiny.

If Lebbeus Woods offers a "radical architecture," then what do Arakawa and Gins propose? This is an urgent and timely question that should occupy the thinking of all contemporary architects whose work has any ethical inflection; it is also a question that should not be answered too readily. Their work as procedural architects finds itself in a complicated situation among and between the three major discourses of ethics, philosophy, and history. Mark Taylor situates it intellectually in a post-Kantian idealism, a phenomenology of perception that "falls between Hegel's phenomenology of spirit and Merleau-Ponty's phenomenology of perception" (128). Yet the greater proximity to the latter is clearly evident in the following comments on Merleau-Ponty by Ignasi Solà-Morales that illustrate cogently the undeniable affinity of *Reversible Destiny* to postwar phenomenological aspirations:

Maurice Merleau-Ponty's *Phenomenologie de la perception* of 1945 offers a synthetic summary of a body of research based on studies of both the structure of behavior and the primacy of perception. This research displaced the merely visual, replacing it with the idea that our experience of the world around us comes from the body in its totality: spatio-temporal, sexual, mobile, and expressive. The visual-tactile dichotomy posited by

Alois Riegl in the early years of the [twentieth] century in order to analyze the various different orders of aesthetic experience was converted by the phenomenologists into a much more general, more basic theory. Even the aesthetic was thus to be understood as that which was connected not with artistic perception but, in a much wider sense, with interactions of every kind between the self and the world (22).

Heidegger's and Merleau-Ponty's separate contributions to architectural theory rest (albeit indirectly) in a common depreciation of the optical paradigm. Both thinkers are also concerned with the recovery of the essential relation of body to labyrinth through the radical proposal that a being's relationship to space is quintessentially one of movement.[22]

*In fact, unless one is in some way enclosed in one [body], one is nothing; but if, on the other hand, one is perfectly truthful, bodies do not exist.*
—St. Augustine, *De vera religione*[23]

Augustine inscribes here a Christian dogma that Arakawa and Gins' *Reversible Destiny* refutes. An architectural body will succeed Augustine's aporial body and be installed in the initiatory premise of procedural architecture as its basic presupposition.[24] It equally eschews Bataille's 1929 definition of architecture as the violent imposition of social order via a calculated monumentality that becomes "the real masters of the world, grouping servile multitudes in their shadows" (quoted in Hollier 53). For Arakawa and Gins, "[a]rchitecture, in anyone's definition of it, exists primarily to be at the service of the body" (*Architectural Body* xi). Bataille, of course, did not endorse his own definition; thinking back to Haussmann and anticipating Albert Speer, he remains alert to the violence at the heart of any monumental aspiration. In the direct lineage of Vitruvian architectural thinking, Bataille connects human to architectural form via a system of projected proportions; to his mind, however, this anthropomorphism results in the petrification of all human activity. Both Constant and Arakawa and Gins are attracted to the benefits of architectural disequilibrium, but Bataille is fascinated by a latent anti-architecture brought about in the purposeful disfiguration of the human form in certain expressionist painting and in children's drawings.

For Arakawa and Gins and non-procedural architects like Robin Evans, who alike see architecture as the construction of the preconditions that govern the way bodies occupy and negotiate space, the question of architectural form and architectural thinking concerns architecture's relation to the scale and matter of human freedom.[25] Arakawa and Gins' singular insight, however, derives from the basic premise that the body is a place, not an identity. Body is local and geographic before it is cognitive and subjective; it is *dasein,* understood as a being "there" in an architectural surround. Moreover, it should be made clear from the outset that their concern with the human body is uncontaminated by intrusive, historical aesthetics. Indeed, their work involves a seminal repudiation not only of Modernist functionality but also of architecture's enduring anthropomorphic paradigm.

In "It and I: Bodies as Objects, Bodies as Subjects," Karen A. Franck offers the useful distinction between designs *for* the body and designs *from* the body, i.e. embodied from transcendental architecting. Designs *from* the body historically led to the anthropomorphic paradigm that governed architecture from Vitruvius to Modernism, precipitating a litany of humanist theories on the relation of human bodily proportions to extrinsic and enveloping dwellings. Liane Lefaivre traces the emergence of the anthropomorphic metaphor (so central to humanist architectural thinking) through three dominant counter-strategies to the patristic conception of buildings as "dangerous bodies." The first, developing in the tenth century, reconfigures the body as the "marvelous body," a repository or magnet attracting a panoply of glittering appurtenances: jewels, cloths, etc. In the twelfth century the "divine" body finds conception, linked to incorporeality, divine luminescence, and geometric proportion and relation. Finally, the "desired" body, conceived as a vital attractor and target of ardor and passionate forces, emerges with Alberti in the fifteenth century.[26] (We have already met with the twentieth century's "itemized body" in Kenneth Goldsmith's *Fidget* in chapter 6.) The anthropomorphic episteme governing the canons of proportion remained pandemic precisely because the measure of man was taken to be the measure of God. This isomorphism of *anthropos* and *theos* granted divine sanction to numerous aberrant architectural feats such as the howling face at Bomarzo, "behind which is a room entered by the mouth lit by the eyes" (Harbison 49).[27]

As well as issuing a carte blanche rejection of anthropomorphism, Modernist architecture also deserted the body as living, projective, and permeable embodiment, losing sight of the fact that bodies inhabit and negotiate space as their primary architecture. This latter fact, quintessential to Arakawa and Gins' procedural praxis, implicates the legacy of phenomenology from Heidegger through Merleau-Ponty up to Karen A. Franck, and equally that "other" tradition of Modernism that includes Frank Lloyd Wright, Alvar Aalto, and Eric Mendelsohn, as noted by Colin St. John.[28] Juhani Pallasmaa comments on the dominating optical paradigm that governed Modernist architecture's obsessive focus on the visible and effected the mental separation of buildings from human bodies: "Modernist design has housed the intellect and the eyes, but it has left the body and other senses, as well as our memories and dreams, homeless" (Pallasmaa 10). This retinal privileging becomes exacerbated in postmodern architecture, which laminated semiotics onto the visual form in order to render architecture "readable" as contrasting codes. It thus seems a curious irony in *Reversible Destiny* that the concern for an architectural body is to a large extent arrived at and disseminated through sophisticated computer generation and cybertechnology but is most readily available through illustrations and documentation in books and magazines. Indeed, at the present stage, Arakawa and Gins' work largely exists in what would have been Constant's dream: the disembodied, immateriality of computer-generated virtual architecture. Franck comments on the physical, servo-mechanistic consequences of a computer screen: engaged in three-dimensional models and interactive computer programs, "[t]he architect's body can remain nearly immobile: there is no need for physical manipulation of materials and tools" (Franck 8). With the additional elimination of tactile and olfactorial sensations, virtual architecting signals the triumph of the visual in a techno-transcendental space of simulacra. Franck's comments can be extended to the dwellers and users of cybernetic spaces where, for designers and users alike, embodiment in a multi-sensory engagement ultimately gives way in the gaze to simulacral sensation. Notwithstanding this irony, the attitude behind Franck's heroic defense of the subjective body is shared by Arakawa and Gins as well as by Juhani Pallasmaa in his architecture designed for sensory stimulation and addressed directly to the body's own systems of orientation.[29] Arakawa and Gins clearly share Pallasmaa's credo that "basic architectural experiences have a verb form rather than being nouns" (44–45) and open up architecture in its verbal form as active "architecting" for lived, experimental experience; to adopt Franck's useful distinction, their focus falls on *how*, not *what*, the body is (Franck 16).

Robert A. Morgan tenders a candid, negative assessment of *Reversible Destiny*:

What is significant about these cybergenerated projects, in spite of their totally fragmented impracticality, is how they represent the current cultural crisis to the extreme. . . . The illusory aspect of the work related to its computer programming. It functions as a digital system, yet has limited applications in terms of actual mind-body involvement. The seduction of virtual time-space gives a convincing display of a virtual environment, but one that is highly self-conscious reflecting a type of narcissistic indulgence.(78)

Morgan's estimation, however, is inaccurate, for it conflates means with ends and fails to credit the project of *Reversible Destiny* with being trenchantly set against the cyberspatial consecration of *ek-stasis* and virtual disembodiment (a topic that concludes chapter 6). Indeed, *Reversible Destiny cannot be experienced merely within texts, images, and cybertechnic representations*. Only when the ratio of simulacra and representation to actual construction widens in favor of the former will Morgan's claims gain in validity.

Constant's decisive shift in emphasis from formal to ambient constructions marks a significant moment in architectural revision. In his "Inaugural Report on the Munich Conference" (1959), he states clearly what he considers to be the architectural issue of the day: "What makes contemporary architecture so boring is its principally formal preoccupations. . . . Even as he uses existing forms and creates new ones, the architect's principle concern has got to become *the effect that it is going to have on the dweller's behavior and existence*" (101, emphasis added). Such a credo, conceived in the last years of the 1950s, lies at the heart of Arakawa and Gins' *Reversible Destiny* project. Their work replaces a lexicon of form with a detailed constellation of new concepts and initially daunting formulations: bioscleave, landing sites, critical holders, and engaging and guiding bars (this latter term has a Kantian antecedent), all of which are designed to explain primary architectural and perceptual effects on the body and senses of the dweller.[30] Rather than repeat the definitions of these important concepts I will refer the reader to published sources, especially to the 2002 *Architectural Body*.[31]

Like Richard Serra's *Clara Clara*, *Reversible Destiny* focuses on the broad issue of spatial tolerance and the more specific matter of proximity with contact and implicit convergences. It seems concordant too with what Manfredo Tafuri calls a "*self-disalienation* launched by negative design" (143). It also confrontationally challenges the ultimate efficacy of behaviorally normative environments.[32] So Arakawa and Gins are not isolated in this proclivity to practical disequilibrium—indeed, their work in part fits into a broad contemporary artistic and architectural inclination. A comparable purposeful disequilibrium obtains in Robert Gober's "pitched" cribs and playpens, where the normally vertical rectangular structures are pitched at a 45° angle and thus rendered nonutilitarian. Gober's work has been compared to Duchamp's readymades and "corrected readymades" but the intended inoperability, when assessed according to the functional paradigm, is clearly a feature shared with some *Reversible Destiny* houses.[33] One need only compare Gober's pitched furniture with the tilted floors of Arakawa and Gins' *Infancy House* and *Transitional House* (*Reversible Destiny* 266–69), where a tilt converts floors into terrains.

Arakawa and Gins describe the counter-habitual effectiveness of the *Infancy House* in the following manner: "Moving through a passageway that prefigures the dining room by mimicking its features, a resident can get the sense of entering the room even before setting foot into it. Bathrooms that exist on three distinct scales at once remain, appropriately enough, tentative and unresolved. Curved walls that lead ever elsewhere and make it difficult to know where to come to rest help strip residents of the dwelling habit" (*Reversible Destiny* 267). For his part, Gerrit Rietveld offers stick chairs that question the nature and function of chairs, thereby inducing a condition in which "the leg meeting the chair isn't two but four entities negotiating a settlement" (Harbison 42). Harbison's own conclusion emphasizes the same qualities of tentativeness and uncertainty that are the defining features of *Reversible Destiny*: "[U]nderlying [the principle of the stick chair] is a sense that nothing is safe or certain [. . .] one can't take even chairs for granted" (Harbison 42). *Reversible Destiny* has also been compared to the strategic "dislocations" advanced by Bernard Tschumi and Rem Koolhaas.[34] Peter Eisenman evinces a similar desire in his plan for the Parc de la Villette where visitors "should sense something else and feel dislocated. That is the important thing—the dislocation from the ordinary expectation of what is a garden" (Eisenman and Derrida 70). But perhaps the works most compellingly comparable to *Reversible Destiny* are the domestic subversions of Günther Feuerstein. Repudiating in 1960 the serial facilities of functional design, Feuerstein, in his plan for "impractical flats," advocated a radical estrangement of the familiar domicile, instead introducing noisy doors, useless locks, and tortuous passages (Sadler 7). Sadler describes the ontological consequences: "[A dweller's home] would no longer protect him from the environment nor the sensations of his own body: ripping out his air conditioning and throwing open his windows, he could swelter, shiver and struggle to hear himself think above the roar of the city; later he might bump and hurt himself against one of the myriad sharp corners in his flat, and sit at his wobbly table and on his uncomfortable sofa" (8). It is as if the abandoned structures and ruined buildings rendered famous in Gordon Matta-Clark's photographic installations are suddenly designed that way for habitation. All of the above examples (and to them we add *New Babylon* and *Reversible Destiny*) are the consanguineous heirs to the Russian Formalist principle of *ostranenie* ("defamiliarization" or "making strange"). Coined by Viktor

Sklovskij as a counter strategy to urban and aesthetic automatism, the principle demands a rejection of the desensitizing effects of habit. Sklovskij writes (perhaps deliberately evokes Rimbaud's famous phrase "too bad for the violin"): "We are like a violinist who has stopped feeling his bow and strings" (quoted in Steiner 49).

Like Constant before them, Arakawa and Gins are attracted to labyrinths as architectural spaces for inducing disequilibrium and imbalance. "It is desirable," they counsel, "to keep the body in a state of imbalance for as long as possible. The actions, the range of actions, possible to the body for righting itself and regaining its balance will both define and reveal the body's essential nature" (*Architecture: Sites of Reversible Destiny* 18). The break with the classic model is unmistakable; imbalance is impossible in the unicursal classical labyrinth where only cognitive uncertainty pertains, and nothing is revealed about the body's essential nature (other than its inevitable death). In another way, however, *New Babylon* and the labyrinths of Arakawa and Gins accord with the central feature of the labyrinth, a feature Wittgenstein attributes to language when he asserted that "language is a labyrinth of paths" (203). Wittgenstein comes close here to specifying the true nature of the labyrinth as a pathway, not an architecture. Labyrinths, in fact, relate less to architecture *per se* than to orchestrated passageways and choreographies; for the essence of labyrinthine experience is the complications and impediments to the body's normative movement in space.

Labyrinths and labyrinthine elements populate *Reversible Destiny* sites. Arakawa and Gins have constructed two single-level labyrinths out of rubber and other materials (*Reversible Destiny* 147); their 1985 *Terrain Study Model No. 2* is redolent in labyrinthine effects induced by the dweller's inability to hold a general and complete plan (*ibid.* 225). In *Antimortality Fractal Zipper City* labyrinth effects find themselves complemented by mirror opposites. "All contours of the city," Arakawa and Gins profess, "have their basis in twin L-shaped labyrinths that abut. Areas selected to be enclosed in one twin remain open public spaces in the other, making two halves of the city complementary opposites in regard to function" (ibid 252–53). The *Inflected Arcade House* (see ibid. 264–65) combines labyrinthine perplexity with inflection. One structure especially, the *Trench House,* recaptures the architectural intimacy and tactility of the classical labyrinth and fuses it with the Situationist vision of an architecture that promulgates desire. As Arakawa and Gins describe it, "[t]he Trench House accommodates and embodies the body's endless desire to draw close to and be in rapport with virtually everything. Trenches cut through surfaces, carving out circular labyrinths. What would normally not be within the body's reach comes to be so.

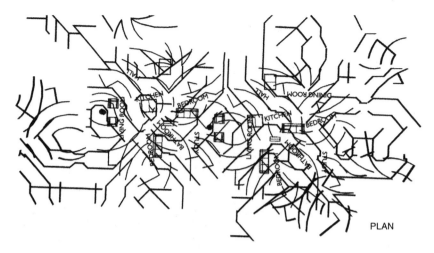

PLAN

Fig. 4. *Plan (part) for Critical Resemblance House* by Arakawa and Gins (Source: Arakawa and Gins *Reversible Destiny*).

A mold of the paths of desire" (*Architecture* 105). All *Reversible Destiny* houses are constructed as "counter dwellings," and like all procedural architecture are designed to foreground landing site activity. Arakawa and Gins describe their important *Critical Resemblance House* as a "reworked labyrinth" that utilizes labyrinth-derived patterns in a binary operation of rectilinear and curvilinear groupings. In its three-level plan, *Critical Resemblance House* clearly anticipates the multilevel labyrinth by offering a comparably torturous negotiation of interior spaces. According to Arakawa and Gins, "[T]he body is invited to move through composite passageways—rectilinear above, curvilinear below—often in two opposing ways at once. It could take several hours to go from the living room to the kitchen. Parts of the kitchen or the living room reappear in the bedroom or bathroom. It might take several days to find everywhere in the house that the dining room turns up" (*Reversible Destiny* 258). Moreover, by featuring "the underside of things," Arakawa and Gins succeed in transposing an imaging landing site into a perceptual one. Although there are undeniable similarities between *Critical Resemblance House* and Feuerstein's "impractical flats," with their non-functioning facilities and deliberate dilapidations, those similarities are superficial. Obviously there is a radical defamiliarization of dwelling common to both. However, the unsettling of the temporal-protentive dimension, which complicates any projected move through time, is distinct to the *Critical Resemblance House*, for this feature expands and maximizes the temporal di-

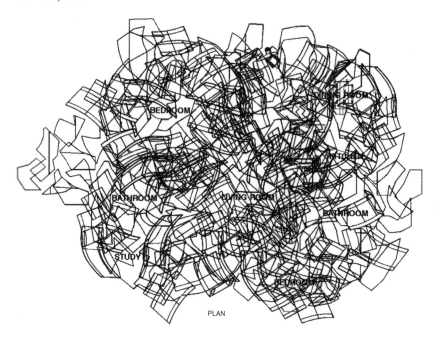

Fig. 5. *Ubiquitous Site House: Plan* by Arakawa and Gins (Source: Arakawa and Gins *Reversible Destiny*).

mension of the classical labyrinth, thus complicating the periphrastic trope of the classical meander with an additional architectural catachresis. Through extending the labyrinth into a chaos to be occupied, the *Ubiquitous Site House* (illus. 1997, 300–301) is the closest *Reversible Destiny* design to fully capture the spirit of *New Babylon* as a dweller-determined architecture. "Shape precludes entry, but entry can occur when a resident forcibly inserts herself into the pliant, half-structured muddle. Room size is proportional to energy expended. . . . [G]enerally each area pushed open constitutes an architectural surround whose every feature lies within touching distance" (*Reversible Destiny* 301).

Arakawa and Gins' multilevel labyrinth is discussed in chapter 8 of their *Architectural Body,* and computer generated images of it form part of the section on landing sites in *Architecture: Sites of Reversible Destiny.* The multilevel labyrinth is proffered as "a prime example of a critical holder," providing its user "with an activating field set up to coordinate and track landing-site dispersal and to depict and augment a person's coordinating skills" (Arakawa and Gins *Architectural Body* 82). Like Constant, they confuse the classical labyrinth with the later maze, attributing to the former "secret passages" and a mandate to puzzle one's way out (ibid. 84).[35] Like its classical ancestor, the multilevel labyrinth, both simple and ingenious, is not difficult to construct; indeed, the recipe provided reads like a Situationist *détourne* of a child's toy:

> Start with a six-inch-thick hula-hoop at hip level. Add enough hula-hoops, all at hip level, to glue together a six-inch plane of them throughout the room. Cut into these fifty or so glued together hula-hoops to make a labyrinth-layer, bending the hoops to vary the curves and occasionally straightening them to make a more direct path. Make two or three distinctly different labyrinth-layers out of the hula-hoop plane. Stacking the labyrinth-layers with one-foot-wide rows of blankness between them, a bit wider proportionately than the blanks accompanying these lines, fill the room with them. (*Architectural Body* 89)

The efficacy of the multilevel labyrinth derives from its blocking rather than facilitating of passage (in this respect it is a radical reversal of the classical model): "How convenient that this labyrinth stops the body proper in its tracks. Within it people will be able to keep track of near and far components of their architectural bodies" (ibid. 84). This blocking and tracking ability derives from the transparent nature of the labyrinth, revised here not as a winding warren of stone wall but as an open "lattice for praxis" (ibid.). The multilevel labyrinth shares the two characteristics of transparency and openness with several of Constant's own multilevel labyrinths. In his envisioned constructions, however, transparency articulates onto the reflective and mirror distortion and, though levels connect, they do not share the intimacy of simultaneous negotiation. Constant's ladder labyrinth resembles an updated hybrid of Piranesi's *carceri* and a 3-D version of the game of *Chutes and Ladders*. Unlike Arakawa and Gins' model, there is little suggestion of a function other than that of play.

In their multilevel labyrinth there is a calculated trade off for this tracking and blocking ability. The physical disequilibrium precipitated by the forced contortions of the human body through non-parallel but simultaneous passages poses a severe threat to any unified sense of identity; it is here, in the lattice of the multilevel labyrinth, that the contestation between "person" and "architectural body" arises in a veritable corporealization of schizopoetics. One might plausibly consider the following description as a textual outtake from Kenneth Goldsmith's *Fidget,* which we previously discussed and sampled in chapter 6: "Bodily inserting every last finger of herself into the multilevel labyrinth, she propels and squeezes her body through it. . . . [S]he elbows and shoulders and elbows, and pushes and pulls, and otherwise insinuates bone and flesh to gain, ever again, traction so as to inch and cram, wedge, and, in full flesh, secrete herself through a lattice that by impinging on her trajectory as a person gives her the many trajectories of an architectural body" (Arakawa and Gins *Architectural Body* 90–1). I refer to a *corporealization* of schizopoetics deliberately, for the consequences desired from the imbalance are not lines of flight but enhanced landing site configurative comportments; it is within the multilevel labyrinth, with its multiple demands for contradictory but simultaneous trajectories, that "the linking of the body proper to an architectural body begins in earnest" (ibid. 84).

## V. Immortality Suite

The Situationists dreamed of an elevation beyond eschatology into the sort of immortality that angels enjoy: "Angels never age, being beautiful children who never become corpses" (Kaufmann 65). Vincent Kaufmann captures the Situationist's attitude to death: "According to the Situationist ideal, even death's ward will be made for life—for living in peace: 'Ward off death, not for dying but for living there in peace.' At its worst, Situationist death is a kind of unjustly slandered mishap, but it comes across more often as a form of serenity. In any event, it never really occurs because there is never any lack of time in the Situationist world" (65). *New Babylon* forgot the body, or at best assumed it to be a package for a child's eternal spirit caught up in a constantly creative flux in which even the dead must move on: "There is no place for tombs in the Situationist city. Consequently, the dead themselves must move about, becoming if not angels then at least phantoms [. . .]" (Kaufmann 65).

For Theseus the labyrinth was a matter of life and death and we have not deserted that theme. The primary purpose of the multilevel labyrinth—as a physical obstacle—is to urge a radical rethinking of human destiny. For Arakawa and Gins procedural architecture is an emergent response to what they consider a primary human need—a crisis ethics as they call it—and their vision embraces nothing less than an architectural and optional reversal of the fate of our species. WE HAVE DECIDED NOT TO DIE. This too was the decision of Theseus in that moment before slaying the man-bull hybrid, but for these new procedural Theseans Death itself is the Minotaur. AN ARCHITECTURE TO HELP KILL DEATH DEAD? Arakawa and Gins believe death is unfashionable and undesirable; their urban call is for "cities without graveyards."[36] Their *Yoro Park* in the Gifu township in Japan offers a taste of the heightened perceptual awareness that architectural imbalance induces. Through such architecture, they hypothe-

Fig. 6. Photograph of ancient cemetery, Okinawa (Source: Rudofsky *Architecture Without Architects: A Short Introduction to Non-Pedigreed Architecture*).

size, human destiny can be reversed, and immortality, rather than a wished-for theological beyond, will be an atheistic matter of individual choice. The design of *Yoro Park* is apt; with its tilts and curvatures it brings to mind a similar constructed terrain: the ancient cemetery on Okinawa. It's hard not to conjecture that the New York-based Arakawa and Gins were familiar with this image, readily available in Bernard Rudofsky's *Architecture Without Architects,* an illustrative catalogue of non-pedigreed architecture prepared for a show at the Museum of Modern Art held from November 9, 1964 to February 7, 1965.[37] And if it was known to them, then it's a marvelous irony that a Japanese necropolis inspired a Japanese park designed for eternal living. (See Elliptical Field, Site of *Reversible Destiny* in Arakawa and Gins, *Reversible Destiny*: 200–201.)

George Lakoff is one of the supporters of Arakawa and Gins' architectural inventions who balk at this post-ontological prospect of "cities without graveyards." He concludes his sympathetic article "Testing the Limits of Brain Plasticity: Or, Why is There a Wall Down the Middle of the Tub?" with an imaginary, tongue-in-cheek Woody Allen scenario:

WOODY: How could the elimination of death itself be disaster? Think if Mozart were still alive! Or Einstein! Or Mr. Weinstein who made the great egg creams!

GEORGE: Or Hitler. Or Stalin. Or Roy Cohn.

WOODY: But think of eternal life! You could watch *Night and Fog* into eternity.

GEORGE: With Alzheimer's? With cancer? You couldn't kill the cells. With no teeth? You couldn't kill the germs in your mouth. Think of how everyone would smell. With my great-aunt Lena? Could you put up with her forever? Dr. Kevorkian has a point.

A few more turns and the scene ends. Woody walks off with a beautiful young girl intent on discussing film theory. They pass a group of old men who look remarkably like Adolph Hitler, Joseph Stalin, and Roy Cohn. (121–22).

Bataille considered death the ultimate human luxury. Since the 1980s science has been telling us that both the terms *life* and *death* are otiose and meaningless, that we have already passed beyond death as a useful concept.[38] Yet death, as human life's ineluctable destiny, as the ultimate and irreversible negativity of human being, still occupies the heart of Western philosophy. Arakawa and Gins have shown a courageous disdain for philosophy, and perhaps rightly so, and yet their procedural architecture occupies a pivotal moment in ontology, arguably the threshold of its end. In a bold negation of the negation, *Reversible Destiny* refuses to embrace the fundamental negativity that has formed the ground of Western metaphysics. They have refused to subscribe to—at least to part of—the binding Heideggerian tenet (of a doubly negative constitution) that sees human being as both a being-towards-language and a being-towards-death. In this manner Arakawa and Gins aspire beyond the ontological project of philosophy to voluntary immortal being. Such a post-ontological destiny would mark the end of being as we understand it and the beginning of a life of endless becoming—in other words the dream of Constant Nieuwenhuys come true.

Assuming that *Reversible Destiny* can be realized, that eventually human death can be overcome, at least two thorny issues remain. To speak of immortality alone is to ignore the issue of the quality of life. Where does pleasure, love, recreation, even evil figure in this vision? Moreover, given our planetary limitations, "to not die" might register on the level of the most selfish project imaginable. As it stands—and never forget that *Reversible Destiny* is an ongoing project—the architectural body, as innovative a concept as it is, remains perilously close to the order of that which Giorgio Agamben terms "naked life." Current juridico-medical ideology embraces this notion as paramount to its efficient operation and at the cost of ignoring the essential forms and qualities of life. Indeed, since Foucault's analyses, we have the evidence to prove the epistemic shift from politics to bio-politics in which bare life is that which should be saved at all costs. Agamben unmasks the insidious force that lies behind all obvious systems of current power: "Biological life, which is the secularized form of naked life and which shares it unutterability and impenetrability, thus constitutes the real forms of life literally as forms of survival: biological life remains inviolate in such forms as that obscure threat that can suddenly actualize itself in violence, in extraneousness, in illnesses, in accidents" (*Means without End* 8). It is in the name of bare, naked life that biopolitics exercises its power, and in which democratic materialism appears in its most essential manifestation. Agamben notes a double trajectory: the preservation of bare life at all costs, and the reduction of forms of life to nakedness in the structure and paralegality of the camp. In Germany (the camp did not originate in Germany, nor did the Nazis create it) such spaces as Dachau, Auschwitz-Birkenau, Buchenwald, and Sachsenhausen gained legitimacy via a suspension of law in certain states of exception *(ausnahmezustanden),* which then became the law outside the Law. (We will have cause to revisit this suspension in a different context in chapter 10.) In 1983 Bernard Cache stated, "It may be possible for us to imagine a radical exteriority that would not be the opposite of an interiority" (37). By the 1980s this virtuality was already haunting cultural memory. Agamben opens up the paradoxical nature of the camp in strikingly similar terms to Cache's ruminated possibility, a nature in which the exception is *"taken outside,* included through its own exclusion" (*Homo Sacer* 170) and offers an image of imbalance and unclarity that fully warrants comparison to the spatial perplications of the labyrinth in its classic and Situationist manifestations. "Whoever entered the camp moved in a zone of indistinction between outside and inside, exception and rule, licit and illicit, in which the very concepts of subjective right and juridical protection no longer make any sense" (ibid.). For Agamben, these comments are not merely historical—far from it. As the inaugural site of modernity, the camp is now firmly entrenched as an instrument of biopolitical power: Kosovo, Kabul, Abu Ghraib, Guantanamo Bay. Agamben is alert to the architectural and urban consequences of this puissance: "This principle [birth] is now adrift: it has entered a process of dislocation in which its functioning is becoming patently impossible and in which we can expect not only new camps but also always new and more delirious normative definitions of the inscription of life in the city. The camp, which is now firmly settled inside it, is the new biopolitical *nomos* of the planet" (*Means without End* 45).

The late philosopher Jean-François Lyotard (also a friend and supporter of the *Reversible Destiny* project) both defines and defends the infantile as "whatever does not permit itself to be written, in writing" (quoted in Harvey and Schehr 25). Perhaps the least visionary and utopian, yet most realizable agenda possible for *Reversible Destiny* would be to prevent the death of the infant by sustaining the form of an inhabitable infancy of architecture along lines sympathetic to the poetics I argue towards the close of chapter 10. The seeds of this are already nascent in the multilevel labyrinth and *Infancy House* where the human body is reversed to the uncoordinated movements of an infant. Indeed, imbalance is a necessary condition of the infant body, the body without writing. There are four full-color pages, presented without text or captions, in *Reversible Destiny* that depict this body without words (179–81). In response to a letter from Lyotard (that great theoretician of infancy) printed in *Reversible Destiny* (11), Arakawa and Gins propose a new hybrid to replace the Minotaur: the less savage concept of the "infant-adult." There is a subtle shift of terms in the correspondence, for in his own letter, Lyotard speaks not of the infant but of the child. And because it was the child that fuelled the architectural hopes of Constant and the SI, *New Babylon* could never have attained that infancy of architecture we find and experience in *Reversible Destiny* sites. Does not this prelinguistic state, this human life before language, return us to the labyrinthine condition that Hollier notes in Bataille's anti-architecture of writing, the state "where oppositions disintegrate and grow complicated . . . where the system on which linguistic function is based disintegrates, but somehow disintegrates by itself, having jammed its own works" (58)? Whatever else *Reversible Destiny* will go on to confront, it must face the infant's entry into the labyrinthine condition that is language. That said, perhaps a lasting (if not *the* lasting) contribution of *Reversible Destiny* is to have returned infancy to the scene of architectural praxis. Moreover, one should be cautious if one concludes that *Reversible Destiny* is an unsuccessful project whose grand *telos* appears currently impractical. One should not dismiss the project outright for perhaps, PERHAPS, like the voyage through the labyrinth, the point is the journey, not the destination.

## Difficult Harmony

The Picturesque Detail in Gilpin, Price, and
Clark Coolidge's *Space*

> *A picture held us captive. And we could not get outside it, for it lay in our*
> *language and language seemed to repeat it to us inexorably.*
> —Wittgenstein, *Philosophical Investigations*

So far there has been no attempt to historicize the work of Clark Coolidge beyond the 1960s; his early work is usually considered inaugural of a minimalist and disjunctive non-referentiality, and he is seen as a pioneer of, or fellow traveler with, Language writing. Jed Rasula's "News and Noise: Poetry and Distortion" is an interesting case in point. Rasula reads Coolidge's *Solution Passages* through the language of information theory (as I do in the case of Jackson Mac Low in chapter 3), remarking that Coolidge's early work comprises a plethora of textual entropy with poems that lack the redundancy necessary to convey meaning through noise. The poems offer a non-redundant randomness in *extremis*, burdening the reader with the daunting task of engaging moments and movements between entropy and message, a veritable "becoming-meaning" as Deleuze would have it, or in Rasula's own biosemiotic terminology, "ripples of order, transitorily charged with sudden unsolicited evidence of life itself" (Rasula 97). At one point Rasula opens up a meditation on the sister arts of poetry and painting: "The relation of signal to noise is as reciprocal as that between figure and ground in the visual field" (98).

Rasula's reflections on these sister arts are neither isolated nor innovative. The humanist doctrine of *ut pictura poesis* ("as is painting so is poetry") can be traced back through Baroque, Mannerism, and the Renaissance to the poetics of Horace and Aristotle.[1] The eighteenth-century poet William Mason, friend and editor of Thomas Gray, chose to write his long poem *The English Garden* in the then unfashionable blank verse for precisely its affinities to natural landscape.[2]

In more recent times critics have drawn attention to the Cubist aspirations behind Stein's *Tender Buttons* as well as William Carlos Williams' *Kora in Hell,* and
to the close parallels between Abstract Expressionism and the poetry of Frank
O'Hara, John Ashbery, and other members of the so-called New York School.[3]
In the present chapter I continue this line of provocation across more historical distance and attempt a rethinking of contemporary disjunctive poetics (here
represented in an early work of Clark Coolidge) along the lines of certain aspects
of eighteenth-century picturesque theory as outlined by its two major theorists,
William Gilpin and Uvedale Price. In this respect my method bears strategic
affinities with Nathaniel Mackey's efforts to break out of predetermined cultural categories by way of purposeful readings across African American and
Euro-American avant-gardes.[4] Where Mackey seeks creative kinships and affinities across ethnic and regional boundaries, I offer a transhistoric reading across
three centuries. My intention, however, is not to mobilize a retrograde aesthetic
theory, nor read a sampling of contemporary disjunctive texts through the taste
and sensibility of a late-eighteenth-century public, but rather to provoke reflection on buried continuities, unavowed patterns, and connections between some
of Gilpin's and Price's aesthetic notions and the radical syntactic, grammatical
disruptions, formal innovation, and minimalist import evident in some of the
early poetry of Clark Coolidge. In this respect the sparse texts that I consider
might be accurately situated within a genealogy of the rough and irregular.[5]

I should state at the outset that this chapter does not exhaust all aspects of picturesque theory, which was designed to advance a mode of vision, a way of grasping reality as a picture.[6] I shall not touch on this wider aspect nor on its relation
to what Baudrillard terms "hyperrealism" but rather focus on its theorizing of
the detail. Discussions of writers along picturesque criteria date back to at least
Ben Jonson.[7] There are also more recent precedents to this appeal to eighteenth-
century models. Marshall McLuhan traces the evidence of its presence in Tennyson's, Rossetti's, and Swinburne's work. More recently Brian McHale comments
on Armand Schwerner's *The Tablets,* whose distinctive form as faux fragments
of an imaginary, ancient text evokes both the eighteenth-century cult of ruins as
well as that same century's predilection for textual hoaxes and fictional authors,
such as Thomas Chatterton's fifteenth-century Bristol monk Thomas Rowley and
James Macpherson's fraudulent translations of the ancient poems of Ossian.[8]

The term *picturesque* derives from the Italian *pittoresco* ("after the manner of
painters") and the picturesque as a movement indisputably grew out of the theories of ideal landscape promulgated by Claude Lorraine and Poussin. Painters and
aesthetic theorists from Titian onward believed in the inherent picturesque quali-

ties of some aspects of nature (see Hussey 9). Emerging in the mid-eighteenth century and cresting in the 1790s and the first two decades of the nineteenth century, the picturesque ruptured the dominant binary of eighteenth-century aesthetic theory, that of the sublime and the beautiful, while at the same time shattering the serpentine criterion laid down in William Hogarth's *Line of Beauty,* the line that insinuates temporality into curvature.[9] In stark contrast, picturesque theory emphasizes the *variety* of particles, *not* their unitary inclination. Gilpin and Price offer a decidedly non-Aristotelian aesthetic of distribution requiring the unsystematic placement of details in a free intermingling that resists uniformity. Most importantly picturesque theory abandons the veridical-representational paradigm in favor of a non-mimetic orchestration of landscape parts in order to arrive at the facture of an aesthetically pleasing picture.[10] While picturesque theory is fundamentally incompatible with panopticality (it repudiates elevated observation and vista control, instead embracing angularity, close-up, and a rich mixture of detail) the picturesque detail itself clearly prefigures the "optical unconscious" whose conceptual emergence is usually credited to Walter Benjamin in his much quoted "The Work of Art in an Age of Mechanical Reproduction," an unconscious whose derepression is made possible through such photographic techniques as close-up and oblique angles sufficient to reveal hitherto unperceived aspects of reality. Initially, however, I want to locate an earlier source for the origin of the picturesque detail.

Robert Hooke's *Micrographia* appeared in 1665 through the auspices of the English Royal Society. Among its brilliantly executed engravings is a microscopic representation of a full stop. What appears to the naked eye as a geometrically symmetrical unit emerges in Hooke's engraving as a chaotic complex of irregularities and rough texture that Hooke himself describes as "smutty daubings" and "a great splatch of London dirt" (quoted in Johns 431). Hooke not only evinces the shock of the detail-within-the-detail, unobtainable by the naked eye, but carries this propensity into the domain of recording all scientific observation, insisting that as much incidental detail as possible be recorded (Johns 433). Hooke's friend, the type-designer Joseph Moxon, realized that alphabetic characters were first and foremost visual details and argued for letters to be deliberately designed according to the architectural rules laid down by the Roman architect Vitruvius. Both Hooke's microscopic revelation and Moxon's recommendation point to an anxiety in the mid-seventeenth century about the epistemological foundations of print culture. The empirical certainty of objects represented in the medium of print is seriously compromised by the limitation of human perception when unaided by prosthetic devices. An ignorance ruled and

Fig. 7. Engraved representation of a period as seen through a microscope (Source: Robert Hooke *Micrographia*).

masqueraded as a false consciousness that could only be improved to decoherence by means of non-human assistance. Moreover when microscopy reveals roughness and irregularity to be not aberrant contingencies but morphologically foundational, the theological doctrine of intelligent design becomes seriously undermined. The Lilliputian paradox is clear: by manifesting a microscopic world, the hegemonic certainty via seeing is called into question and the retinal episteme is radically destabilized, thereby undermining the very foundations of human understanding.[11]

Barbara Stafford admirably traces the popular rise of microscopy through the eighteenth century. By Gilpin's time such popular books as Martin Frobène Ledermüller's *Amusements microscopiques* (1768), together with the commercially availability of Wilson Hand microscopes, helped bring this scientific instrument into the purlieu of the middle-class domestic sitting room. As early as 1721 we find Joseph Addison extolling the power of the microscope to reveal "a green leaf swarm[ing] with millions of animals" (quoted in Stafford 349). The microscope had sufficiently entered the eighteenth-century imaginary for its user to be "the secular priest of the Enlightenment" (Stafford 345). For the purposes of this chapter, however, I will argue that Hooke's microscopic discoveries— specifically his magnification of a typeset period—simultaneously undermined the credibility of mimesis and print culture in general and inaugurated a set of visual criteria that subsequently find aesthetic accommodation in the theory of the picturesque detail. Martin Price offers the evidence to support this claim: "The picturesque in general recommends *the rough or rugged, the crumbling form,* the complex or difficult harmony. It seeks a tension between the disorderly or irrelevant and the perfected form. Its favorite scenes are those in which form emerges only with study or is at the point of dissolution. . . . Where it concentrates upon a particular object, the aesthetic interest lies . . . in *the internal conflict between the centrifugal forces of dissolution and the centripetal pull of form*" (277, emphases added). Putting aside the evocations in this tensional aesthetics (so redolent of New Critical sensibility), Price's observations capture exactly Clark Coolidge's early poetic aspirations to attain the effects that Price specifies as being arrived at by means of "a conception of structure based upon the overthrow of limited ideas of unity" (Price 279). Unlike the oneiric detail of the Pre-Raphaelites, the impetus for the picturesque detail is found within a scientific detection of change, *not* a reaching out to a sur-materiality whose dominant effect is wonder. A dictionary of the picturesque would include such words as "rugged," "uneven," "asymmetric," "shaggy," "rough," "incrustated," "eroded," "intricate," "angular," and "irregular"—words equally applicable to both quantum mechanics and several of the plates in Hooke's *Micrographia*.[12]

The Freudian *ichspaltung,* that foundational fracturing of the ego permitting the fetishistic substitution of parts for a repressed entirety—heel, the toe, the nose etc.—is a preeminent criterion for the picturesque in a singular way. This substitution for the whole by a detail invokes of course the figural regimen of synecdoche, metonymy, and metaphor: three literary tropes that are central not only to psychic fetishism but also to the variety-assemblages envisioned through picturesque theory. Some aspects of picturesque theory promote a celebration of insignificancies, a spreading out of the sensible according to the paradigm of mixed detail and loose neighborhood, thereby offering an aesthetics of fracture, *crudescence*, and erosion, "of garnished rocks [and] shattered Precipices" (Gilpin quoted in Barbier 109). Most significantly picturesque theory (and perhaps most so in Gilpin) both resists the uniformity of perfection and promotes instant creativity over imitation.

Whereas Gilpin formulates his version of the picturesque as an addition to the category of beauty (speaking of "picturesque beauty"), Uvedale Price advances it as a distinct third aesthetic category located between the sublime and the beautiful.[13] Its presiding characteristics moreover are diametrically opposed to those of the beautiful and sublime. In stark contrast to the unitary "over-awe" and astonishment brought on by the sublime, the picturesque emphasizes those capricious sensory benefits deriving from an experience of diversity, intricacy, and partial obfuscation: pleasures that stimulate active curiosity and a playful encounter with details. Price remains, however, in broad concurrence with Gilpin in specifying the most efficient causes of picturesque effect to be "the opposite qualities of roughness and of variation, joined to that of irregularity" (Price 61). Like Gilpin, Price offers a materialist and essentialist theory in which picturesqueness constitutes an inherent quality in certain objects and details. The architectural ruin (Gilpin's own penchant is for ruined castles) transforms regular form into a variety of irregular details that give incidental elements their due. A temporal transition occurs from beauty to picturesque via erosion and decay. In a passage taken almost verbatim from Gilpin, Price offers a vivid description of this temporal accumulation of detail: "Observe the process by which time (the great author of such changes) converts a beautiful object into a picturesque one. First, by means of weather stains, partial incrustations, mosses etc.; it at the same time takes off from the uniformity of its surface and of its color; that is, gives it a degree of roughness, and variety of tint" (62).[14] Such picturesque details are contingent and subject to birth and modification through time. Beauty, one might say, is a being-towards-the-picturesque with erosion functioning as a decelerated catalyst to accidental details, resulting in an ordered variety not unlike the vortical dynamics at the base of Pound's revised theory of the image.[15] Price's description of hollow lanes and byroads is worthy of Thoreau: "[T]he turns are sudden and unprepared; the banks sometimes broken and abrupt; sometimes smooth, and gently but not uniformly sloping; now wildly over-hung with thickets and trees and bushes; now loosely skirted with wood; no regular verge of grass, no cut edges, no distinct lines of separation; all is mixed and blended together" (I, 29). At times his descriptions anticipate the effects brought on by that technological liberator of the "optical unconscious," the cinematic zoom: "on some [branches] the knots and protuberances add to the ruggedness of their twisted trunks; in others, the deep hollow of the inside, the mosses on the bark, the rich yellow of the touch-wood, with the blackness of decayed substance, afford such variety of tints" (ibid. 33). Both theorists are attracted to the haptic, that type of space that effectively removes the subordination of hand or eye in their complex, reciprocal relation, thereby demolishing the figure-ground relation and blurring the distinction of sight from touch.[16] The haptic–optic zoom, which brings about the tactile, spatial isolation that produces the detail, is central to the picturesque's theory of proximity; it anticipates too Cézanne's notion of "iridescent chaos" achieved when the artist paints at close range and too close to an object to represent it.[17] A detail is an intensity apprehended in a larger composite; it resists integration. The detail is not, however, the "unformed" or "deformed" in Kant's dynamical sublime; the detail undermines but does not collapse the object-form. In this respect, it offers a landscape of teeming particulars that force their volatile presence beneath the conceptualized object-form.

I choose the following passage from George Meredith's "The Day of the Daughter of Hades" as exemplary of Pricean picturesque:

And the steeps of the forest she crossed,
On its dry red sheddings and cones
Up the paths by roots green-mossed,
Spotted amber, and old mossed stones.
Then out where the brook-torrent starts
To her leap, and from bend to curve
A hurrying elbow darts
For the instant-glancing swerve,
Decisive, with violent will
In the action formed . . . (49)

Meredith complements a metric breathlessness with a poetics of close and rugged detail to produce a passage in which vista does not obtrude and picturesque detail dominates: "dry sheddings," "mossed stones," "roots," "brook-torrent," "spotted amber," and "instant-glancing swerve." Such details territorialize attention in a constantly moving panoply in which the dominant active mood is that of a temporal "jerk." In exemplary picturesque manner, the passage gestures back to those singularities that lie outside of the leveling concept of the "general idea" that forms the basis of Johnson's aesthetic, as outlined in *Rasselas*.

Gilpin's own theory of the picturesque lies scattered among his drawings, writings, and vast accumulation of correspondence (much to Sir George Beaumont), but from them clear aesthetic preferences emerge. Roughness is the *sine qua non* of Gilpinian picturesque, marking the ascendancy of proximity and detail in late eighteenth-century aesthetic theory. Not surprisingly, Gilpin prefers highly fractured forms to unitary shapes. A broken rock, for instance, facilitates prismatic reflections, the aleatoric dance of light upon irregular surfaces. Gilpin is at his most microscopic in books such as *Remarks on Forest Scenery* (one of his popular picturesque guides) in which details are not merely enumerated but subjected to complex diagrammatic analysis. His own accompanying sketches are meta-topographies offering imaginary landscapes. Paul Barbier offers a succinct description of Gilpin's disjunctive method of pictorial composition of objects: "Instead of the continuous line, which is formal and structural, his pen consistently breaks up the surfaces and seeks their roughness, for therein lies the whole representational value of an object. Even when he treats a fairly smooth surface, such as a rock-face or a gentle slope, the line will be broken up in dots and dashes like a Morse code" (105). Joshua Reynolds famously disparaged the "minute attention" and "petty particularities" of not only Dutch realist painting but also the fussy moral canvases of William Hogarth; by implication he would look askance at such attention to "minute particulars" (Blake's phrase) so evident in the passages I cite above. For Reynolds, the incomparably superior "grand style" in painting (with its embrace of the invariant and general) is incompatible with an aesthetic of the detail.[18]

At this point I would like to present two opposing criteria for grammatical consequence en route to my discussion of some of Coolidge's early texts. The first is a short quotation from Wittgenstein's *Zettel*: "Like everything metaphysical the harmony between thought and reality is to be found in the grammar of the language" (55). The second I take from Heidegger's famous comments on metaphysics in his "Letter on Humanism": "In this regard 'subject' and 'object' are inappropriate terms of metaphysics, which very early on in the form of Occidental 'logic' and 'grammar' seized control of the interpretation of language. We today can only begin to descry what is concealed in that occurrence. The liberation of language from grammar into a more essential framework is reserved for thought and poetic creation" (218). Where Wittgenstein enshrines grammar as the guarantor of a harmonic equation between thinking and the real, Heidegger lends philosophic legitimation to the poetics of grammatical disruption that Coolidge inherits less from Charles Olson than from the systematic chance-generated texts of Jackson Mac Low (discussed in chapter 3) and earlier from Italian Futurism's *parole in libertà* (words in freedom). John Cage in the famous analogy he drew between grammar and the army observed that any attack on grammar is an attack on the sentence and unitary closure. Cage ignores, however, the cross-disciplinary analogy of the sentence to pictorial perspective, the fact that grammar organizes meaning in a manner precisely homologous to the vanishing point in perspective painting, with the grammatically orthodox sentence conducting the mind along a line to a semantic completion.[19]

The balance of this chapter examines two of Clark Coolidge's minimalist poems gathered in an early book from 1970, *Space*. Despite his inclusion in Ron Padgett's and David Shapiro's definitive anthology of New York poets, Coolidge registers as a curious anomaly to such a localized gathering. I say this because his work contains no indications of O'Hara's personalism with its "I do this, I do that" agenda; neither does his work display the coterie conversational tonalities nor the surrealistic collage method we find in Ashbery's early collection *The Tennis Court Oath*.[20] Indeed, Coolidge's early texts are so minimal and subreferential as to appear inassimilable into any poetics of the New York School.[21] Coolidge's abstract, non-representational texts seemingly embrace Stein's Cubist precept for composition that we find in her poem "A carafe that is a blind glass": "an arrangement in a system to pointing. All this and not ordinary, not unordered in not resembling" (Stein 3). There is, however, one crucial difference: Coolidge jettisons Stein's deictic imperative and counters visual order with semantic roughness—the jagged ruination of the semantic picturesque.

The jacket copy for *Space* emphasizes the book's reductive structure, the removal of syntax leaving the reader's attention "open to the ways in which words can become instruments of a verbal order." The book as a whole moves from a relatively packed page toward the disintegration of linguistic units stacked in an austere vertical column. Despite its progressive reductionism, *Space* consistently offers linguistic details that never stabilize in representation. Although the historical legitimation of *ut pictura poesis* is indisputable, the book's application raises obvious critical issues for comparative analysis. How does one apply the criteria of representational art to a non-representational practice like Coolidge's (or Cage's)? What comprises genuine "roughness" in the textual? How does lexemic "variety" manifest, and how do we apply the criteria of landscape to textual composition? Additionally, Coolidge's self-confessed indebtedness to improvisatory jazz is well known and, given his scrupulous avoidance of ekphrastic sorties or imagistic propensities of any kind, it may seem ironic to approach his early work through an aesthetic theory of the visual arts. Yet such an approach is neither gratuitous nor unwarranted. Coolidge himself writes of his attempt "to peer through the lines into [a] possible Word Art Landscape, work within it & return Wordscapes, Word objects to refresh the mind so currently overloaded with centuries of medial language-tape" (quoted in Carroll 149). "Wordscapes" are constructed by exploiting such material aspects of language as lay outside the purlieu of description: "Hardness, Density, SoundShape, vector-force, & degree of Transparency/Opacity"—qualities and predilections Coolidge sees (not surprisingly) in the work of Gertrude Stein who, in her play *Four Saints in Three Acts,* strove to make the saints the landscape (quoted in Carroll 149). However, this list also enumerates those picturesque features evoked by Gilpin and Price. At times Coolidge can even discuss his choice of vocabulary in terms strikingly consonant with the picturesque. Speaking of his choice of the word "trilobite" in a 1966 composition, Coolidge refers to it as an "angular, uneven, heavy word" (Coolidge "Arrangement" 162).

Charles Bernstein and Barrett Watten both draw attention to the quality of "landscape" in Coolidge's early poetry. Watten notes that the poems in *Space* present "imponderable landscapes" (93) while Bernstein comments on the "[r]epeating [of] particular words of a word mine like counting off the cities and towns of a landscape, a wordscape" (265). It might seem that Coolidge aspires not only to completing the Objectivist agenda and the skewed referential texts of Stein via a poetic that is less lexically than morphemically based, but also to the marriage of word and page to arranged vista. Let me examine such a wordscape in the following text, the final page of "AD," a nineteen-page poem that progresses from multiple word lines grouped in recognizable stanzas (of similar obduracy) to a stark minimalism borne out in the kind presented here.

> erything
> eral
> stantly
> ined
> ards
> cal
> nize

Coolidge is apparently using the same vertical reading strategy of page edges developed in his poem "Cabinet Voltaire" and included in his 1968 volume *Ing*. There, Coolidge sought and transcribed the second parts of words broken by the edge of the prose block in certain texts that Robert Motherwell included in his 1951 anthology *The Dada Painters and Poets*.[22] Section 3 of "Cabinet Voltaire" is excavated from Hugo Ball's "Dada Fragments" and opens with transcriptions of the opening word parts of lines 2 and 20 respectively:

tradict

Theless

Section 4 drives from paragrammatic transcriptions from Kurt Schwitters *Merz* (the bracketed numbers are added by me to indicate the respective line in Coolidge's source text):

rose (2)
gressed (7)
pedient (14)

trary (27) that (21) parison (23)
tramine (45)

Regardless of his manner of composition (which aligns him with the work of Johnson, Mac Low, and Cage) the effects are identical. Coolidge shatters the representational paradigm governing all picturesque theory by transposing the picturesque onto a textual plane of minimal to zero signification. A textual proximity is constructed below the level of the word to situate the language material within the potential turbulence of word parts, thereby allowing them to resonate both as entities and events. In the famous words of Heraclitus, the reader becomes estranged from that which is most familiar. At the same time Coolidge transposes Gilpin's own complication of the optical complacency occasioned by Claudian perspective (complete with its *repoussoir,* proportionate staffage, and depth progression from front through middle to far distance) into a linguistic complication on the levels of diminished syntax and demolished lexeme. Coolidge does not advance a utilized language that offers itself to intentional experience; rather he offers language unmitigatingly materialized.

Given the paragrammatic method of "unconventional" reading that Coolidge employs, the following passage from Bruce Andrews' first book, *Edge* (1973), illustrates not only his own poetic but also Coolidge's: "Most of my stuff is based on fragmentation and the qualities of words other than (and along with) their meaning. The words aren't related at the center but by their edges (connotations, etc.)—like the interrelated pieces of a non-representational ceramic sculpture. . . . I like the edges, discreteness, fragments, collision" (11). Craig Dworkin notes the marvelous transposition obtained by this method in which "Coolidge transforms the carnival of the Cabaret Voltaire into a cabinet of linguistic curiosities" (161). A linguistic *Wunderkammer* no doubt, but Charles Bernstein further detects the quality of a stark frontality in Coolidge's work, an eschewal of distance. Coolidge's is "a poetry of elimination: stripping away any thing that distances, a reducing to bare form" (Bernstein 262). Although Bernstein's assessment presupposes a preexisting, normative notion of language and linguistic matter from which Coolidge deviates (hence "stripping" and "reduction"), the refusal to utilize distancing effects (description, representation, referentiality in general, as well as a coherent speaking subject) situates this poem within the broad aesthetic of picturesque proximity. Barbier recovers a piece of rare Gilpin ephemera that is pertinent to Coolidge's text, a specimen comment pasted to a sepia mount beneath a landscape: "The rock on the right, joined to a piece of ground, which advances a little nearer the eye, on which a group of cattle, in the shade, were happily opposed to a light ground at the bottom of the rock. The landscape admitted no distance" (95).[23] By denying the reader a recession into mimetic distance or logical clarity, while at the same time relying on the impossibility of referential separation or attaining a destination outside the textual field of the linguistic signs, Coolidge renders this poem both tangibly "present" and semiologically disturbing. Just as picturesque practice rejects Reynolds' grand style in order to focus on arranging descriptive minutiae (for example, lichen, gnarled roots, and broken stems) so too does Coolidge's text of subsemantic parts suggest an eroded text, broken, rough, and as a consequence prismatic. The common issue in picturesque theory and Coolidge's poem—one that raises major complexities in non-linear productive-receptive negotiation—is how to successfully make connections between details when syntax and grammar are abandoned. This blend of the uncanny with residual picturesque elements together yield cognitive uncertainty and therefore might evoke that cerebral disequilibrium brought on by defamilarization, or perhaps suggest a purposefully manufactured "ruin" in the eighteenth-century spirit of the ruins of Charles-Louis Clérisseau or the manufactured ruined castle of the Landgraf of Kassel. However, Coolidge's work opens up to less affective responses or fanciful receptions. Coolidge does not offer a descriptive poem of disconnected but comprehendible phrases but rather a hypolexemic listing that seems to invite "completion." This minimalist piece yields little in semantic content yet remains susceptible to a reader's own productive desire. In this respect it cannily connects not only to the productive reader of the open work (valorized by Language writing) but also with the dominant philosophical doctrine of the late-eighteenth century: associationism. Despite the lines being printed flush left and thus complicating their status as verbal fragments, Coolidge's morphemes nonetheless invite completion by their inherent suggestiveness. We are tempted to insert a missing *ev-* before *erything*, treat *eral* by association as the last four letters of the words *several* or *mineral*, add *in* or *con* to the page–event *stantly*—in other words indulge in a playful pastime of filling-in-the-blank. The poem's invitation to the reader inflects the picturesque aesthetic quality of prismaticality, which is brought on by roughness, with roughness here understand as the semiotic incompleteness offered by each line.

But isn't this type of readerly "production" little more than a titillation on a tawdry level? Can it not be considered an application in *extremis* of Mallarmé's counsel that words should not mean but suggest? If so, does it not compare with Ball's poems-without-words discussed in chapter 1? The reader is challenged to engage words *outside* the regime and expectancies of descriptive and propositional language, words in a condition that we might consider as prior to meaning. Whether we approach the text as an opportunity to "complete" its sublexemic provocations, or as an affective response to semio-material obfuscation, it nonetheless remains a verbal landscape without perspective or vanishing point.

This aspiration to poetic landscape is evident in another page from *Space:* ["of about"]

 

 

of                          about

 

 

 

since                 dot

 

The page here consists of three syncategoramatic terms ("of," "about," and "since") and one three-letter word ("dot") of ambiguous status (do we read "dot" as a noun or as a verb?) Unable to serve as either subjects or predicates when standing by themselves, "of," "about," and "since" have no referential functionality, and their stark arrangement and absence of syntax make the poem semantically unyielding (that building upon the fragment toward meaning that we noted in the early poems is not available here). The lexical arrangement of the page seriously inhibits any perceptual sequencing on the reader's part. (Are words here placed or suspended?) Although it deprives the reader of grammatical connections and prosodic enjambment, thus leaving the reader in a state of depleted cognition, the poem still offers its *pictorial* status for us to ruminate and engage. If we pay attention to its visual effect as a wordscape, we note that its four words form the angles of a frame that contain a potentially charged absence. Avoiding linearity and depth, Coolidge creates the boundary to an absent topography in which syntax gives way to terminals and corners. Moreover, the four words are placed such that the last two form a triangle with the page number (80) at the bottom, thereby drawing a paratextual element into the word-page composition. Clearly the placement and nature of the words indicate a visual syntax at work in which words do not articulate so much as separate and draw critical attention away from meaning *per se* and toward their own roles as elements in meaning and such non-semantic issues as what constitutes a terminus or corner and what is a verbal relation outside of grammar and syntax.

No ideas but in things? The two poems considered above hardly exemplify the notion of epistemic *embodiment* that William's famous call inspires. The aesthetic proximity is perfectly in accord with the doctrine of "no ideas but in things," yet where we precisely locate "things" in *Space* is a fraught question. "Things" are no doubt present (in the very "event" of words), but they lack intellectual impregnation. The last pages of *Space* offer a morphemic rather than a verbal poetry, one that instead of advancing epistemological uncertainty refuses the semantic exchange-value on which knowledge depends. One might at this point be tempted to appeal to the aesthetic sentiments of a late-Victorian critic and claim that through layout and content Coolidge comes close to realizing that quality Arthur Symons isolated in the short lyrics of Robert Bridges in which we are "nearest in words to silence" (207). Such a silence in words will occupy a central place in my final chapter; here, let me emphasize the constructedness of this poetry: it is not the stripped-down version of a post-Romantic meditation, nor the Benjaminian fragment offering itself as allegory, but the monstration of semantic parsimony that causes us, its readers, to tenant the unhomely. Paradoxically to read such imageless poems brings the reader close to experiencing that cleavage Levinas ascribed to both the image in general and his own facial picturesque: both a sign and thing, both a self and a stranger to itself.[24] There is a process of symbolic reversal, or to use Levinas' more accurate term, a "symbol in reverse" that draws attention to the surface where language finds itself inscribed (quite literally) at the edge of its own limits. It's tempting at this point to invoke the ghost of Hölderlin, for Coolidge, like his German predecessor, "directs his language to the fundamental gap in the signifier, that transforms lyricism into delirium, . . . work into the absence of a work" (Foucault 17). Coolidge's trajectory however is atheological; it flies neither from the gods, nor from the absent father. The effect of Coolidge's texts suggests the same uncertainty of language evoked by the later poems of Paul Celan; language is unavailable as a plenitude of eloquent resource.[25]

Barrett Watten astutely draws attention to "a syntactic basis in a 'regard for certain arrangement of objects'" in Coolidge's early work; he notes "a mimicking of the painterly surface" in a manner similar, though not identical, to the first generation of New York School poets (88–89). (Arrangement presupposes a spatial separation between details and it was, of course, the constructive principle of arrangement that attracted Pound to the Chinese ideogram.) Watten's reading is persuasive in light of the fact that Coolidge himself has admitted to a predilection for "arrangement" as a concept rather than "composition" or "structure" (Coolidge 144). Starting not with rules but materials, he investigates the non-relationship of assemblage and the pressure between elemental linguistic parts. Watten also attests that Coolidge "extends art into language" (468) yet, in a certain sense, the extension is reversed.

Above all, the picturesque moment endorses a poetics of sensation rather than interpretation or reflection. Uvedale Price theorizes the capricious sensory benefits of the picturesque in comparison to the unitary "overawe" brought on by the sublime: "Again, by its variety, its intricacy, its partial concealments, it excites that active curiosity which gives play to the mind, loosening those iron bonds with which astonishment chains up the faculties" (I: 106). Price does not call for evaluation but rather for a mental flâneurism, a playful encounter with detail and curiosity. (Here we are not far from both a poetry of pure affect and a poetry of readerly productive involvement.) Such encounters can also bring about a collapse of language, an inarticulate response that approximates both an infant renaissance and a sigilistic reflex. I take the following passage from an anonymous journal of a picturesque tour through Wales in the summer of 1795: "we hardly ever spoke! or if we did it was only between long pauses that involuntarily we cried out sometimes all together, did you ever?—no never—[until] fatigued with our own barren exclamations . . . we all agreed to be *quite silent*"

(Quoted in Andrews 11). Do we judge this reaction, this collective retreat into silence, as an instance of Pricean "overawe" before the sublime, or does it perhaps open aesthetics to an unforeseen ontological dimension (touched upon in chapter 8) that of infancy?

Ruminating on Ovid's version of the myth of Narcissus, Maurice Blanchot arrives at the image of a marvelous child who is dying. Narcissus, "having turned into an image . . . dissolves in the immobile dissolution of the imaginary, where he is washed away without knowing it, *losing a life he does not have*" (126, emphasis added). This lost life that the infant never had marks a singular passage and an ineluctable destiny for human being: to die into language without knowing it. Heidegger famously posits a double negative constitution of being: a being toward death and a being toward language. Both inclinations are unavoidable and irreversible, and somewhere in that transit is a stage named infancy. Infancy inflects pre-subjective intensities into what Deleuze judges to be "a pure immediate consciousness with neither object nor self" (26). It similarly inflects the more portentous advent of language precisely as an infant's death. A child emerges from an infant corpse still warm outside and at the limit of a life's indebtedness to living language: already belated, this infant is a not yet something. Moreover, infancy has no survivors precisely because infancy is the non-ground of language, withholding that secret of language that "language" can never recover. This scenario, of course, which constitutes a primal scene, is the happening of a non-event, an impossible event because the infant occupies the space of the imaginary. In this context, the phrase "an infant is being killed" is of the order of a phantasmatic designation that refers to a passage in which there is a death of an infant and a one who survives. The disinherited child suspended between two worlds "to whom no longer what's been, and not yet what's coming belongs" (Agamben 43) is a recurrent them in Rilke's poetry. This theme remarks the interstitial space of infancy, a brief epoch condemned from the start to death.

Let me try to outline a poetics of infancy—a poetics haunted by a death into language—by way of an interrogation. What would it mean to desire illiteracy as an intense, ephemeral condition of being without language? The meaning would be to "wish" for infancy. The question invokes not only Malcolm Andrews's anonymous picturesque-seeking travelers, but rephrases the desire to abandon the order of words that reverberates through the shattered Halls of Mirrors of twentieth-century-avant-garde practice: Ball's *lautgedicht* and Kruchenykh's *zaum* (discussed in chapter 1), Nepomucin Miller's and Karl Reuterswald's punctuation poems, and the gestural calligraphy of Henri Michaux's *Mouvements*. This desire, of course, has its precedents, as we have seen in the marbled page of

Sterne's *Tristram Shandy* (the subject of chapter 5). Indeed, from Aristophanes' bird language, through Shakespeare's *chough*, Cage's mesostic erosions, and Beat poet Michael McClure's "beast language," the evidence of numerous attempts to escape the regime of the signifier are sufficient to constitute a literary counter-tradition. To recover a state outside adult parlance, a state before language, and return to an *en-fans* is the common *telos* behind this tradition. Can an encounter with the material proximity that makes up Coolidge's *Space* register as an infant experience? Does the uncertainty of what is before us, the uncanniness on each page, leave certainty simultaneously bereft and exposed? According to Agamben, "Experience is incompatible with certainty, and once an experience has become measurable and certain, it immediately loses its authority as the heterological adversary of knowledge" (*Infancy* 17–18).

Let's return to our travelers who hardly ever spoke, and did so, if at all, only after long pauses, with their cries and barren exclamations coming without volition and their binding compact to be "quite silent." In *Love's Body* Norman O. Brown offers a brief account of an infant word, a *verbum infans,* ineffable but nonetheless a state in which silence and speech are reconciled (257). This may be worth pondering in relation to the silence of our travelers after the fatigue induced by their otiose exclamations: the infant state within the picturesque moment; it also invokes the assemblage of morphemes and white space that characterize the majestic, minimal conclusion of Coolidge's *Space.* To have nothing to say and to say it and in that way utter poetry is a different sigilism from that of our travelers. For underlying Cage's notorious definition of poetry (made in his 1949 "Lecture on Nothing") is not only the poet's insight that silence is the scream on the most effective side of the dictionary, but also the inflection of the ethical implications of raw orality. I believe we have an urgent need for an alliance between creativity and philosophy for the sake of ethics. This is an old call made most recently by Gerald L. Bruns but traceable through Levinas and Kierkegaard back at least to Kant.[26] If not unethical in itself, writing nonetheless evades the fundamental ethical encounter, which is not a self-addressed categorical imperative as Kant would have us believe, but the exposed encounter of two faces and a reader and a text. The necessary link here latches ethics onto both immediacy and proximity and proximity to the infancy of encounter. It is a frequent link on occasions: on first encountering *Tender Buttons,* or *Finnegans Wake,* or Jackson MacLow's *Stanzas for Iris Lezak,* or Welsh mountains, or the Twin Towers disaster of September 11, 2001, or Clark Coolidge's *Space.* Lyotard describes this infancy as a "welcome extended to the marvel that (something) is happening, the respect for the event" (quoted in Harvey and Schehr 49). This infancy arrived at through encounter unfolds of necessity another matter—the infancy of ethics.

In conclusion, what is the cultural valence of evocation? Furthermore, how feasible is this transhistoric confluence of Gilpin, Price, and Coolidge? Like Heidegger I believe in the volatility of origins, a notion of beginning figured not as a fixed punctum but as a recurring eruption, a turbulence, an iterant wave. Such a theory of origin introduces a chiasmic consequence: historical ideas and moments are contemporized while at the same time contemporary issues are historicized. The destiny of twentieth-century poetics has been the political, and through its embrace of the latter it avowed a major linguistic infelicity, embracing an unclear concept of the political as indistinguishable from social immanence. Along the way "aesthetic" became a suburb of the undesirable, the anomaly, an unwanted remainder. Hopefully the parallels I've drawn (and which I could extend) from a minor eighteenth-century aesthetic moment open up a contemporary line of thinking around disjunction and irregularity and demonstrate if nothing else that the picturesque remains one of contemporary poetry's unexorcised ghosts.

# The 'Pataphysics of Auschwitz

*This chapter will proceed to open as a wound to be sutured somewhere between a telephone and a bathroom door.*

## Part I: The Fraternal Contaminant: A Definition Followed by an Entertaining Prelude

Ever since the mind developed as a machine to think without fingers, 'pataphysics, the science of imaginary solutions, has been around as a renegade rationality whose project has been the ludic anamorphosization of truth, science, and their reactionary structures, regulatory ideals, and compromise formations. Ludic? By all means ludic, yet a strict tenet of imperturbability is fundamental to all 'pataphysical endeavors. 'Pataphysics is *serious,* for to effectively debunk the serious it must itself be taken seriously. Neither parodic nor partaking of the logic of the absurd, 'pataphysics operates as a decidedly unofficial contaminant, generated within, and as a part of, all or any scientific production. Installing itself within those rational endeavors of syllogism, ratiocination, and truth production, it asserts its own status as an essential and part-constitutional pollutant. Operating within these patriarchal terms, 'pataphysics eludes the power of both the scientific and the rational; it subverts their scope and complicates the limits of their dominance, subjecting them to a festive pulverization that opens up the implications of their discourse and thereby relativizes their dispensations. Locating its activity in the membranous space between scientific and artistic spheres, 'pataphysics continuously resuscitates a rational impertinence, a fulguration against the cogito. 'Pataphysics does not describe an historic moment but rather marks a transhistoric state of mind in which the covering law of 'pataphysics is totality. Everything is 'pataphysics, either conscious or unconscious. 'Pataphysics and its presidential choreography of the inclination ensure that the 'pataphysical is and always will be the rogue operative among scientific endeavor.

And so be it. 'Pataphysics historically and consciously originates within the mind of Alfred Jarry (1873–1907) whose own definition of the term occurs in Book II of his neo-scientific novel *The Exploits and Opinions of Doctor Faustroll Pataphysician,* which was published posthumously (three years before Stein's *Tender Buttons*) in 1911. Jarry writes:

> 'Pataphysics, whose etymological spelling should be ἐπὶ (μετὰ τὰ φυσικά) [*epi (meta ta phusika)*] and actual orthography 'pataphysics, preceded by an apostrophe so as to avoid a simple pun [patte à physique], is the science of that which is superinduced upon metaphysics, whether within or beyond the latter's limitations, extending as far beyond metaphysics as the latter extends beyond physics. Ex: an epiphenomenon being often accidental, 'pataphysics will be, above all, the science of the particular, despite the common opinion that the only science is that of the general. 'Pataphysics will examine the laws which govern exceptions, and will explain the universe supplementary to this one; or, less ambitiously, will describe a universe which can be—and perhaps should be—envisaged in the place of the traditional one, since the laws which are supposed to have been discovered in the traditional universe are also correlations of exceptions, albeit more frequent ones, but in any case accidental data which, reduced to the status of the unexceptional exceptions, possess no longer even the virtue of originality. (*Selected Works* 192)

"'Pata" invokes a subtle declension on the general order of the prefix—from "meta" through "para," beyond and beside, to their fusion in a spatial logic that demolishes alike (as will be soon disclosed) in the revolutions of a "physic-stick" and the historic moment named Auschwitz.

As the science of the particular aimed at examining laws that govern exceptions, 'pataphysics operates under the strict aegis of two appropriated laws: those of the *syzygy* and the *clinamen,* both of which pertain to the broad relationship of matter to motion. In its astronomical use *syzygy* refers to a conjunction or opposition of the systems of two planets in their orbit around a third; in biology it denotes the conjunction of two organisms without the loss of identity. As a governing law of 'pataphysical methodology, *syzygy* promotes those momentary oppositions as conjunctions in verbal meanings (such as puns and portmanteaux) that always characterize the scientific discourse of imaginary solutions. Jarry's most famous contribution in this area is the semantic conjunction of space and time, *ether* and *eternity,* to produce the semantic twin of "ethernity," which is a momentary conjunction in a logical space that carries along with it the cataclysmic breakdown of a coupled opposition.

The *clinamen* derives from Lucretius' Roman version of classical Greek atomic theory. Lucretius (ca. 95–55 C.E.) describes the phenomenon of the *clinamen atomorum* in Book II of his scientific poem *De Rerum Natura:*

> . . . so that the mind itself may not be subject
> To inner necessity in what it does—
> And fetch and carry like a captive slave—
> The tiny swerve of atoms plays its part
> At unanticipated times and places (113)

The literary appearance of this term is rare after Lucretius, yet its emergent moments are important because they suggest a conceptual continuation. De Quincey overtly attributes the term to Lucretius in his "Letter to a Young Man" (*Works* 85), and Coleridge speaks of a "*lene clinamen,* the gentle bias" in his *Aids to Reflection.* The *clinamen* became a central preoccupation in the resurgence of interest in Lucretius' thinking in the 1980s and '90s (in the writings of Serres, Nancy, Derrida, and Baudrillard for instance). Michel Serres describes it as "the minimal angle in a laminar flow" that "initiates a turbulence . . . the angle interrupts the stoic chain, breaks the *foedera fati,* the endless series of causes and relations. It disturbs, in fact, the laws of nature" (153). Nancy writes: "one cannot create a world with simple atoms. There has to be a *clinamen.* There has to be an inclination or an inclining from one toward the other, of one by the other, or from one to the other. Community is at least the *clinamen* of the 'individual'" (3–4). For his part, Harold Bloom adopts it in 1973 as the first of his six revisionary ratios.

The *clinamen* then, marks an atom's deviation from its path, its aberration from a stable flow and its consequent collision to produce a new formation. Whereas science (that "totality of the world's legends" as Serres so aptly puts it) would harness any deviance to the logical perimeters of its own dyadic ontology, 'pataphysics (as the science of imaginary solutions) inscribes and articulates the moment, condition, and the place where *the law is insufficient to prevent the clinamen.* That the origin of the concept of atomic declension can be traced beyond Lucretius to Greek Epicurean philosophy is a noteworthy fact if for no other reason than it betrays the belatedness of Jarry's science.[1] Indeed, to a pre-microscopic culture the existence of the atom, let alone an atomic swerve, could only be hypothe-sized but never proved; hence, this aspect of Epicureanism is patently an imagi-nary science and 'pataphysical from its very inception.

My own argument focuses mainly on the application and pertinence of Jarry's second law of declension: the *syzygy*. If the *clinamen* disturbs the laws of nature, then the *syzygy* reinforces those laws pertaining to exceptions, for it brings about a confraternity of two anomalies. Moreover, the fusion and dis-appearance of oppositions are brought about not by way of a concordat but by a sacrificial conjunction. Both the economy and outcomes of a *syzygy* are pro-foundly chiasmic, producing simultaneously a conjunction of opposites: affir-mation and negation, truth and untruth, "the possibility of the incompossible" (Bök 41). Jarry's own 'pataphysical theory of gravity obtains by way of *syzygy* so that "the fall of a body towards a center" is exactly the same as "the ascen-sion of a vacuum towards a periphery" (*Selected Works* 193). Are we passing into night or retreating out of day? This is a question that expurgates the festive and lethal simultaneity of 'pataphysical *syzygy*. Jarry also describes a practical in-ducement of *syzygia* in the form of a mundane toilet brush he calls the "physic-stick"; in its 'pataphysical reincarnation, it serves as an efficient agent of revo-lution (*Selected Works* 245). Spinning around its axis induces a heraldic blazon of paralogical choreography whereby "in each quarter of every one rotation . . . you form a cross with yourself" (111). Whether Jarry's physic-stick inspired Du-champ's readymade remains a moot point; however it may be fruitful to rethink the *objet-trouvé* through the kinetics of the *syzygy*. Does not the act of appro-priating, renaming, and recontexualizing a bottle rack or a snow shovel effect both an oppositional conjunction of art and utility and at the same time effec-tively demolish the bar that separates equipment from aesthetic object?[2] More-over, the rationale for the readymade is inherent in the notorious postulate of "'pataphysical equivalence" advanced by I. L. Sandomir: "There is thus no differ-ence whatsoever, either of nature or degree, between different minds, any more than there is any difference between their products, or indeed between one thing or another. For the Complete Pataphysician the most banal graffito equals the most consummate book, even the *Exploits and Opinions of Dr. Faustroll* them-selves, and the humblest mass-produced saucepan equals the *Nativity* of Altdor-fer" (179). The *syzygy* enjoys an esteemed lineage. It is latent in Aristotle's claim "that Contraries, when set beside each other, make the strongest appearance,"[3] and reappears throughout history: in the *coniunctio oppositorum* of Avicenna, for instance, and the concordant discord that structured much of seventeenth-century aesthetics. There is also a marked similarity between the *syzygy* and the

Stoic conception of lived temporality as *cairos*. The latter relates to *syzygy* not as its conceptual enantiomorph but as a practical development out of it, for *cairos* signals "the abrupt and sudden conjunction where decision grasps opportunity and life is fulfilled in the moment" (Agamben 101). This would appear to endorse the spontaneous social assemblages of the Situationists, the later Happenings, and a broader poetics of *bricolage* that operates as a superinducement upon what is at hand.[4] Moreover, it is *syzygy* that, as a momentary conjunction of opposites, superinduces temporality and motion into the surreal image. Through a 'pataphysical redaction those famous and familiar definitions of the Surreal image reemerge in slightly modified form. Now it is as "[b]eautiful as the chance *and fleeting* encounter on a dissection table of a sewing machine and an umbrella" (Lautréamont) and "a *momentary* bringing together of two more or less distant realities" (Reverdy) and yet again "[t]he *transitory* joining of two apparently unjoinable realities" (Ernst).[5] By inducing a *temporary* conjunction of opposites, the *syzygy* introduces a complexity of kinetics and temporality into the assemblage of impossibles. Together, the *clinamen* and *syzygy* ensure that our universe will be 'pataphysical, that existence is shattered and constructed by means of the simultaneous agency of declensional and conjunctive oppositional forces.

## The Collegium 'Pataphysicum

To the 'pataphysical disposition, all scientific problems reduce to issues of administration and classification. There is a central and theoretical need to produce and institute a complex bureaucratic terrain; there is an impulse to reclassify all classification by shifting the ground of taxonomy from a traditional base in matter and substance (in other words "what is done") to an attitudinal base ("how it's done"). Founded in 1948 the present *College of 'Pataphysics* consists of more than ninety commissions and sub-commissions, all of which have precisely differentiated functions, but which ultimately fall under the binding rule of 'pataphysical *equivalence.*

Under the *Commission for Licities and Harmonies* is the *Sub-Commission of Imaginary Solutions,* the function of which is the infinite provision of "semi-virtualities" for any subject, and the *Sub-Commission of Probabilities,* which specializes in statistical and logical operations. Under the *Commission of Unpredictabilities* (whose ordinary function is to uphold or instantiate the principle that only the unpredictable exists) are several important sub-commissions including the one of *Glory and Protuberances.* Set up as a socio-medical "organism" to diagnose "evil" and to work in conjunction with the *Sub-Commission of Imagi-*

*nary Solutions,* the *Sub-Commission of Glory and Protuberances* controls three "Intermissions:" *Apotheoses* (which handles changes of opinion, canonizations, panegyrics and obituaries), *Fine and Foul Arts* (which handles doxoscopic matters), and the *Intermission of Ornaments and Ideas.* The *Commission of Drafts and Minutes* has under its jurisdiction the *Lalalogical Sub-Commission,* which deals with all post-Babelian matters (the confusion and profusion of tongues, imaginary languages, etc.) and with definitions, "indefinitions," and subsumptions. (Its memorial president is James Joyce.) Other sub-commissions under the *Drafts and Minutes* include those of *Orpheons, Cliques and Claques, Paremiography, Hypotheses and Pedestals, Apostils, Paraphrases, Cercopsies,* and *Plagiarisms.*

The *Commission of Order and Time* controls the *Sub-Commission of the Ordinary and the Small Extraordinary,* which itself regulates, assesses, and generally problematizes the ratio of predictabilities to unpredictabilities. The *Sub-Commission of Obliquities* specializes in oblique solutions, artifices, and subterfuges. (In this capacity it could have supervised both the Bolshevik Revolution and the 1958 Eurovision Song Contest.) The *Commission of Transquinite Processions* controls the *Sub-Commission for Pope Marcellus,* which has the specific duty of supporting, repairing, and supplementing any defective sub-commission. The numerous sub-commissions under the control of the *Commission of Order and Time* include *Parapomps and Escorts, Funiculars, Pads and Stamps, Nardigraph, Ordnance and Berthings, Metastases, Assumptions, Diadoses,* and *Rotations.*

Regulating all suspicious cases, dubious operations, defective nomenclatures, and various and sundry difficulties in conduct and appearance is the *Commission of Ellipses, Eclipses, and Anesthetics.* Its *Sub-Commission of Anachronism and Local Color* supervises the relation and interface of both these terms as 'pataphysical points of reference. Other sub-commissions under the jurisdiction of this commission include *Impredictables and Epithets, Canons and Paragons, Implied Moralities, Inadequations,* and *Paralyses and Anesthetics.* The *Collegium 'Pataphysicum* similarly supports numerous occupied chairs: *Lyricopathology, Military and Strategic Eristics, Applied Mental Alienation, Catachemistry and 'Pataphysics of the Inexact Sciences, Erotics and Pornosophy, Crocodilology, Applied Alcoholism, Applied Experimental Necrobiosis, Spoonerism, Applied Blablabla and Meteology, General 'Pataphysics and Dialectics of the Useless Sciences, Pedology and Adelphism, Cinematographology and Oneirocriticism,* and the Chair of Comparative Atrocities. Among the college's many achievements, I am permitted to mention only its radical abolition of the Gregorian calendar in favor of the 'pataphysical perpetual calendar. The 'Pataphysical Era (P.E.) began on September 8, 1873 (the birthday of Alfred Jarry), which instantly became the first day of the month Absolu of the year 1 (1 Absolu 1 P.E.) The 'pataphysical calendar divides the year into thirteen months (twelve of 28 days, one of 29). The months are (in order from the old September 8): Absolu, Haha, Sable, Décervalage, Gueules, Pédale, Clinamen, Palotin, Merdre (anglicized as Pshit), Gidouille (29 days), Tatne, and Phalle. The thirteenth of each month is always a Friday. In its accompanying transformation of feast days, the college implemented two significant changes. The old Christmas became the Feast of the Nativity of the Acheopteryx and the old New Year is celebrated as the Feast of Décervelage (unbraining).

## 'Patacedents

Permit me to trace this spirit of permanent 'pataphysics in a few examples that originate before the 'Pataphysical Era (they comprise what Oulipians would call plagiarisms by anticipation). The claim of Plutarch of Chaeronea to a specifically 'pataphysical recognition comes through a short treatise contained in his monumental gathering of theosophy, philosophy, anecdotes, and precepts known as *The Moralia.* It is a speculative essay upon the origin and meaning of the letter *E* (epsilon) inscribed above the door of the temple of Apollo at Delphi. Plutarch proposes several theories (all of them sequentially dismissed.) In his first argument, Plutarch suggests that the *epsilon,* holding fifth place in the Greek alphabet and additionally signifying the number five, represents the composite dedication to the oracle of the five original sophists: Chilon, Thales, Solon, Bias, and Pittacus. His second argument has a similar form of development. The epsilon, being second in place of the vowels, represents Apollo in his planetary embodiment as the sun that holds second place among the planets after the moon. The third argument is less syntactic and more grammatical. Arguing from the sound of the epsilon (*ay-ee*), Plutarch develops the theory that the letter notates the original form of oracular address as both the notes of interrogation and exclamation. A fourth argument proposes a logical basis for the letter's presence. The sound of the epsilon is "ay-ee," which signifies the word *if,* whose use and presence are indispensable to the formulation of a syllogism. Plutarch then proposes a fifth, numerical, solution: the epsilon, as the number five, signifies the initial "marriage" of the first even number (two) and the first odd (three). Plutarch then reads a certain sexual implication in this imaginary solution: "For in case of divisions into equal parts, the even number being every way parted asunder, leaves behind a receptive principle, as it were, in itself, and a space; but when the odd is treated in the same way, a middle part still survives that is productive of division; in which way it is more generative than the other" (181). Plutarch finally concludes in favor of the invocationary argument: "Neither number, therefore, nor rank, nor conjunction, nor any other of the remaining parts of speech, I think, does the letter signify, but that it is an address to the god, or an invocation, complete in itself, that together with the utterance thereof puts the speaker in mind of the power of the deity" (190). Jarry's own lettristic speculations are best demonstrated in chapter 6 of *Dr. Faustroll* in the section, "Concerning Some Further and More Evident Meanings of the Word 'Ha Ha.'" The arguments are remarkably Plutarchian and in sections anticipate Derrida's concept of *différance*:

> In the first instance, it is more judicious to use the orthography AA, for the aspiration *h* was never written in the ancient languages of the world. . . . A juxtaposed to A, with the former obviously equal to the latter, is the formula of the principle of identity: a thing is itself. It is at the same time the most excellent refutation of this proposition, since the two A's differ in space, when we write them, if not indeed in time, just as two twins are never born together. . . . The first A was perhaps congruent to the second, and we will therefore willingly write thus: A = A.
>
> Pronounced quickly enough, until the letters become confounded, it is the idea of unity. Pronounced slowly, it is the idea of duality, of echo, of distance, of symmetry, of greatness and duration, of the two principles of good and evil. . . . It would be a complicated problem to study, in addition, whether the first A was the efficient cause of the second (*Selected Works* 228–29).

## Bladders and Clinamen

John Taylor (1580–1653), grand lalologist, self-styled "Water Poet," inventor of the Barmoodan tongue and scriptor of several utopian languages, ranks as a true typology of the later Dr. Faustroll. He worked as a boatsman running a ferry between the Surrey and Middlesex sides of the Thames. Of his many 'pataphysical exploits, one in particular demands our attention. In 1623, as the sedate Iaggard and Blount printed the sedate first folio of Shakespeare's works, Taylor—in the ceremonious company of Roger Bird, a vintner (happily)—sailed from London to Queensborough in a paper boat of their own construction with two stockfish tied to two canes serving as oars. After three miles the paper bottom disintegrated and Taylor was forced to resort to eight full-blown bladders for floatation. The boat survived in this condition from Saturday evening to Monday morning when they finally reached Queensborough.

The comparison to Jarry's own version of Odysseus, Dr. Faustroll, is worth noting. In Book I, chapter 6 of *The Exploits and Opinions of Dr. Faustroll,* Jarry describes the doctor's boat as a sieve dipped in melted paraffin. Faustroll himself explains the method of floatation: "When I place my sieve on the river, the water's skin tautens against the holes, and the liquid flowing underneath cannot penetrate unless the skin breaks" (Book 6 Chapter 1). To complete this incomplete genealogical patchwork, let me link these journeys to the voyage of Mallarmé's *Yole,* described in *Le Nénuphar blanc* ("The White Water Lily"): "I had rowed a great deal, with a vast, clear, drowsy motion, my eyes fixed within on the entire forgetfulness of movement, as the hour's laughter flowed around. So much motionlessness idled away the time that brushed by a dull sound into which there half slipped the skiff, I only confirmed the halt by the steady sparkling of initials on the uncovered oars, which recalled me to my worldly identity" (145). Of 'pataphysical note here is the precise operation of the clinamen in the boat's half-veering, which causes a return to identity through an implosion of word and thing, signifier and referent, the steady sparkling of initials on the raised oars.

Isaac D'Israeli cites several examples of early 'pataphysics in his *Curiosities of Literature.* His description of the *cento* form of poetic composition clearly points to 'pataphysical implications:

A *Cento* primarily signifies a cloak made of patches. In poetry it denotes a work wholly composed of verses, or passages promiscuously taken from other authors, only disposed in a new form of order, so as to compose a new work and a new meaning. Ausonius has laid down the rules to be observed in composing *Centos.* The pieces may be taken either from the same poet, or from several; and the verses may be taken either entire, or divided into two; one half to be connected with another half taken from elsewhere; but two verses are never to be taken together. Agreeable to these rules he has made a pleasant nuptial *Cento* from Virgil. (112)

The clinamen lies at the basis of the *cento* as that swerve of textual elements away from one to another context and the inclination of meaning into its own semantic difference. It is the matrix of found poetry and treated text that postmodernism provides countless examples of. However, the range of 'pataphysical displacement and equivalence is perhaps best seen in the work of the Empress Eudoxia, who wrote a life of Christ in *centos* taken entirely from Homer.

D'Israeli gives additional accounts of early madcap Irish antiquaries who mention the existence of public libraries before the flood, others who compiled an exact catalogue of an astronomical library in the ark of Noah, and a certain Paul Christian Ilsker who compiled a precise catalogue of Adam's library in Paradise. Mention also should be made of Thomas Hood, the early-nineteenth-century humorist, who at the request of the Duke of Devonshire submitted a list of "imaginary" titles for the spines of "sham books" to be constructed at the entrance to the ducal library staircase at Chatsworth in 1831–32. Of the hundreds of these 'pataphysical non-publications I will mention the following: Johnson's *Contradictionary, John Knox on "Death's Door," Chronological Account of the Date Tree, The Scottish Boccaccio* by D. Cameron, Shelley's *Complete Conchologist,* and Blaine on *Equestrian Burglary; or the Breaking-in of Horses (Notes* 311).

## Charles Fourier (1772–1837)

Fourier might honestly be labeled as history's most delightful and endearing psycho-ceramicist (psycho-ceramics being the 'pataphysical study of crackpots). Sublime, vatic, absurd, obsessive in matters of detail, pathological in his prognoses and desires for social reform, Fourier's theories and schemes based upon a principle of universal passional attraction (itself conceived as a socio-moral parallel to Newton's theory of gravity) range from the impossible to the irresistible. The scope of his thinking and writings is too broad to be dealt with adequately in this superluminal resumé, yet a few of his cosmological, evolutionary, and social theories call for mention. Fourier's entire opus may be read as a vast play of systematics without a system, communicated through a terminology without metonymic investment. He reinvents the universe as a universe of precise, calculable parts whose productive force is pleasure. Through a constant struggle to realize his thinking in a hypostasized locale where thinking had never gone, Fourier became the first 'pataphysician to articulate the *erotic* limits of meaning. His triumph is the dissolution of the boundaries demarking all logical empires, permitting the real and the unreal to recombine and reorganize inside a non-Aristotelian space that produces the *marvelous.* Consider, for example, the following proposal (worthy of any Italian Futurist) to replace the moon by artificial "nocturnal furnishings" that will be "considerably assorted and composed of our vivid and variously colored moons, next to which Phoebe will appear as what she is, a pale ghost, a sepulchral lamp, a Swiss cheese." Another example is his proposal to perpetuate warfare by replacing mortal with culinary combat. Disputes were to be settled by "thesis meals," and Fourier proposed the use of forty-four "systems of tiny pastries"; these included pastries "anathematized by the council" and pastries "adopted by the Council of Babylon." Here is his lovable scheme to pay off the French debt to England entirely in hens' eggs.

Fourier likewise inaugurates the 'pataphysical immersion in accountancy, navigating numbers into the previously unknown and uncharted oceans of insanity, bound by an authoritative and pompous discursive pressure: he informs us, for instance, that in Rome during the time of Varro there were 278 contradictory opinions concerning true happiness. Among Fourier's 'pataphysical prognostications is the calculated height of "Harmonian man," which will be precisely eighty-four thumbs, or seven feet. He justifies this seemingly arbitrary unit of measure by informing us that he adopted as a natural measure the foot of the king of Paris; it has this property precisely because the regal foot is equal to the 32nd part of the water level in suction pumps. Fourier lists, neologizes, and enumerates; his semantics is a utopian one of intersections, recombinations, inversions, of bizarre logical neighborhoods, rationalized maverick vectors, linguistic geometries, and *pleasures.* The erotics of precise calculation are omnipresent. There are, for instance, 810 passions in each sex; within these are four basic passions and three distributive passions. The Composite passion is the passion for excess; the Butterfly passion demands a change of direction every two hours. There are twelve radical passions plus a thirteenth that Fourier calls "Unity-ness."

But Fourier's utopian production through a 'pataphysical method is perhaps best seen in his cosmological scheme, outlined in his first major opus, the *Theorie des quatre mouvements* of 1808. Fourier presents here a major theory of "universal analogy," positing that the universe is a unified system of hidden correspondences in which nothing escapes, nor exhausts, the analogical operation.[6] The twelve radical human passions are each represented by its own color, musical note, geometrical shape, and celestial body. The stars and planets all have sexual lives analogous to human ones and pass through stages of infancy, youth, maturity, and decline to eventually die in dotage. The average life of a planet is 80,000 years, half of which comprises "upward vibrations" and the other half "descending" ones. The moon, argues Fourier, contracted a fever from the earth and died a little before the Flood. The Earth's own life span will be distributed between thirty-two periods (our present being the fifth). On reaching the eighth period, the Earth will enter into "Harmony," Fourier's age of social utopia. In the Harmonian age, people will develop tails equipped with eyes and corpses will convert into aromatic clouds and drift purified through interstellar regions. Six new moons will appear to replace the current single one and numerous analogical "anti-species" will develop to replace all existing harmful creatures (there will be anti-lions, anti-sharks, etc.) The most memorable event promised during this period will be a geothermal phenomenon that Fourier terms the "Polar Crown." As a consequence of the coagulation of the Northern Lights, a ring will form around the North Pole. Remaining in perpetual contact with solar emissions and continually reflecting light through the northern latitudes, the polar ice caps will melt and the geological syntax of the Earth will be redistributed in a species of Bakhtinian carnival. Siberia will be warmer than Florence; oranges will grow in Warsaw ("the Polish tangerine"), and the northern seas—losing their salinity and being disinfected by a fluid emanating from the polar ice caps—will turn into "a sort of lemonade." "I am an inventor," he proclaimed, "not an orator." In his old age Fourier surrounded himself with cats and flowers. He was found dead in 1827, kneeling among his beloved flowerpots in his dressing gown. According to Barthes, Fourier read De Sade.

Toronto, 13 Gidouille, 114 'P. E.

## Part II: The 'Pataphysics of Auschwitz

In 1994 Jean Baudrillard invoked a millennial 'pataphysics for the contemporary era, an epoch characterized by the unreality of the real, the disappearance of history and the historical subject, and the emergence of a radical skepticism about the general reality of events.[7] The topic of what follows might well touch on millennial history but only by way of a detour back through a middle decade of the nineteenth century. This part is also written against the broad background of a single interrogation that is locational rather than epistemological in its nature: not *what* is but *where* is 'pataphysics? Where are its territorial emergences and historical interventions?

Traditionally and dismissively considered to be a ludic vacation, the cognitive diversion of adult children as my 'patacedents may suggest Jarry's minor science has not been taken seriously. At its best 'pataphysics is commonly thought of as ratiocination on vacation with King Logic, a monarch neither deposed, *abscondite,* nor assassinated but rather euphrosynally carnivalized. But thanks to William Anastasi's credible research we are now beginning to understand the profound influence of Jarry's thoughts and writings on the work of both Duchamp and Joyce.[8]

Situationist Asgar Jorn prophetically declared in 1961 that 'pataphysics was primed "to galvanize human thought and action in about two hundred years time." We yet await the year 2161 for proof or otherwise of Jorn's prediction; suffice to say that he sees 'pataphysics as the third great stage in Western religions. Following the natural epoch that ended with the Bronze Age and our current Judeo-Christian materialist age, the world awaits its third age, which will be 'pataphysical. Jorn was the first to realize the potentiality of Jarry's minor science as a weapon against metaphysics. Arguing the 'pataphysical premise of equivalence facilitates the development and dissemination of "organized absurdities" (that is to say games), Jorn co-opts 'pataphysical absurdities into the Situationist agenda for the promulgation of situations. The regime of organized absurdities marks "the pataphysical overture to the world" (Jorn). Gilles Deleuze presents a similar, though less theological argument, drawing attention to 'pataphysics' serious dimension in a short comparison with Heidegger.[9] As a superinducement upon metaphysics, 'pataphysics yields a ready asymptosis toward the Heideggerean project, and Deleuze focuses on three appositional preoccupations: technology and the machine, the sign, and their common critique of metaphysics. However the precursory reverberations of another key aspect of Jarry's science of imaginary solutions is absent from his discussion. Avoiding an outright assertion, Deleuze raises the question of Heidegger's speculations around the transition of technique into art: "Could one also say that Heidegger sees a transition toward art in the national socialist machine?" (195). I intend to pursue this line of thinking indirectly by examining a haunting apposition between the general law of 'pataphysics and that National Socialist "machine" termed *der lager*.

The fact that I am writing this as a founding member of the *Collegium 'Pataphysicum Canadensis* grants no authority to what I am about to say, and what I do write, when I start to write it, should be assessed, and quite brutally assessed, against Jarry's claim that everything is 'pataphysics. Let us revisit Jarry's definition: "'pataphysics will be, above all, the science of the particular, despite the common opinion that the only science is that of the general. 'pataphysics will examine the laws which govern exceptions. . . ." Now keep this in mind as we turn to the Nazi Final Solution. "Auschwitz," attests Georgio Agamben, "marks the end and the ruin of every ethics of dignity and conformity to a norm" (*Remnants* 69), but does this make it 'pataphysical? Like National Socialism, Jarry's minor science is less the repudiation than the culmination of a project named Reason; both encounter the condition of the exception and both respond with solutions—the one imaginary, the other "final." It is surely coincidental, in the specific form of coincidence that is syzygial, that Jarry's science, launched in a novel and a cycle of plays, emerged during the same historical period as the concentration camp, whose origin remains contested between British and Spanish imperialism at the end of the nineteenth century, and whose prevalence dates from World War I.[10] To argue a causal link between 'pataphysics and the camp would be laughingly impertinent, but the rule of chance legitimates this oppositional conjunction in a world whose very essence and cultural memory is, to say the least and the most, 'pataphysical.

Agamben's inestimable value in *Homo Sacer* is to have examined the juridico-political structure that made—and makes—an Auschwitz possible. Not born of orthodox law, the camp emerges from the substitution of martial law to cover a state deemed to be an exception. Let us review some pertinent historical facts. At the beginning of the 1850s Prussia legally implemented both protective custody *(Schutzhaft),* and the "protection of private freedom" *(Schutz der persönlichen Freiheit)* as a measure designed to meet a state of emergency and such a degree of social unrest as to be declared a state of exception *(Ausnahmezustand).* The insidious novelty within the Nazi resuscitation of this already trenchant institution within the governments of the Weimar lies in a subtly nuanced rewording of the German Constitution. No mention is made of a "state of exception," and the previously "provisional suspension of the Constitutional articles protecting personal rights" is now rendered "suspended until further notice" (*Homo Sacer* 168).

Let me introduce at this juncture the early Weimar political theorist and proto-fascist constitutional lawyer Carl Schmitt (1888–1985). Since September 11, 2001 America and much of Europe has been living out the political effects of the legacy of Schmitt's political theories with regard to a state of protracted exception (the death of Osama bin Laden on May 2, 2011 notwithstanding). Schmitt's theory of sovereignty and the exception is laid out preeminently and concisely in his book *Political Theology* (1922, revised 1934). Clearly emerging from the neo-Kantian rubble of 1918 (preeminently the work of Ernst Cassirer), Schmitt sought a radical alternative to universal norms and rules. Sovereignty for Schmitt marks the essence of the political and manifests in a specific situational decision: He is Sovereign who decides which case is an exception. (The German word for "exception" is *Ausnahmezustand,* which is normally translated "state of emergency.") Sovereignty pertains to situational decisions, not to norms. Its central question is "the question of the decision on the exception" (9). "What characterizes an exception is principally unlimited authority, which means the suspension of the entire existing order" (12); as such, it monopolizes not the gamut of coercion or even law, but the range and absolute, unquestionable declaration. Sovereignty is fundamentally non-representative; the sovereign does not represent a "general will" but manifests within the exception, as the declaration of the latter's very existence.

Schmitt is more timely than original; he is clearly the heir of Thomas Hobbes (both Schmitt and his student Leo Strauss wrote books on Hobbes), and *Political Theology* resuscitates two tenets of *Leviathan:* that the relation of a norm to a decision is an entirely pragmatic relation, and that law is made by sovereign power, not truth. Tellingly, Schmitt likens the exception in jurisprudence to the miracle in theology (36). Indeed, beyond this isolated similitude, Schmitt's entire theory of sovereignty is constructed on the premise that political concepts are secular versions of theological ones. (Jarry's own secularizing of theology took the form of a reconsideration of Christ's passion as an uphill bicycle race.) The archive of Western history documents many sovereign declarations, such as: Article 14 of the French Charter of 1815, which granted sovereign power to the monarch, and article 48 of the 1919 German Constitution, which granted sovereign power of declaration to the president of the Reich. Personally, and, closer to my former home, the 1970 War Measures Act, hastily pushed through by Canadian Prime Minister Pierre Elliott Trudeau in response to the terrorist activities of the Front Libération Québec, resuscitated an act first passed in August 1914 that authorized the internment of thousands of Ukrainians and east Europeans in twenty-four concentration camps across Canada. William Scheuerman remarks (quoted in the *Boston Review* 2001) that there are sufficient emergency measures in the United States today to allow the American administration free-reign to arrest and incarcerate indiscriminately without trial; ditto the United Kingdom. The full albeit brief history of such political states of exception can be consulted in Agamben's book of the same name (*State of Exception*); suffice to say here that the current state conditioning the United States is neither egregious nor inaugural but rather symptomatic of an episodic appeal to the anomaly as a paradigm of government since the late eighteenth century. The effects of such sovereign declarations of exception are paradoxical to say the least: the temporary suspension of civil liberties and human freedoms and the proliferation of surveillance and coercive totalitarian measures all for the sake of the protection of human freedom.

If we revisit Jarry's own description of the trajectory of his minor science, then the link of 'pataphysics to a Schmittian notion of sovereignty becomes obvious: "'pataphysics will be, above all, the science of the particular, despite the common opinion that the only science is that of the general. 'Pataphysics will examine the laws which govern exceptions . . . ." There are several passages in *Political Theology* that, when isolated, read like quotations from Jarry: "The exception is more interesting than the rule," and "The rule proves nothing; the exception proves everything."

Schmitt is not alone in his theorization of sovereignty and the state of exception at this historical point in time. It is known that Walter Benjamin showed interest in Schmitt's theory of sovereignty, although in their final intellectual formulations they seem like polar opposites.[11] In "Curriculum Vitae (III)," Benjamin linked his ongoing aims as well as his intentions in *The Origins of German Tragic Drama* (the *Trauerspiel*) to those of Schmitt's political theories, stating their similar claims on anti-territoriality: "This task ['destroying the doctrine of the territorial character of art'], one that I had already undertaken on a large scale in *Ursprung des deutschen Trauerspiels*, was linked on the one hand to the methodological ideas of Alois Riegl, especially his doctrine of the *Kunstwollen*, and on the other hand to the contemporary work done by Carl Schmitt, who in his analysis of political phenomena has made a similar attempt to integrate phenomena whose apparent territorial distinctness is an allusion" (*Selected Writings* 78). This articulation of Riegl onto Schmitt is fortuitous in that it links aesthetic issues onto politics. However in the *Trauerspiel* itself Benjamin advances nothing less than an uncompromising reversal of Schmitt's theory in which the baroque sovereign crisis exposes an inability to decide: "The antithesis between the power of the ruler and his capacity to rule led to a feature peculiar to the *Trauerspiel* which is, however, only apparently a generic feature and which can be illuminated only against the background of the theory of sovereignty. This is the indecisiveness of the tyrant. The prince, who is responsible for making the decision to proclaim a state of emergency, reveals, at the first opportunity, that he is almost incapable of making a decision" (Benjamin *The Origin of German Tragic Drama* 70–71). In "Critique of Violence" Benjamin investigates the judicial means to implement force as well as the possibility of forms of violence that elude juridical sanction, arriving at the conclusion that a "pure" (i.e. revolutionary) violence can exist outside the law. Benjaminian violence in the state of exception clearly gestures toward a different destiny than Schmitt's protofascism; as specified in the eighth thesis of Benjamin's "Theses on the Philosophy of History" (completed in the spring of 1940), it opens outside of the law certain possibilities within historical materialism: "The tradition of the oppressed teaches us that the 'state of emergency' in which we live is not the exception but the rule. We must attain to a conception of history that is in keeping with this insight. Then we shall clearly realize that it is our task to bring about a real state of emergency, and this will improve our struggle against Fascism" (Benjamin *Illuminations* 256). The dark present of the contemporary seems to have ushered in as its *nomos* not Benjamin's optimistic revolutionary force but Schmitt's version of the state of exception.

Agamben notes the consequences: "*The state of exception thus ceases to be referred to as an external and provisional state of factual danger and comes to be confused with juridical rule itself*" (168). One Nazi jurist, Werner Spohr, described this new state of immanent exception as a "state of willed exception," an aptly paradoxical phrase that equally describes the atomic clinamen. The 'pataphysical origins of the camp can be readily inferred from Agamben's own chilling analysis:

> The camp is the space that is opened when the state of exception begins to become the rule. . . . What is excluded in the camp is, according to the etymological sense of the term "exception" *(ex-capere), taken outside,* included through its own exclusion. But what is first of all taken into the juridical order is the state of exception itself. Insofar as the state of exception is "willed," it inaugurates a new juridico-political paradigm in which the norm becomes indistinguishable from the exception. (*Homo Sacer* 169)

As a superinducement of 'pataphysics into the space of the camp, this remarks both the culmination and the disinvagination of a juridico-'pataphysical dimension, for the law that governs the exception disappears precisely because a state of exception becomes the law outside the law. Agamben offers a sobering image of the *syzygial,* and arguably postmodern, contemporary nature of life in the camp as a complex, moebial conjunction of opposites: "Whoever entered the camp moved in a zone of indistinction between outside and inside, exception and rule, licit and illicit, in which the very concepts of subjective right and juridical protection no longer make any sense" (*Homo Sacer* 170).

Despite the grand 'pataphysician I. L. Sandomir's assurance that "[t]he World is one great aberrance which, additionally, universally, is based upon an infinity of other aberrations" (178), the dimensions, and dilations of the 'pataphysical aberration still remain. I do not presume to explain a Nazi Final Solution via the science of imaginary solutions, nor try to realize the grand 'pataphysical dream of projecting history into the fourth dimension, yet I am attempting to expose a 'pataphysical dimension within a part of the internment camp's practical execution that proffers somber consequences. And if Agamben's postulate that the camp is central to the project of biopolitics, indeed, that "the camp is the new biopolitical *nomos* of the planet" (*Means Without End* 45), then this chapter could have been titled "The 'Pataphysics of Guantanamo Bay" or "Suspended until Further Notice." With his novel *The Supermale,* Jarry left 'pataphysics behind to pursue the open vista of possibilities beyond Being, a pursuit of great intrigue to Deleuze.

Jarry's belovedly despicable character Père Ubu (that aberrant fusion of Rabelais' Panurge and H. G. Wells, and the character whom Jarry's translator Cyril Connolly dubbed the Santa Claus of the Atomic Age) outlines the final solution to his own 'pataphysical mission: "We shall not have succeeded in demolishing everything unless we demolish the ruins as well. But the only way I can see of doing that is to use them to put up a lot of fine, well-designed buildings" (quoted in Anastasi "Jarry, Joyce, Duchamp & Cage"). The neatly ordered architectural plan of Auschwitz is readily available to American audiences on the cover of the English translation of *Homo Sacer,* and we can see Ubu's demolish-to-rebuild scenario being played out as I write in the ruins of Fallujah and Mosul. 'Pataphysics is not over, its mission not accomplished, its imaginary desires still not fulfilled, and its fourth-dimensional historiography is perhaps still to be written beyond Benjamin, Schmitt, and the phenomenon of the anomaly in the historical realities of today and beyond.

# 11

## The Instrumental Nightingale

### Some Counter-Musical Inflections in Poetry from Gray to Celan

*For me music isn't a superior expression of the individual. I prefer poetry.*
—Otto Han

*Mine are songs for people who cannot sing to sing.*
—Robert Duncan, *Notebook 31*

*When the mode of the music changes the walls of the city shake.*
—Plato

*Man speaks by being silent.*
—Martin Heidegger, *What is Called Thinking?*

My argument in this chapter presupposes the validity of a crucial distinction between the semiotics and the acoustics of poetic music; the former is evident in
the discovery by English poetry (largely via Swinburne and Tennyson) of an ac-
cumulative continuity through symphonic syntax, which is found residually in
much subsequent procedural and normative poetry (in Zukofsky's deployment
of fugal structures, for instance, and in Basil Bunting's attempt to incorporate
the violent contrasts of the sonata form). However, the acoustics of this verbal
music require a different tracking from pre-romantic proclivities through English Romanticism, to the twentieth-century avant-garde; it is left to the reader
to decide whether or not this chapter constitutes a transhistoric perlustration or
a germinal genealogy of poetic counter-musicality that transects current arguments around periodicity.

Paul H. Fry observes that "sound supercedes music as the poetic occasion" in
several Romantic texts, texts in which "[i]t is not music that poetry hears . . . but
rather sound, with its emphasis on resonance, pitch, and timbre, and an impli-

cation even of monotony: 'The murmurous haunt of flies on summer eves'" (Fry 45). Rather than valorize and elevate the *musical* like their German counterparts, certain British Romantic and pre-romantic poets adopted a hostile, even negative attitude toward it. For example, this attitude is noticeable in the shift in natural musical acoustics from birdsong to insect noise in some of Thomas Gray's and William Collins's poems, and in a consciously ambiguous relation to the *musical* in some of Keats's and Wordsworth's odes. A consistently negative disposition to music can be detected that might be best described as an apophatic turn in the acoustic paradigm. This turn clarifies Gray's, Collins's, and Keats's genealogical position as the vaunt-couriers, if not the prophets, of such avant-garde manifestations as the Dada sound poem, the Italian Futurist *parole in libertà*, and the Russian Futurist *zaum*. Not surprisingly, this acoustic apophatic drift becomes politicized in music after Auschwitz, so I finish this chapter with a discussion of a concrete poem by Eugen Gomringer and a poem of Paul Celan to conclude with a reflection on the ethical burden of any post–1945 music.

It is precisely music's intransigent refusal to yield conceptual profit that leads both Lessing and Kant to its disavowal.[1] However, the fate of music changes with the advent of German Romanticism when an essential link is established between music and a general expressionist theory of art. "The aim of music," claims Johann Georg Sulzer, "is to arouse the emotions; this it does by means of sequences of sounds that are appropriate to the natural expression of the emotion; and its application must suitably conform to the intentions of nature in emotional matters" (quoted in Hermand and Gilbert 33). Sulzer, Herder, E. T. Hoffman, Tieck, Novalis, A. W. Schlegel, and Wackenroder alike praise the nonrepresentational character of music as offering the paradigm of a minimally mediated expression of feeling.

By contrast, in England there emerges, from the mid-1740s onward, a discernible disposition to the counter-musical that is not evident in its German affiliate. Starting with the new genre of the allegorical ode in Collins's 1747 *Odes on Several Descriptive and Allegorical Subjects*—whose revolutionary rhythmic variations and unrhymed cadences inaugurated a new order in poetic listening—there is a noticeable shift in emphasis from birdsong to insect noise in the targeted referential zones of sonority. The "Ode to Evening" opens with a magisterial interlacing of lyric audition and physical respiration that effectively blends the human and nonhuman:

> If aught of oaten stop, or pastoral song,
> May hope, chaste eve, to soothe thy modest ear,

Like thy own solemn springs,
Thy springs, and dying gales,

O nymph reserved, while now the bright-haired sun
Sits in yon western tent, whose cloudy skirts,
    With brede ethereal wove,
    O'erhang his wavy bed

Now air is hushed, save where the weak-eyed bat
With short shrill shriek flits by on leathern wing,
    Or where the beetle winds
    His small but sullen horn,

As of the rises 'midst the twilight path,
Against the pilgrim borne in needless hum:
    Now teach me, maid composed
    To breathe some softened strain. (52–53)

In this opening Collins constructs an illbient environment, a weightless, measureless condition induced by ambient sound samplings in which sonic data appear and fade away beyond the listener's control. And if Collins establishes a conventional Hellenic locus for music at the start of the poem, it is in order to deviate from it with the melopoeia that escorts the reader to non-musical, even barely acoustic, terrains. The movement of the first three stanzas goes from music to insect noise to silent breathing, after which the subject of music never appears again, muted by the masterly interface of sonorous verbal effects.

Insects figure emblematically in Gray's 1748 "Ode on the Spring" as a moralistic marker of time and ephemerality. The poem opens with a decidedly ornithological thrust. After a formulaic introduction of conventional mythological staffage ("rosy-bosomed Hours" and "Fair Venus' train") attention moves at line five to a more natural ornithological scenario: "The Attic warbler pours her throat,/ Responsive to the cuckow's note,/ The untaught harmony of spring[.]" However, a marked shift occurs in the third stanza. At a moment of calm we are introduced to a different, if not alien, aerial populous:

Still is the toiling hand of Care:
The panting herd repose:
Yet, hark, how thro' the peopled air

The busy murmur glows!
The insect youth are on the wing,
Eager to taste the honied spring,
And float amid the liquid noon:
Some lightly o'er the current skim,
Some shew their gaily-gilded trim
Quick-glancing to the sun (4).

We know Gray developed a scientific interest in entomology, evident here in his use of details.[2] Unlike the static call and response of the warbler and cuckoo, Gray's insect youth are on the move in a varied ephemerality and delight that Gray utilizes to advance a *carpe diem* theme to the speaker-moralist of the poem. Granted the power of speech, the insect populous appropriate the proper moral tenor and rectify the moralist's own theoretical attitude.

Methinks I hear in accents low
The sportive kind reply:
Poor moralist! and what art though?
A solitary fly!
..............................................
On hasty wings thy youth is flown;
Thy sun is set, thy spring is gone—
We frolick, while 'tis May. (4)

Gray chooses the metallic sounds of bells (both as curfew signals and sheep accoutrement) to open his 1751 "Elegy Written in a Country Churchyard" and to invoke a socioeconomic terminus in the poem's setting: the end of a working day. (We must wait until 1850 for Tennyson's *In Memoriam* to give us the image of ringing bells as the voices of strangers.) Music barely figures in Gray's poem, whose somber themes are those of class disparity, obscurity, and death (with the latter perhaps a subtle nod to the 1746 massacre of the Scots at Culloden). Music in its brief appearance is associated with aristocratic pride:

Nor you, ye Proud, impute to These the fault,
If Memr'y o'er their Tomb no Trophies raise,
Where through the long-drawn isle and fretted vault
The pealing anthem swells the note of praise (39).

The poem's final stanza, which describes the burial procession, moves the reader quickly from a listening ear to a reading eye: "The next with dirges due in sad array/ Slow thro' the church-way path we saw him borne. / Approach and read (for thou can'st read) the lay, / Grav'd on the stone beneath yon aged thorn" (42). This draws the poem to its conclusion in the tactile, epitaphic silence of a mute writing rather than a choric anthem. Against this diminishing sonic horizon Gray introduces insect sound (as he did in the "Ode to the Spring") at a pivotal point of stillness: "Now fades the glimmering landscape on the sight,/ And all the air a solemn stillness holds, Save where the beetle wheels his droning flight" (37). The dominant mood in both Gray and Collins is entropy, a movement into stasis and equilibrium in which the non-human sounds of birds and insects register as brief negentropic moments in the state Fry chooses to call the ostensive moment.

This shift from musical themes intensifies in Keats. More than once the poet draws attention to a paradoxical, sonorous component within silence. In his poem "I stood tip-toe upon a little hill" occurs the "little noiseless noise among the leaves, / Born of the very sigh that silence heaves." Likewise, the "Ode to Psyche" presents "tuneless numbers," and the melodies in "Ode on a Grecian Urn" are sweeter precisely because they elude audition:

> Heard melodies are sweet, but those unheard
> Are sweeter; therefore, ye soft pipes, play on;
> Not to the sensual ear, but, more endear'd,
> Pipe to the spirit ditties of no tone.

"Ode to Psyche" frames its titular goddess inside an actual negation of the musical: "[No] virgin-choir to make delicious moan / Upon the midnight hours; / No voice, no lute, no pipe . . ." and although the subsequent stanza offers a desirable rectification of the situation—"So let me be thy choir, and make a moan" exults the speaker—this move to music is immediately annulled in the concluding reference to the poet's mind, whose complex, indeterminate interiority is figured as both a "wild quietness" and the equally tacit "wreathed trellis of a waking brain" (261–64). The dominant mood of the "Grecian Urn" is a cold, pastoral silence consequent to the statuesque fixity of all vital signs by the power that Büchner's Lenz calls "a Medusa's head"[3] and in the representational space Levinas admonishingly names "the meanwhile."[4]

The acoustic and structural connections to ethereality and flight, traceable from Kepler to Dryden, are themselves attempts at reconnecting to earlier theories of a musical universe based on mathematics, proportion, and an aerial power of flight. Birds attracted St. Francis of Assisi through their symbolic gentleness. On the other hand Peirekius has a more practical attraction to the effect on humans of the passionless peace in the melody of birds, where the prevalence of sedate, quiet harmony supposedly promotes in humans a contemplative mode.[5]

If the "Ode to a Nightingale" consecrates the historical continuity of a single bird's song, it ends dramatically with a radically different acoustic effect: "Forlorn! the very word is like a bell / To toll me back from thee to the sole self!" (260). This is clearly not a wedding bell, nor a signal of danger or alarm, but the index of an ontological interpellation and the termination of ecstatic flight. After Keats, the cultural investment in the nightingale as the acme of poetic birdsong finds itself in a precarious state; indeed in the minor Romantic poet Thomas Lovell Beddoes's 1837 poem "The New Cecilia" it reaches effective cancellation. Reflecting on the lost powers of her dead husband, Saint Gingulph, (Beddoes adopts Byron's abbreviation to St. Gingo) his gypsy wife declares:

> "He no more can work wonder
> Than a clyster-pipe thunder
> or I sing a psalm with my nether end."
> As she spoke it, her breakfast beginning on
> a tankard of homebrewed inviting ale.
> Lo! the part she was sitting & sinning on
> struck the 100th psalm up like a nightingale.
> Loud as birds in an Indian forest, or
> A mystic memnonian marble in
> The desert at daybreak, that chorister
> breathed forth its Aeolian warbling[.] (*The Ivory Gate* 27)

Courtesy Beddoes' masterly Rabelasian, lower displacement—Beddoes himself admits it to be "a very nasty objectionable piece of foolery" (*The Letters* 220)—Keats' "light-winged Dryad of the trees" fades away beyond the forest dim into a sonic whiff of gypsy afflatus that is itself a parodic reversal of hymning.

But if music finds a ready referent in birdsong it is unsettled and problematized by insect sound. This focal shift from ornithological to entomological acoustics has been noted already in Collins and Gray, and in "Ode to a Nightingale" it manifests as the "murmurous haunt of flies on summer eves" (259). Fry recognizes in this "a-signifying" buzzing of nature both "a permanent resource of poetry" and a perennial ostensive instrument—for him, that "mesmerization by sound of the will to signify" defines poetry's ostensive moment (Fry 45–46) and hints at a cogent diachronic trajectory: Homer's droning flies around the milk pail, the buzzing cicadas of the Greek Anthology, Milton's gray-fly, Shakespeare's "shad-borne beetle with his drowsy hum" in *Macbeth*. To this list, one might add John Clare's "songs of the clumsy brown-beetle and bee," his "cricket twittering o'er its dream," (*Village Minstrel* II 31, I 14), Thomas Burbidge's "dazzling gnats" (*Ambervalia* 113), and perhaps most famously Proust's protracted meditation on the wasp and the orchid in *Remembrance of Things Past* and Gregor Samsa's becoming-cockroach in Kafka's *The Metamorphosis*.

The evidence gathered to support this historically persistent entomological phenomenon is consistent: all of Fry's examples of "buzzing" derive from the sounds and sounding of an exclusively insect world. (In passing, we might add to Fry's catena the buzzing that invades the character of Mouth in Beckett's *Not I*. It's tempting too to recall André Breton's urge to "[p]ut your trust in the inexhaustible nature of the murmur" [quoted in Kittler 227]). However a comment of Deleuze and Guattari's best elucidates the significance of this entomological counter-musicality as the registration of molecular becoming: "the reign of birds seems to have been replaced by the age of insects, with its much more molecular vibrations, chirping, rustling, buzzing, clicking, scratching and scraping. Birds are vocal but insects are instrumental.... The insect is closer, better able to make audible the truth that all becomings are molecular" (308). We might note too that for Derrida "differential vibration" is a response to desire constituting a bliss caught in alterity (*Points* 137). Canadian soundscape scholar and composer R. Murray Schafer adds a prophetic, machinic complexity to Deleuze and Guattari's observation, remarking that one general unmusical effect of insect sounds is to "give the impression of being steady-state or flat-line sounds [reaching the ear as] a continuous, unvarying monotony. Like the straight line in space, the flat line in sound rarely occurs in nature, and we will not encounter it again until the Industrial Revolution introduces the modern engine" (36).[6]

If Dryden's "Alexander's Feast" belatedly celebrates the Pythagorean and post–Pythagorean *musica mundana* as harmonic proportion, then Wordsworth's late ode "On the Power of Sound"—in its shifting of attention from the semiotics of music to the acoustic materiality of voice  occupies a pivotal position between William Collins and the Dada *lautgedicht*.[7] I wish to read Wordsworth's ode against Deleuze and Guattari's claim that "we must make a different distinction: the face with its visual correlates (eyes) concerns painting; the voice with its auditory correlates (the ear is itself a refrain, it is shaped like one) concerns music"

(302). Wordsworth's own antipathy to actual music is well documented, but in his ode "On the Power of Sound" a reduction of musicality follows a precise trajectory through voice and listening into sound and noise. When Wordsworth does introduce the topic of music it is to celebrate not music *per se* but the force of sound within the musical and its capacity to spiritually move the agent and auditor alike. "By Ear he said," that famous hortation of Olson's, precessionally haunts Wordsworth's poem as a genius loci. The poem not only starts with the ear but ends with it and, despite traveling by contractions and dilations through a vast and varied itinerary, we never leave that auditory organ.[8] Symmetrical descriptions of tympanic effects establish a persistent rhythm throughout. The beginning describes an abreaction of internalized sonic data prior to linguistic formulation and acted out entirely in the architectural space of the ear:

> a Spirit aërial
> Informs the cell of Hearing, dark and blind;
> Intricate labyrinth, more dread for thought
> To enter the oracular cave;
> Strict passage, through which sighs are brought,
> And whispers for the heart, their slave;
> And shrieks, that revel in abuse
> Of shivering flesh . . ." (211).

From cell through labyrinth to oracular cave, Wordsworth maps the territory of affiliations that the rest of the poem unfolds. The ear is recalled in "the sky's blue caves" and "the milder echo from their cells" of Stanza III. But toward the end of this stanza there is a redirection from a description of the ear to an itemization of the therapeutic benefits of music and demotic lyricism: "Happy milkmaids, one by one/ Scattering a ditty each to her desire" and

> Blest be the song that brightens
> The blind man's gloom, exalts the veteran's mirth;
> Unscorned the peasant's whistling breath, that lightens
> His duteous toil[.] (213)

But this apparent shift only temporarily forestalls the advance of the auricular image bank. In stanza five, "Inspiration"—and we should remain alert to its polysemic registration—"travels like a blast/ Piping through cave" (214).

In his description of the idiot's "mouldy vaults of brain"—in a passage prescient of the late-nineteenth-century psycho-physical discovery that "A roaring in the ears and the roaring of trains are equally capable of providing disordered brains with assonances, alliterations and rhymes" (Kittler 219)—Wordsworth chooses to emphasize the physical impact of sound by way of the inner architectonics of the listener's ear:

> Convulsed as by a jarring din;
> And then aghast, as at the world
> Of reason partially let in
> By concords winding with a sway
> terrible for sense and soul! (215)

Stanza IX constructs a parabola starting with music but ending with a plea to return listening to the non-musical realities within sounds. Opening with a brief description of the mythic Arion's transformative musical powers, the stanza develops this mythic framing of music with Pan pipes and Fauns and Satyrs beating "the ground in cadence." In fact, we are not far from that state of frozen suspension of sound and form already noted in Keats's "Ode to a Grecian Urn" and essential to all classical representation and ekphrasis in general. This cryogenic mimesis, however, is set up only to be toppled:

> To life, to *life* give back thine ear:
> You who are longing to be rid
> Of fable, though to truth subservient, hear
> The little sprinkling of cold earth that fell
> Echoed from the coffin-lid;
> The convict's summons in the shepherd's knell;
> "The vain distress-gun," from a leeward shore,
> repeated—heard, and heard no more! (216)

The coffin-lid recalls the ear's inner cavity as a double recipient of both acoustic life and death; the silence is the dead sound after the echo in the coffin of the ear.

The majestic Stanza XI presents a reality inhabited by "wandering utterances," evocative not of the *musica mundana* of Pythagoras, but of James Macpherson's perambulatory Ossianic voices. (Incidentally the bird song encountered by the speaker in Wordsworth's poem "To the Cuckoo" is described as a "wandering Voice" [87].) The question posed in the ode "To the Power of Sound" is whether "a scale of moral music" brings unity to a seeming world of *alea*. Complicit with univocity, the speaker avers that "all things are controlled [by] one pervading spirit/ Of tones and numbers" (217), and though harmonics return in the last stanza they connect not to musical proportion but to "[a] Voice [that] to Light gave Being." It would appear that conventional Judeo-Christian onto-genesis returns in the call to the familiar divine *fiat,* yet a haunting indetermi-nacy remains. Is the divine command the primal and ultimate achievement of Voice, or are God's works—his photic clearings—the voice's paradigm produc-tion? In the preceding stanza the ear returns to listening but the auditory organ, central to poetic and musical experience alike, is at that point the ear of God, an ear prior to the utterance of any *fiat.* Reflecting on the propositional violence within all discourses deploying "a system of knowledge that tends to ignore lis-tening processes," Gemma Fiumara suggests that "we could start out by admit-ting that there could be no saying without hearing, no speaking which is not also an integral part of listening, no speech which is not somehow received" (1).

Music enjoys an undeniable referential status in this ode of Wordsworth's, dominant at times, but consistently subordinated to the binding regimen of the sonorous and its reception in listening. (It's always Mercy who "listens," and even God comes equipped with an ear.) At its conclusion the ode rests on the cor-related organs of voice and ear transposed to the power of divinity. This macro-poetic circuitry, however, occurs inside the micropoetic circumscription of the ear—and the ear distorts and duplicates: "Ye Voices, and ye Shadows/ And Im-ages of voice—" (Wordsworth 212). Voice never appears in lucid self-certainty until the end; rather the pernicious doubling that Levinas calls a reality and its shadow always contaminates it. But if the ode does not constitute an outright re-pudiation of music, it does represent a serious enervation in, and relegation of, the primacy of the musical. The effectiveness of "On the Power of Sound" derives from its indiscriminate mixing of musical and non-musical sounds while main-taining all the while the ear as the paramount site of auditory invasion—this demonstrates what poetry and music have in common: the interiorizing agency of the subject's ear as a poetic and critical desire on the other side of projection. Keats's attraction to the "spirit ditties of no tone" is hardly prophetic of Schoen-berg, and though his claim that "heard melodies are sweet, but those unheard are sweeter" may not anticipate Cagean silence, the two sentiments do nonethe-less testify to an overt hostility to music within certain elements of English Ro-manticism.

The counter-musical turn in Collins, Gray, Keats, and Wordsworth may strike us as surprising considering the Romantic investment in expressive theory and even more so if we consider Carlyle's equating of poetry with "musical thinking" in his "The Hero as Poet:"

> All speech, even the commonest speech, has something of song in it . . . . Observe too how all passionate language does of itself become musical. All deep things are Song. It seems somehow the very essence of us, Song . . . . The primal essence of us; of us and of all things, the Greeks fabled Sphere-Harmonies: it was the feeling they had of the inner structure of Nature; that the soul of all her voices and utterances was perfect music. Poetry, therefore, we will call *musical Thought*. The Poet is he who *thinks* in that manner. (quoted in Duncan 83)

These sentiments absorb a rich lineage through Kepler, Ficino, Ptolemy, Aristotle, and Plato back to Pythagoras, and find congruent substantiation in Wordsworth's preference for the language of the common man and Whitman's praise of the inherent poeticality of slang; they also anticipate the work of Dirac and Schrödinger in mathematics, William Carlos Williams' speech-based poetics, and Zukofsky's terse tenet that "[c]ondensed speech is most of the method of poetry" (28). At the same time, there is something in Carlyle's claim closer to a fissure in that smooth space of concurrence, for his contention, that in states of powerful emotion we move naturally into song, registers as a perhaps surprising anticipation of the similar and primary rationale for the transgressive linguistic condensations effected in the twentieth-century avant-garde projects of *zaum* and words in freedom.

Much of what follows negotiates a single question: how do we discriminate between the voice that sings and the voice that speaks? Speech, in all languages, as architect Daniel Libeskind tells us, "is itself constructed out of geometries, out of consonants and vowels. It has even led some to believe that speech is a secret form of music that has been forgotten" (51). More famously Walter Benjamin avers that "written language grows out of music and not directly from the sounds of the spoken word" (214). However, music separates from speech at the point of song whose origin is easy to explain. Song arises out of speech through an extension of the ictus, holding a primary stress that foregrounds a tone. In other words, song is not born out of states of passional and emotional intensity but at the moment that meaning is made to halt or stammer, with the separation of sound from meaning both inaugurating and contaminating the musical at the precise moment when vocality emerges as an evanescent entropy.[9]

When Basil Bunting ruminated on the perplexing fact that when a banal, unoriginal phrase of Horace's ("O fons Bandusiae") is read it provokes unfailingly a powerful, authentic, emotional response, he concluded that "[t]he emotion was aroused by the sound of the words [and] had next to nothing to do with their meaning" (38). In relegating the semantic to a lower order in poetic experience, Bunting demands a radical asymmetric relation of a word's sound to its meaning. Reversing Pope's hallowed dictate that sound be echo to the sense, Bunting insists that sense impede the impact of the purely sonic. This marks a pivotal, recursive moment in poetics, a moment that can be labeled sacrificial, for at the core of Bunting's claim lies the strategic sacrifice of poetic meaning to the sensuous materiality of its language, to what the little known eighteenth-century Welsh philologist Rowland Jones terms "acoustic desire." But, as will soon become apparent, Bunting's proclivity for sound is inscribed here chronologically out of place, an Anglophonic echo of earlier Futurist and Dadaist aspirations.

As already noted, the significance of sound is central to Fry's notion of poetry's ostensive moment in which semantic underdetermination "temporarily releases consciousness from its dependence on the signifying process" (4). Given Fry's claim that the ostensive moment is "revealed in the release from the compulsion to signify" (11), it is curious that the sound poem eludes his consideration, doubly so given the fact that Fry presents a detailed and insightful analysis of an avant-garde text by Eugen Gomringer. If the ostensive moment bemoans the entrapment of poetry in the material-ideality of the arbitrary signification of language, and if Fry's claim is correct that a form of "interart envy results in the reduction of music to sound," then *zaum, parole in libertà* and *lautgedichte* (discussed in chapter 1) commonly deserve their place in Fry's august and transhistoric pantheon.

It is the concerted desire to rescue linguistic sonority from signification that connects the sonopoetic innovations of the classic avant-garde to Fry's theory of the ostensive moment. In his experimental *zaum* or "transrational language" the Russian Futurist Alexei Kruchenykh grants sound an autonomous value. The target of his attack is not the word as such but the normative word's semantic and grammatical subordination to the mandate to mean something. In his famous assertion that the "word is broader than its meaning" Kruchenykh uncouples the binding relation of signifier to signified not to demolish but rather expand the functions and dimensions of the word. In the stead of conventional words in his *zaumist* texts are numerous paraverbal "poetic irregularities"—clipped lexemes, lexical hybrids, neologisms, and fragments—that recast the word as a flexible organization of phonematic material capable of translogical, but nonetheless emotional, communication.

> dyr bul shchyl
> ubeshchur
> skum
> vy so by
> r lez (60)

As his argument in "Explodity" indicates (and not without a certain epochal irony) Kruchenykh's rationale for *zaum* accords exactly with Carlyle's for musical thinking. "Emotional experience cannot be put into words (frozen words, concepts), word-tortures, gnoseological isolation. Therefore, we strive for a transrational language . . . that is the language people resort to at crucial moments" (Kruchenykh 65).

There is a similar sensibility at work in the Italian branch of Futurism. Fillipo Tomasso Marinetti (1876–1944), the core architect of the Italian Futurist movement, launched his *parole in libertà* (words in freedom) in 1912 as an attempt at a radical syntactic explosion designed to liberate the word from all linear and grammatical bondage. (His comprehensive and uncompromising list of prohibitions includes syntax, adjectives, adverbs, conjunctions, and punctuation). Like Carlyle and Kruchenhyk, Marinetti's rationale for such linguistic diremption is predicated on the judged ineffectiveness of grammar and syntax to convey states of emotional excitation. Indeed, as offerings of unmediated emotional expression, both *zaum* and *parole in libertà* propose an Augustinian blackout against Wordsworthian lyric strategies of emotive deferral. Marinetti describes this ineluctable abandonment of syntactic regimen and grammatical constraint in non-poetic states of excitement and emotional intensity. Placed in intense conditions, such as war or earthquakes, a person will resort to violent methods of expression, "brutally destroying the syntax of . . . speech. . . . The rush of steam-emotion will burst the sentence's steam pipe, the valves of punctuation, and the adjectival clamp" (quoted in Apollonio 98). Marinetti laid heavy stress in performance upon onomatopoeic structures arrived at by the deliberate distortion of words. "[L]yrical intoxication allows us, or rather forces us, to deform and reshape words; to lengthen and shorten them; to reinforce their center or their extremities by increasing or diminishing the number of vowels and consonants" (quoted in Clough 50). In light of Kruchenhyk's and Marinetti's rationale for lyric intoxication we can consider Wordsworth's famous recipe for poetic composition (emotions recollected in tranquility) as a desired prophylactic against *zaumist* expletive.

An attempt to find a basic connection between an object and its verbal sign, predicated upon the efficacy of the sonic as a direct, unmediated force, lies at the base of words in freedom. *Paroliberismo,* like that of fellow Futurist musician Luigi Russolo's art of noise, aims at the mimophonic representation of ambient technology and the kinetics of urban simultaneity by means of verbal anamorphosis, predominantly martial industrial rhythmic sound and strident onomatopoeia. For many Futurists the discrete partition between music and poetry required abolition; as a result several Futurist "texts" blur the boundary between printed poem and musical score. The beginning of Giacomo Balla's "Onomatopea Rumorista Macchina Tipografica" (Onomatopoeic Noise Canzone for Printing Press) for twelve simultaneous speakers offers an example of this:

1° settesettesettesettesettesette
2° nennenennenennenennenennenenne
3° vùùùùmmùùvùùùùùmmùùvùù
4° tè.tè.tè.tè.tè.tè.tè.tè.tè.tè.tè.tè.tè.
(quoted in Rasula and McCaffery 110)

Such is the return and revenge of insect noise with the advent of the modern engine that Schafer speaks of.

As discussed in chapter 1, the Dadaist *lautgedicht* (sound poem) or *verse ohne worte* (poetry without words) actively courts a more mystical and prophylactic quality. In actuality, Ball's sound poems (like their predecessors "Kroklokwafzi" 1905 by Christian Morgenstern and Paul Scheerbart's 1897 "Kikakoku") commonly present a morphological experience together with an *abscondite* meaning—yet they register a "meaning-effect" and can be accurately described as specimens of virtual semantics. To substantiate this claim, compare these brief excerpts from Ball's and Scheerbart's sound poems:

Kikakoku!
Ekoralaps!
Wîso kollipánda opolôsa.
Ipasatta îh fûo.
Kikakokú proklínthe petêh.

Nikifilí mopa Léxio intipáschi benakáffro - própsa pî! própsa pî!
*Scheerbart* (quoted in Rasula and McCaffery, 104)

gadji beri bimba glandridi lauli lonni cadori
gadjama gramma berida bimbala glandri galassassa laulitalomini
gadji beri bin blassa glassala lauli lonni cadorsu sassala bim
gadjamatuffm i zimzalla binban gligla wowolimal bin beri ban
o katalominal rhinozerossola hopsamen laulitalomini hoooo
gadjama rhinozerossola hopsamen
bluku terullala blaulala loooo
*Ball* (quoted in Bohn 37)

Neither poem ranks as a splendid instance of Pound's dance of the intellect among words but both nonetheless offer a veritable orgy of words stripped down to their individual sonic materiality, a state in which music finds itself in a contractual transit where song loans voice to noise.[10] If Collins and the Romantics conduct us away from music back to natural sound without significance, Ball's sound poems take us along that trajectory of desire that Foucault ascribes to the logophiliac Jean-Pierre Brisset—a restoration of "words to the noises that gave birth to words, and to reanimate the gestures, assaults and violences of which words stand as the now silent blazons" (quoted in Deleuze 149 n40).

If the mandate of Futurism is to work free the word from a binding semantic regimen and syntactic-grammatical constraints, to redirect a sensed energy from themes and message into matter and force, then the slim corpus of Dadaist sound poetry remains a stubbornly word-bound practice. All of them preserve a readily detectable morphological patterning in their sonic gymnastics that upholds the aural presence of largely inaccessible semantemes—but semantemes nevertheless. Ball's poems consistently conjure up a xenoglossic presence, a sense of texts whose meanings are inherent but defy comprehension, and his poetry without words testifies to the omnipresent possibility in cacophony and gibberish for language to return as either recognizable words or in a comprehensible "syntax" that suggests an unknown language. Certeau describes the experience of such heteroglossia as "voices" haunting a plurality of boundaries and interstices: "The voice moves, in effect, in a space between the body and language, but only in a moment of passage from one to the other and as if in their weakest difference" (230).

Let me return to our ornithological theme by way of the following question: how do Ball's texts differ from the transcription of birdsong? We left feathered chatter at a seeming terminus with the supercession of insect noise and mapped out an august and profound lineage for the latter in literature, attaining its machinic manifestation in *paroliberismo*. However, the history of the sound poem in its transcribed form, and our poetic legacy in general, indicate that literature has never been entirely free from the attraction to bird vocalization. From the birds in Aristophanes' cloud-cuckoo land, through the "lhude singe cu cu" of the anonymous medieval lyricist and the owl's "Tu—whit! Tu—woo!" that opens "Christabel," to *The Waste Land*'s "Twit twit twit Jug jug jug jug" of the nightingale, it seems that the prevalent desire to attain birdsong beyond mere thematic capture is equally the permanent poetic resource that Fry claims of insect noise. One of the earliest recorded examples of literary onomatopoeia dates back to Aristophanes' play *The Birds* where a purported phonetic transcription of birdsong serves as an effective parody of Socratic discourse:

> Tio tio tio tio
> Tio tio tio tio
> Trio to trio to totobrix
> Toro toro toro torotix
> Tio tio tio tinx
> Trio trio trio totobrix
> Epopoi
> Poi
> Popoi
> Torotorotorotorotix
> Kikkabau kikkabau
>       (quoted in Rasula and McCaffery 101)

Notwithstanding Aristophanes' parodic intention and conscious depreciation of the written word (he does this by introducing, as William V. Harris notes, "fraudulent oracles with emphasis on the fact that they are in writing" [90]), his transcription is no different than serious efforts by ornithologists to notate bird vocalization phonetically. For example, Nicholson and Koch offer a charming array of neologisms to notate variant bird vocalizations—none of which would be out of place in a Dada verse without words:

> Hawfinch: Deak . . . waree-ree-ree Tche . . . tche . . . tur-wee-wee
> Greenfinch: wah-wah-wah-wah-chow-chow-chow-chow-tu-we-we
> Pied Flycatcher: Tchéetle, tchéetle, tchéetle, diddle-diddle-dée

Corncrake: crex-crex, krek-krek, rerp-rerp
Common Snipe: tzit-tzit tzit, trui, trui, trui (quoted in Schafer 30)

Out of context, yet in light of the sonopoetics of the avant-garde, the question emerges as to what distinguishes the literary from the scientific in the above notations and also why birds don't sing now at Dachau?

In "Diapsalmata," the opening section of *Either/ Or,* Kierkegaard defines the poet as "[a]n unhappy man who in his heart harbors a deep anguish, but whose lips are so fashioned that the moans and cries which pass over them are transformed into ravishing music" (19). The intimate link established between music and suffering, and the overwhelming gap between human origin and aesthetic effect, quickly lead Kierkegaard to a genealogy of infernal musical machines. The poet's fate of radical asymmetry he likens to "the unfortunate victims whom the tyrant Phalaris imprisoned in a brazen bull, and slowly tortured over a steady fire; their cries could not reach the tyrant's ears so as to strike terror into his heart; when they reached his ears they sounded like sweet music" (ibid.). By comparison this Kafka-like image offers a heterological sobriety to the Aeolian harp, which was famously seized upon by the Romantic poets as a ready emblem for the inherent source of music in nature.[11] Kierkegaard alerts us to the historical bonds between music, realpolitik, terror, and tyranny. In conclusion I wish to extend this Kierkegaardian reflection on aesthetic sound and suffering to the fate of music after Auschwitz.[12]

> Be for a little while eternal,
> singing with all the songs in your body
> but making no sound.
>> Horace Gregory, *O Mors Aeterna*

> Al-'Ayn dhat al-jafn al-ma 'daniyah
> ("the eye with an eyelid")
>> Sherif Hetata

> And now the music means "forget."
>> Andrew Lang

In a context of kettledrums, elephants, Prussian cabinets, petty Germans, Greiswald men, and onomatopoeic forests, Heinrich Heine offers an acerbic and prescient observation that will form the backdrop to the balance of this chapter.

"Gentlemen, the earth is a barrel, and men are pins stuck seemingly at random on its surface; but the barrel turns, and the pins strike and give a sound, a few frequently, the rest seldom, and this produces a curious complicated music which is called history" (80). If Dadaist and Futurist endeavors reach the zenith of the counter-musical, albeit via an uncanny reconnection to avian-song, then the thematic departure from music and a concomitant move into political silence comes in a famous untitled concrete poem by Bolivian-born Eugen Gomringer.

```
silencio silencio silencio
silencio silencio silencio
silencio         silencio
silencio silencio silencio
silencio silencio silencio
```

Written in the early 1950s, the poem first appeared in the above Spanish version in 1954 (the same year as Gomringer's influential statement on concrete poetics, "from line to constellation"); it was reprinted along with the German original to facilitate comparison in 1963. (In this chapter I'll refer to its Spanish version, "Silencio.") Although critical commentary on this poem is plentiful, almost all of it focuses on the aesthetic issues that "Silencio" raises, especially the aesthetic paradox it stages and best summarized in poet Carla Harryman's terse interrogation: "Does delicious silence hear delicious silence written?"[13] Liselotte Gumpel, while presenting both Spanish and German versions and drawing attention to the problematic of its translation, ignores the poem's rich historical nuance. Classifying it as an "optic-semantic tautology" that aspires to a supranational comprehension, Gumpel directs her exclusive attentions toward the semantic-iconic relation that the poem exploits. The white space in the center that underwrites the absence of the word "assumes a kind of ironic eloquence, since the black signs 'tell' what the white space 'means.' . . . Semantically, 'silence' signifies what the space *is* and the word is *not*" (Gumpel 95).[14] Michael Webster commits to an equally apolitical, formalist reading when claiming that "the space in the middle of the poem gains meaning from the words surrounding it; the space presents ironically the meaning of the word. To take the space away impoverishes the whole construction; the poem forms an isomorphic *gestalt* of visual, verbal, and vocal parts. The relation between space and word is not tautological, as some have imagined the relation between image and word in Apollinaire's *calligrammes*, but isomorphic, or that of a single entity in which the visual element assumes a form analogous to the verbal meaning" (142).

Helmut Heissenbuttel offers the first intimation of the political dimension in Gomringer's poetry in his introduction to Gomringer's 1969 collection of constellations *worte sind schatten (words are shadows),* arguing that the playful poem "ping pong" "produced for him [Gomringer] the effect of a 'liberation' after the 'sluggishness' *(Erschlaffen)* experienced in Germany at war's end" (quoted in Gumpel 92). Paul Celan too writes of the state of the German *Muttersprache* in a 1958 questionnaire: "with most sinister events in its memory, . . . it can no longer speak the language which many willing ears seems to expect. . . . It distrusts 'beauty.' It tries to be truthful . . . a 'greyer' language, a language which wants to locate even its 'musicality' in such a way that it has nothing in common with the 'euphony' which more or less blithely continued to sound alongside the greatest horrors" (Celan *Collected Prose* 15–16). Until Paul Fry's astute reading there has been a critical somnolence or myopia around the poem's political ramifications and the historicized hermeneutic enrichments that pragmatic and speech act theory might offer. Indeed, given the ideological context of the composition of "Silencio"—in the shadow of post–war Germany—the poem demands to be read politically within the caustic radiation emitted by Adorno's proclamation that "[a]fter Auschwitz there is no word tinged from on high, not even a theological one, that has any right unless it underwent a transformation" (367). The original German version replaces *silencio* with the more complexly nuanced *schweigen,* a word that can be read as either descriptive of an acoustic condition or as a performative utterance in the imperative mood. The poem's extra-aesthetic connotations explode in a veritable *Sprachgitter:* "tais-toi," "shut up," "keep quiet," and "let's not speak."[15]

```
schweigen schweigen schweigen
schweigen schweigen schweigen
schweigen                schweigen
schweigen schweigen schweigen
schweigen schweigen schweigen
```

Accommodating the word as, on one hand, a descriptive term not requiring a speaker, and on the other a powerful over-coded utterance, preserves the poem from overwhelmingly formalist, aesthetic encroachments.[16] Moreover, taking the word in its multiple registers positions it effectively in its authentic historical context, a context, Fry notes, in which the question of a national silence and the failure to render an objective account of mass exterminations is instantly and unavoidably invoked.[17] (Heidegger's own notorious taciturnity around the issue may be held as synecdochal of the German nation at the time Gomringer writes this poem in the early 1950s.)[18] Replacing the non-locutional Spanish version with the original German *schweigen* shifts textual centrality to the compelling semantic triplet of an empowered voice of command, a silenced voice of the victim, and a collective silence of complicity, a triplet matched in the poems lateral structure of three repeated words.[19] Given that at the time of composing "Silencio" Gomringer was theorizing an ekphrastic, spatialist poetry that would register as a picture, thereby facilitating its visual perception "as a whole as in its parts," is it fanciful to note that the pattern of Gomringer's rectangle utilizes the same elemental forms as the swastika, or to see in it a schematized, aerial view of a death camp or a parliamentary gathering of the bund?[20] Can we read the silence at the poem's wordless center not only as an indictment in absentia of the historian's reticence to write the victim's absent testimonial, but also as a concrete and savagely ironic textual transposition of Hitler's 1937 demand for a *volkloser Raum* (a space empty of people)?[21] This extraordinary call for a peopleless space "names the driving force of the camp understood as a biopolitical machine that, once established in a determinate geographical space, transforms it into an absolute biopolitical space," at which point Death "is a simple epiphenomenon" (Agamben Remnants 85–86).

In 1897 Ernst von Wildenbruch became the first German poet to record his own voice on a wax cylinder. He recorded a poem he wrote especially for the occasion and in which he claims the phonograph forces the past to speak.[22] There is an easy shift from silence into amnesia and in the light of this Germanic episode within the broader history of acoustic technology the paradoxical claim can be advanced that Gomringer's silent poem has realized a phonographic destiny for visual poetry. Hearing, insists Rudolph Bultmann, "is the means by which God is apprehended . . . hearing is a sense of being encountered, of the distance being abolished, the acknowledgement of a speaker's claim on us" (quoted in Lyotard *The Lyotard Reader* 96). If we grant credence to Bultmann's assertion, then the white space registers an absence of hearing that further marks the absence of God. Commenting on Bultmann (in a discussion of the people of Israel) Lyotard poses the rhetorical question: "How then can deicide be present in their religion?" and immediately supplies an answer: "In the form of writing. Hearing is the sense of absence of the dead God. The ear listens to writing. Writing is the word of the dead father" (ibid. 96). "I have nothing to say and I am saying it and that is poetry." John Cage's famous testimonial that proffers a veritable negative poetics of a saying without a said, of a degree zero of empty locution, offers a hinge between Bultmann's claim on listening and Kafka's harsh rendition of colonial law. Indeed, "The Penal Colony" offers a concatenating fable that links torture and writing to the law in which the latter is inscribed by the harrow, meridian like, around the middle of the victim's body. The rest of the body is covered in calligraphic flourishes. After the Law is written there is nothing to write but the act of writing. Kafka offers a written parallel to Cage's poetics transposed to the judicial and punitive realm. The flourish is a purely gestural act of the body through writing, and what joins the torturer to the victim is a scribble without content, an asemia, an unmediated incision that results in a periphrastic excess utterly alien to discourse. On a conceptual level too Kafka's fable and Cage's poetics present photographic and sonographic negative reversals of Gomringer's constellation. All three, in linked yet different ways, return their readers to that state of infancy, to that body without language I delineate in chapter 9. But unlike Kafka's torturous and illegible writing, Gomringer's white rectangular silence offers itself as an empty space to be read. Barthes draws attention to the growing importance of the empty space of the signified (169). Unlike the imperial palace at the heart of Tokyo that is experienced as an empty center, the heart of "Silencio" is minimal but charged.[23] At the rectangular heart of its silence, both bitterly and elegantly ironic, Gomringer's poem screams out its indictment.

But the history of this fascinatingly misunderstood poem is not complete. In the mid-1980s Harry Warschauer's Hebrew translation appeared as number 16 in John Furnival's Openings Press Card Series. The Hebrew character translates as the sound "sh" and thus in the translator's own copy at least, the central space gains an additional complexity. Gomringer was persuaded to sign his name in the center of the silence. On the verso of this copy the publisher adds a note to Warschauer (dated December 1988): "I got Prof. Gomringer to shatter the silence of your version of his silence for you when I was in Brasil [sic] this summer." Alan Halsey, a poet, bookseller, and friend of Warschauer provides some clues to his intentions: "I'm sure Harry saw it as a political poem. As a Jewish kid he was got out of Germany & via eastern Europe into England in the early war years by the Quakers—what was that scheme called, the Kinderbus? Kindersomething. [The term used was *Kindertransport*.] He became a tabloid journalist, mostly run of the mill stuff but involved himself in investigations into Holocaust denial, Nazi revivalism & so on."[24] I have remarked upon the rector of the University of Freiburg's post–war silence regarding the death camps; now let me bring him to speak. In the section of *Being and Time* called "Dasein's Attestation of an Authentic Potentiality-for-Being, and Resoluteness," Heidegger describes the manner in which conscience, rising above the hub-hub of quotidian idle talk, calls to itself. "But how are we to determine *what is said in the talk* that belongs

Fig. 8. *Silencio* translated into Hebrew by Harry Warschauer (Source: Openings Press Card Series).

to this kind of discourse? Taken strictly, nothing. The call asserts nothing, gives no information about world-events, has nothing to tell. . . . The call dispenses with any kind of utterance. It does not put itself into words at all; yet it remains nothing less than obscure and indefinite. *Conscience discourses solely and constantly in the mode of keeping silent"* (Heidegger, *Being and Time* 318). I will purposefully betray the context of Heidegger's discussion in order to redirect it as a commentary on Gomringer's poem. The call (*Ruf*) of conscience is silent and is figured in the poem in the central empty rectangle, and the potentiality aroused is that in Heidegger and Germany at large to break their silence about another silence. Lyotard comments on the historical unphrasablility of this other silence: "The silence surrounding the phrase: *Auschwitz was the camp of annihilation* is not a state of the soul; it is the sign that something that is not phrased and that is not determined remains to be phrased. This sign brings about a linkage of phrases. The indetermination of meanings left unformulated, the annihilation of the means to determine them, the shadow of negation emptying reality out to the point of dissipating it, in one word, the injustice done to victims that condemns them to silence—it is this and not a state of soul that calls out to unknown phrases to link up with the name of Auschwitz" (quoted in Carroll 171–72).

"Silencio" however, enfolds a more ancient Jewish heritage found in a curious aspect of the Hebrew language. Aleph, the first letter in the Hebrew alphabet, is the only letter that is unpronounceable. Spinoza describes it as being the originary glossal event prior to speaking, as "the beginning of sound in the throat that is heard by its opening," a description that Daniel Heller-Roazen claims to be overly positive (Heller-Roazen 20). In the modern Hebrew phonic assemblage, Aleph is not the commencement of sound but a silence, the letter being "treated as the silent support for the vowels it bears, deprived of even non-sound, the interruption in articulation, it is thought to have once expressed" (Heller-Roazen 20). In *The Zohar*'s account of priorities in the divine letter-creation of the world, it is Bet (the second letter in the alphabet and the sign of the blessed, or blessing) that God grants the right to initiate the mundane creation. Aleph (and bear in mind that all Hebrew letters are feminine) refuses to come forward during God's decision as to which letter will assume the task of creation. "Aleph, Aleph," inquires the Holy One, "why did you not come forward before me like all the other letters?" "Master of the World," she replies, "I saw all the other letters come before you to no end, and what was I to do? Moreover, you have already given this precious gift to the letter Bet, and it is not proper for the great King to take back the gift that He has just given to one servant to give it to another" (Heller-Roazen 21). Rather than rebuking Aleph, God grants her primacy among the letters and gives to her sole unity to serve as the primary constructive principle. We can now construct our interpretation. The central absence in "Silencio" that marks the poem's silence is precisely the space of the unpronounceable Aleph, which is unpronounceable owing to the fact that it represents silence, quiet, peace, no noise—in other words the silence of the lambs. Significantly Aleph is absent from the repeated words that make up both the Spanish, English, German, and Hebrew versions of Gomringer's poem. Like the function the Holy One assigned to Aleph, it is the central blank that truly unifies "Silencio."

The status and nature of Aleph is discussed at some length in the opening part of the *Midrash Rabbah* (a prominent ancient rabbinic commentary on the Torah). One interpretation holds the Holy One would never allow a world to be created by a curse—only by a blessing, a *Bet*. Thus we have a blessed instead of a cursed world, a conclusion that, in the light of the *Shoah,* reads bitterly ironic. Heller-Roazen concludes his short meditation on the letter Aleph with a sentence I find remarkably apposite to Gomringer's "Silencio": "The sole material of divine speech, the silent letter marks the forgetting from which all language emerges. Aleph guards the place of oblivion at the inception of every alphabet" (25).

Derrida reminds us that apophasis is the modality of the voiceless voice that manifests in the form of a negative declaration to God beyond being and from the consciousness of restricted ontological parameters (*On the Name* 35). Less aporetic, and perhaps more fitting, might be the following cheerless facts that John Felstiner provides: "Not far from Czernowitz, at the Janowska camp in

Lemberg (now Lvov) an SS lieutenant ordered Jewish fiddlers to play a tango with new lyrics, called 'Death Tango,' for use during marches, tortures, grave digging, and executions. Then, before liquidating the camp, the SS shot the whole orchestra. This 'Todestango,' of which a recording exists, was based on the Argentine Eduardo Bianco's greatest prewar hit. . . . [In 1939 Bianco and his band] . . . entertained Hitler and Goebbels, who preferred the tango to the 'decadence' of Negro jazz" (28–30).[25] Paul Celan (living in Paris at the time of Bianco's visit) answered with his own poem to ~~music~~, "*Todesfuge*" (Deathfugue):

> Black milk of daybreak we drink it at evening
> We drink it at midday and morning we drink it at night
> We drink and we drink
> We shovel a grave in the air where you won't lie too cramped
> A man lives in the house he plays with his vipers he writes
> He writes when it grows dark to Deutschland your golden hair Margareta
> He writes it and steps out of doors and the stars are all sparkling
> He whistles his hounds to come close
> He whistles his Jews into rows has them shovel a grave in the ground
> He commands us play up for the dance
> ...................................................
> He shouts jab this earth deeper you lot there you others sing up and play
> He grabs for the rod in his belt he swings it his eyes are so blue
> Jab your spades deeper you lot there you others play on for the dancing
> (quoted in Felstiner 31)

This memorable poem, written prior to Celan's famous mutilations of the German language, serves as a grim parallel to the Nazi ritual of "Totenehrung" (homage to the dead), which is described by Frederic Spotts as the "catechism" of the Nazis, "a recitation of the names of party members and 'heroes' who had 'sealed their loyalty to the Führer and nation with their heart's blood'" (64). Felstiner aptly and most movingly calls the poem in which music figures as a critical torture both "the *Guernica* of postwar European literature" and "the benchmark for poetry 'after Auschwitz'" (26). It is beyond contention that "Todesfuge" marks a limit point in the history and territory of the lyric, that most musical of poetic forms. Its opening image inscribes the twisted paradox of music after the Wannsee Conference and its complicity in the final solution, hinting too at the functional destiny of piano wires—a twisted musical metamorphosis and metataxis whose antecedent typology is Phalaris's bull.[26] To listen to music is perhaps to read beyond writing in a form of listening that recovers to experience that which Plato names *chora,* a paradoxical ur-place that is a non-space, a place of primary imprint that cannot be specified as mind, body, sensibilia, or idea.

But does this claim uphold in the light of death fugues? And if not, how do we meditate the state and fate of music after Auschwitz? The early Nietzsche—the Nietzsche of *The Birth of Tragedy*—situates music within that essence of the tragic that stands antipathetic to both narrative and mimesis. However, Nietzsche's meditation was on pre-Euripidean Greece, not Nazi Germany, and given this chronological incongruence I might offer a final conjecture that perhaps Adorno's proclamation on the word should be extended to music in the contemporary world. For after Auschwitz there is no music tinged from on high, not even a theological music that has any right unless it undergoes a transformation.

A short reflection by Lyotard in *Soundproof Room* on an incident between two brothers recounted in André Malraux's great text, *Man's Fate,* conveys Lyotard's acrid comments on the larval existence of certain literate social members; it also encapsulates the critical desires and hopes of this chapter in a stark manner that return us to its entomological theme. "In the Shangai schoolyard that Katow crosses to get to the locomotive firebox into which he will be tossed alive, stretched out among the doomed men, Kyo feels bodies rise up through his throat, a clamor that is barely audible, inform [*sic*] 'quavering . . . buzzing . . . murmur.' . . . Concealed beneath the dispersed, disparate community of connoisseurs, readers, and spectators lies, in actuality, an aggregate of insects convulsively clinging to 'their' sign" (Lyotard *Soundproof Room* 94).

## Coda

*while a man has voice he may recover music*
—Louis MacNeice, *Collected Poems* 60

A coda and not a codicil, for there is no last will or testament in the case of what follows. Agamben's *Remnants of Auschwitz* offers an apt coda to "Silencio." The book's moving investigation into archive and testimony emerged as a personal imperative after certain public accusations were laid against its author. What follows are Agamben's words: "Several years ago when I published an article on the concentration camps in a French newspaper, someone wrote a letter to the editor in which, among other crimes, I was accused of having sought to 'ruin the unique and unsayable character of Auschwitz.' I have often asked myself what the author of the letter could have had in mind. The phenomenon of Auschwitz is unique (certainly in the past, and we can only hope for the future). . . . But why unsayable? Why confer on extermination the prestige of the mystical?" (31–32). Agamben's trenchant refusal to admit the ineffability of Auschwitz leads him into an extended analysis of the paradoxical logic governing all testimony to this historical event. In the case of Auschwitz, "the value of testimony lies essentially in what it lacks; at its center it contains something that cannot be borne witness to and that discharges the survivors of authority. The 'true' witness, the 'complete witnesses,' are those who did not bear witness and could not bear witness" (34). It is not the dead that constitute the core of this lacuna but those who reached their ontological nadir—"touched bottom" is Primo Levi's phrase—and are described in survivor testimonials and in the rare case of their own survival. The name assigned to them by camp guards and inmates alike was *Muselmänner* (Muslims), a descriptive euphemism that calls upon the similarity of the uncoordinated movements of their bodies in states of malnutrition and hypothermia to those of healthy Muslims at prayer. (Seen from afar "one had the impression of seeing Arabs praying" [Ryn and Klodzinski, quoted in Agamben *Remants* 42]). Sofski lists the variant names used in the other camps: "donkeys" in Majdanek, "cretins" in Dachau, "cripples" in Stutthoff, "swimmers" in Mauthausen, "camels" in Neuengamme, and "tired sheiks" in Buchenwald. In Ravensbrück the women were called both "female Muslims" and "trinkets" (quoted in Agamben 44). Other less euphemistic names included mummy-men, living dead, and staggering corpses.

In the light of Agamben's ethical desire to speak for those who cannot speak, for the true witnesses that cannot bear witness, and by bringing to light the crucial position of the *Muselmann* in the assessment of the "unsayable event" that is Auschwitz, the absent space that marks the structural core of "Silencio" can at last be filled with a historical specificity, and the poem can be elevated to an ethical and deaestheticized plane partly hinted at in these final words and perhaps not even contemplated by Eugen Gomringer: "Auschwitz marks the end and the ruin of every ethics of dignity and conformity to a norm. . . . The *Muselmann*, who is its most extreme expression [i.e. degradation], is the guard on the threshold of a new ethics, an ethics of a form of life that begins where dignity ends" (Agamben 69).

# Notes

## Introduction

1. To hypothesize a reiterative history is not novel; Marx discusses its anachronistic construction in his *Eighteenth Brumaire of Louis Bonaparte* where he proposes a reiterative model with a changed valence: "Hegel remarks somewhere that all great events and historical personages occur, as it were, twice. He forgot to add: the first time as tragedy, the second as farce," (Marx and Engels 115). Similarly the circular model of historic epochs has been presented variously by Vico and Spengler; it has appeared as well as the trope of the second coming, which forms the foundation of much Christian thinking.

2. I take the phrase "Archeology of the New" from the Irish poet Fergal Gaynor who mentioned it in conversation on the topic of this book.

3. The implications of palindromic time are taken up in Stewart Home's anthology *Plagiarism: Art as Commodity and Strategies for its Negation.*

4. Canguilhem offers a discerning discussion of anomaly in the context of the biological sciences. See 125–149 (especially 131–37).

## Chapter 1

1. Ball himself supplies the evidence for Barzun's and Divoire's precedence in his summary of the first cabaret at his new club. "And, at Mr Tristan Tzara's instigation, Messrs Tzara, Huelsenbeck and Janco performed (for the very first time in Zurich and in the whole world) simultaneous verses from Messrs Henri Barzun and Fernand Divoire, as well as a simultaneous poem of his own composition." (See Ball, "Cabaret Voltaire," 20.) In actual fact Barzun's "*Chants Simultanés*" were first performed in 1912.

2. See Higgins, *Horizons: The Poetics and Theory of the Intermedia*).

3. T. J. Demos interprets the poem politically as an attack on military authority and, while noting that the theme of homelessness articulates onto the poem's use of multiple and mutually invasive languages, fails to note in this an important antecedent to both *The Waste Land* and *Finnegans Wake*. See Demos, "Zurich Dada: The Aesthetics of Exile," 7–29. Although the poem clearly alludes to the Great War (then in progress), I do not concur with Demos' interpretation but see instead a more local cause, a veritable coterie joke. Huelsenbeck recalls that the Cabaret Voltaire took over the premises of the former Cabaret Pantagruel at Spiegelgasse I, a century-old building, owned at the time by the ex-sailor Jan Ephraim, "now berthed in Zurich" (Huelsenbeck 4).

4. It seems Huelsenbeck incorporated genuine language following a felicitous discussion with the proprietor of the Cabaret Voltaire, Jan Ephraim, who was familiar with the South Pacific and African coasts as a sailor where he had acquired knowledge of some authentic African songs. Ephraim supplied Huelsenbeck with this brief passage:

> Trabadya La Modjere
> Magamore Magagere
> Trabadja Bono
> (Huelsenbeck 8–9)

According to Huelsenbeck when his authentic negro poems were presented at the Cabaret Voltaire "the audience thought they were wonderful" (9). Why Huelsenbeck refers to them in the plural is somewhat puzzling because he only mentions the three lines above. Moreover, evidence from Ball indicates that Huelsenbeck performed only two such songs on March 30. A Maori song "Toto Vaco" was included, however, in his 1920 anthology *Dada Almanach* and was probably supplied to him by Ephraim.

5. Morgenstern's pithy description of his song, as well as both poems are reprinted (in their entirety) in Rasula and McCaffery, 104–5. Scheerbart's text first appeared in his 1900 novel *Ein Eisenbahnroman, ich liebe dich (A Railway Novel, I Love You)*. While both poems utilize question and exclamation marks, Morgenstern complicates a purely phonetic reading by adding unreadable "passages," such as a semicolon enclosed in parentheses (;) and a blank space within brackets [ ]. It is interesting to note that Morgenstern's own spiritual and mystical propensities (he was strongly influenced by Rudolph Steiner's theosophical thinking) cannily accord with those of Ball. I discuss Scheerbart's poem "Kikakoku" in relation to Ball's own "gadji beri bimba" in *Prior to Meaning*, 166–67.

6. Ball volunteered to enlist in the German army but was turned down because of ill health. He did, however, personally travel to observe the war in Belgium, and his reactions are discussed later in this chapter.

7. Yeats' plans for revising Irish Theater along the lines of Japanese Noh theater leads him to remark in 1916 that "[t]he human voice can only become louder by being less articulate, by discovering some new musical sort of roar and scream" (Yeats iv). This remarkable congruence of Yeats' emerging theatrical theories with Ball's attraction to Eastern dramaturgy and such Zurich Dada manifestations as the *lautgedicht* remains to be researched.

8. The influence of Kandinsky's dramatic theories on Ball's thinking about expressionist theater is well known. (See Ball 7–10; Huelsenbeck xvi.) However, Kandinsky seems a palpable theoretical force behind the *lautgedicht* (especially the materialization of the phonic for spiritual ends) as this passage from his "On the Question of Form" evinces: "Matter is a kind of larder from which the spirit chooses what is *necessary* for itself, much as a cook would. . . . Sound, therefore, is the soul of form, which only comes alive through sound and which works from the inside out" (Kandinsky 147, 149).

9. Independence is stifled by the false need for consensual acceptance "[b]ecause democracy denies the writer the means of existence, because it encourages the monstrous tyranny of journalists" (Ball 26).

10. On Ball's antagonism to the printing press it may be of interest to note that the Italian Futurist Giacomo Balla wrote an "Onomatopoeic Noise Poem for the Printing

Press" two years prior to Ball's sound poems. Part of the poem is reproduced in chapter 11. Fortunato Depero also wrote a "Canzone Rumorista" (noise song) in the same year as Ball's *lautgedicht* was conceived. Ball was certainly aware of Italian Futurism—he had received a copy of *Parole in Libertà* from Marinetti himself (see Ball 25) and his own assessment of that movement creates for Ball a broader problematic: "There is no language anymore" (ibid.). Cocteau draws attention to the didactic values to be drawn from the machine on grounds thoroughly consonant with Futurist poetics: "It is a weakness not to comprehend the beauty of the machine. The fault lies in depicting machines instead of taking from them a lesson in rhythm, in stripping away the superfluous" (quoted in Sitwell 184–85).

11. Ball's dissatisfaction with journalistic language dates to well before this famous proclamation. In July 1915 he laments that "[t]he word has been abandoned, it used to dwell among us. The word has become commodity. The word should be left alone. The word has lost all dignity" (26).

12. Andrey Bely argues for an intuitive drive to neologistic constructions (themselves precipitating cognitive innovations) occasioned by the auditory reception of speech: "When we hear living speech . . . it kindles our imagination with the fire of new creations, that is, with the fires of new word constructions. And a new word construction is always the beginning of the acquisitions of new acts of cognition." (Bely 97.)

13. Ball's avowed idiosyncrasy and his belief in the basic individuality of human beings leads him to reject philosophical abstraction. "Abstract idealism is itself only a cliché. Living beings are never identical and never act identically, unless they are trained and prepared for the Procrustean bed of culture" (Ball 47). It is important not to confuse Ball's repudiation of abstract idealism with aesthetic abstraction, which he believes is the necessary movement of all art from representational to non-representational form. (See Ball 55 for his ruminations on the beneficial retreat of art from figuration.) On these grounds I believe Hans Richter is correct in characterizing the *lautgedichte* as abstract phonetic poetry.

14. See Jolas 405–20.

15. It is interesting to compare the following sentiment articulated two decades before Ball's work by the *Yellow Book* contributor Richard Le Gallienne: "The idea, then, of a nation, is a grandiloquent fallacy in the interests of commerce and ambitions, political and military." (Le Gallienne 157.)

16. Ball's attempts are worth comparing with those of the German political theorist Carl Schmitt, whose own version of political theology and his related theory of sovereignty is discussed in chapter 10.

17. For more on this relation see my chapter "The Elsewhere of Meaning" on the *Jappements* of Claude Gauvreau in *North of Intention*, 170–77. Interestingly, Levinas argues that sound (as distinct from the experience of noise) is inseparable from the verbal. "[T]he sound is symbol *par excellence*—a reaching beyond the given. If, however, sound can appear as a phenomenon, as *here,* it is because its function of transcendence only as-

serts itself in the verbal sound. The sounds and noises of nature are words that disappoint us. To really hear a sound is to hear a word. Pure sound is the word" (Levinas 148).

18. Writing of Paul Verlaine, Arthur Symons claims that "[w]ords serve him with so absolute a negation that he can write *Romances sans Paroles*—songs without words, in which scarcely a sense of the interference of human speech remains" (quoted in Sitwell 228).

19. Doesburg published his "lettersoundconstructs" under the pseudonym of I. K. Bonset. For an example, see Rasula and McCaffery 14. Hausmann's poem can be found in Bohn 97.

20. Ball's "Elefanten Karawane" is accessible under the tile "Karawane" in Bohn 36. My version restores the original title but removes the typographical varieties that are a striking feature of the 1917 version.

21. See Gilman. Leah Dickerman (29–30) further claims that Lombroso's theories are precursors to Dada.

22. It's thus surprising to find Worringer absent from the seminal anthology *Symposium of the Whole: A Range of Discourse Toward an Ethnopoetics,* ed. Jerome and Diane Rothenberg (Berkeley: University of California Press, 1983).

23. It is well know that several Dadaists (Harp, Huelsenbeck, and Tzara) avoided or delayed military conscription by convincingly feigning their insanity. For details see Dickerman 23, 40 n67.

24. See von Humboldt 34.

25. Apparently Wundt's *Völkerpsychologie: Eine Unter der Entwicklunggesetze von Sprache, Mythus und Sitte* was a relatively popular book given that after its initial publication in 1900 a second edition was called for in 1904 and a third appearing in 1911 (with a Russian translation in 1912)—this lends credence to the possibility that the book was seminal not only to Ball's own theories but also to those of the Russian Zaumniks Khlebnikov and Kruchenhyk. There is however no mention of Wundt in the abridged English edition of Ball's diaries.

26. Ball's propensity to self-representation results in numerous fascinating equations. The fate of Ball the poet is the fate of Germany (Ball 30); he reckons his life script is the same as the biblical Daniel's (34) and at other times the same as Stephen the protomartyr (49). Steinke quotes passages from two of Ball's adolescent poems that indicate "a capacity for being seized and carried away by forces greater than himself" (23).

27. Benjamin traces a parallel trajectory of the phonic in the career of the Viennese poet-satirist Karl Krauss and detects a dissolution of the instrumental word into "a merely animal voice" (Benjamin *Reflections* 264).

28. This defense of the individual—outside democracy or community—attunes with Tzara's own reflections on the socio-emotive origins of Dada. "So DADA was born of a desire for independence, of a distrust of the community." (Tzara 125). Ball's mantic speculations will be developed extensively by Eugene Jolas in his investigations into Vertigralism, paramyth, alchemical poetics, the theory of the mantic compost, and his

language of night. All are outlined in *Transition* 23 (1934–35), which also includes a short piece by Ball himself on gnostic magic (86–87). Ball's attraction to magic is hardly anomalous. Indeed, we can trace a general attraction to magic and the occult back at least to the late 1880s. Yeats for one became a member of the Order of the Golden Dawn in 1890 and fell under the influence of the writings of Eliphas Lévi (l'Abbé Constant) and Stanislas de Guaïta. Richard Ellman offers a colorful account of the fin de siècle attraction to the occult in his biography of Yeats *The Man and the Masks*. It should also be noted that a decade before the invention of the *lautgedicht* Alexandr Blok, in a 1906 essay "The Poetry of Exorcisms and Curses," offers the following example of magic songs and secret words to ward off evil spirits:

> Ai, ai, shikharda kavda!
> Shivda, vnoza, itta, minogam,
> Kalandi, indi, yakutashma bitash,
> Okutomi mi nuffan, zidima (quoted in Janacek 47)

29. Tzara, for his part, will remove the *ds* in DADA to form his new independent movement of "Aaism" (Tzara 115).

## Chapter 2

1. A teasing intimation of an after "modern" occurs in the twelfth-century clerk Walter Map's *De Nugis Curialium* (Courtiers' Trifles): "I give the name of modern period (modernity) to the hundred years which have passed, and not to those which are to come, although they may have the same right to the name, by reason of their nearness, since the past hath to do with narration and the future with divination" (75).

2. Considered as a term of containment and as a referential frame, postmodernism operates with the same flexibility as did the term "restoration" in the seventeenth century. For details see Jose 67–71. By the early 1970s postmodernism already enjoyed a flourishing magazine dedicated to that term: *Boundary 2: A Journal of Postmodern Literature*.

3. See Hutcheon.

4. Rexroth 100–101.

5. Olson first employs the term in a letter to Cid Corman dated 13 June (1952) and published in *Letters for Origin* on page 102. Maud's alteration to "archaic postmodern" derives from his sense of Olson's recursivity and recovery of the past. For full details see Maude 126–37.

6. See Schneidau.

7. See especially Altieri's *Enlarging the Temple*, 15–25.

8. This discussion, of course, eludes the other thorny issue of how to reevaluate modernism, especially the heterogeneity of the period, the "coherent" modernism of Eliot and Pound, alongside the decoherent modernism of Stein and Joyce, and the non-canonic

modernism that would include, among others, Bob Brown, Bernard DeVoto, Eugene Jolas, Abraham Lincoln Gillespie, the Baroness Elsa von Freytag-Loringhoven, and Alfred Kreymborg. Do we maintain a modernist/postmodernist great divide and uphold the term "postmodern" as infinitely catalyzable or replace it with a more apposite term, and if so which?

9. A tradition of deletional poetics would include the eighteenth-century minor theorist Peter Walkden Fogg whose *Elementa Anglicana* (1792–96) contains a theory of unspoken music detectable in the length and caesura of straight black lines that replace the verbal spacing of a chosen poem. Also admissible would be Man Ray's notorious 1924 "Sound Poem" that appears to block out with thick black lines—in an identical manner to Fogg—all words of a text, leaving the syntactic spacing between, Bob Brown's *Gems,* a Victorian novel *A,* Joan Retallack's 1995 *Afterrimages,* Ann Hamilton's 1993–94 installation *tropos,* John Cage's "writings through," *Finnegans Wake,* and Jackson Mac Low's numerous systematic chance selections and deletions from Pound's *Cantos* and other texts. Johnson was also familiar with British artist Tom Philips's text-sifting art that culminated in his *A Humument* (a treatment of William Hurrell Mallock's Victorian novel *A Human Document*), which employs a similar corrosive poetics. (See Alpert 556.) *Radi os* can be considered "deconstructive" in so far as it codifies the interplay between presence and absence. Johnson's relief composition grants its source text the status of a trace in the sense outlined by Derrida in *Speech and Phenomena,* as a utopic, dislocating simulacrum of a presence constituted by effacement. This seems to capture both the philosophical and canonical relation of Johnson's and Milton's respective texts. See Derrida, *Speech and Phenomena,* 156.

10. *Radi os* was published without pagination.

11. See O'Leary "An Interview with Ronald Johnson." It goes without saying that this tenet of a latent reality under a manifest appearance is central to both Freudian and Marxist method as well as to the method of the paragrammatic readings of Mac Low and Cage discussed in chapters 3 and 4 respectively.

12. Relief engraving was not invented by Blake—there are sixteenth-century examples of relief xylography known as the "white-line" woodcut in which the background is left in relief. See for example the title page of Pelbart's *Stellarium Coronae Benedict Marie Virginis,* published by J. Otmar, Augsburg, 1502. Closer to Blake's time is Thomas Bewick (1753–1828), some of whose famous woodcuts were realized by the same relief method.

13. Although Nicholas Lawrence in a thoughtful essay flags Blake's illuminated books as "perhaps the most important predecessor for *Radi os*" (287) he does not examine the connection in full detail. See Lawrence 282–91.

14. Interestingly, Brian McHale does not draw attention to a methodological affinity here to some of Susan Howe's poetry: "it is as if Howe had dipped some source text in an acid bath until everything had dissolved away except these few resistant nuggets of language." The passage describes perfectly Johnson's "negative" poetics of composing not the words but the holes. See McHale 211.

15. See my essay "Insufficiency of Theory to Poetical Economy" in *Prior to Meaning: the Protosemantic and Poetics*, 3–14. Certeau's delineation of tactic and strategy as two distinct logics of action is not new and goes back at least to Clement of Alexandria (obit. ca 215CE) and his discussion in *Stromateis* Book I of the relation of "control" *(taktikon)* to "command" *(strategikon)*. For a full discussion see O'Donovan 32.

16. See, for example, Jenkins, especially pages 62–63.

17. For various discussions of the paragram see Starobinski, Kristeva, and Steve McCaffery, "*The Martyrology* as Paragram" in *North of Intention: Critical Writings 1973–1986*, 58–76.

18. Lawrence 282–91.

19. Some recent medieval scholarship links this practice of recirculation to a conscious medieval analogy of fecal excretion and creativity. Addressing the marginal imagery in medieval illuminated manuscripts, Michael Camille comments, "On an even more general level we might think of fecal product as creative power. Just as scholars of the fabliaux [e.g. R. Howard Bloch in his *The Scandal of the Fabliaux*, University of Chicago Press, 1986] have begun to see excrement-making as a trope of fiction itself, the *recirculation of dead matter*, these latrines of fecal form swirling at the edges of the pages can similarly evoke the artist's power to make forms from the 'clay' of the earth" (115 emphasis added). Although citing the *Poetria Nova* on the previous page, Camille fails to note the critical role of textual recycling and resuscitation in Geoffrey's own treatise.

20. Initial burnishing would have normally involved a preliminary grinding followed by a light abrazing, then a wiping with recently kindled charcoal and a quenching in cold water.

21. In her *Pythagorean Silence*, Susan Howe similarly suppresses paginated serialization to render textual space a version of pictorial space; in Johnson's case a plate, in Howe's a canvas. Jerome McGann offers an ebullient metaphorization of Howe's nonlinear textual materiality in an ecstatic response: "We gaze at it much as one gazes at a night sky, scanning its reaches no longer being told where to begin or where to go" (McGann *Black Riders* 102).

22. In "From *Hurrah for Euphony*," Johnson recalls the impression Sewell's book made on him: "When I read . . . *The Orphic Voice*, I knew I wanted to be of that order of writer she talks about."

## Chapter 3

1. Karl Young relates that Mac Low in conversation admits to having performed the entire text once and parts of it several times. See Young 134.

2. Saussure's research into the paragram (or moving gram) can be consulted in Starobinski and my own "*The Martyrology* as Paragram" in *North of Intention: Critical Writings 1973–1986*, 58–76. Mac Low's optical poetics (felt in its pursuit of letters, not sounds) can be traced back through Arnaut Daniel's *rhymes estrampas* (rhymes out of place) and the optical bias of Isidore of Seville to the early Irish Scribes. For the latter see

Parkes. The former is explored by Agamben in *The End of the Poem: Studies in Poetics* 31–32 and 83 (the latter making possible a reading of Mac Low's method as a version of dictation).

3. See Moles.

4. All of Mac Low's methods of systematic-chance generation are open for all rewarding subjects, and this brings up the possibility for numerous strategic readings that can be highly charged. A survivor of the Shoah for example might choose "Auschwitz" as a theme word and trace it through Hitler's *Mein Kampf*, or the Bible, or the *Merchant of Venice*. A feminist might take "Molly Bloom" and read through *Ulysses* to reorganize it along the axis of that theme name.

## Chapter 4

1. Jean Starobinski has written five articles on the subject (see *Words upon Words* ix), one of which, "Le texte dans le texte," proved seminal to Julia Kristeva's related study "Towards a Semiology of Paragrams." Transphenomenal textual endeavors similar to Saussure's can be consulted in Joseph de Maistre's obscure collection, *Soirées de Saint Pétersburg*. De Maistre conjectures morphological derivation in Latin by way of paragrammatic articulation of separate suffixes and prefixes. "[F]rom these three words, *CAro DAta VERmibus* they have formed the word *CA-DA-VER,* 'meat abandoned to the worms.' From two other words, *MAgis* and *voLO,* they have made *MALO* and *NOLO,* two splendid verbs that every language, Greek included, can envy Latin" (quoted in Eco 104).

2. Saussure's hypograms bear comparison to that other practice of the hidden name outlined in the thirteenth century *Cabala of the Names* of Abraham Abulafia and which "begin by combining this name, namely, YHWH, at the beginning alone, and examining all its combinations and move it, turn it about like a wheel, returning around, front and back, front and back, like a scroll, and do not let it rest." (See Idel, 21.) Abulafia terms this procedure *Hokhmath ha-Tseruf* or the "science of letter combination." Unlike Cage's "writing-through" Abulafia's is a permutational method for combining the sacred letters in all their possible configurations. In disagreement with both Saussure and Starobinski, Jean Baudrillard contends that repetition and accumulation do not occur via the hypogram but rather through diffraction (break-up and dispersal) with a consequent destruction of the theme-name: a symbolic act equivalent to the sacrificial extermination of God or the hero. For the full discussion see chapter 6, "The Extermination of the Name of God," in Baudrillard, *Symbolic Exchange and Death,* 195–242.

3. The term "paragram" first occurs in a notebook dedicated to a phonemic analysis of Lucretius' *De Rerum Natura* (Ms. fr. 3964. See Starobinski 18.) Coincidentally, Lucretius in the same work draws the analogy of atoms in movement to letters in transposition. There is clear evidence in Saussure's research of vacillation in his terminology. He explains his rationale for choosing "paragram" over "anagram" in Ms. fr. 3964: "Anagram, as opposed to Paragram, will be reserved for instances in which the author wishes to amass in a small space, in one or two words, all the elements of the theme-word, more

or less as in the definition of 'anagram'—a figure which has a very restricted importance among the phenomena presenting themselves for study, and which, in general, represents only a part, or an accident of the Paragram." Ironically, Saussure does not advance a clear definition of the paragram but suggests in the passage above a more "scattered" and telestic phenomenon. His sense is clearly not the one contained in the definition tendered by the OED ("A kind of play on words, consisting in the alteration of one letter or group of letters in a word") but closer to Leon Roudiez's description of paragrammatic action as a non-linear agency that produces an infinite network of significatory possibilities. A text is paragrammatic, he writes, "in the sense that its organization of words (and their denotations), grammar, and syntax is challenged by the infinite possibilities provided by letters or phonemes of combining to form networks of signification not accessible through conventional [i.e. linear] reading habits" ("Twelve Points from Tel Quel," *l'Esprit Créateur* [Winter 1974], 14[2]: 300. Quoted in Kristeva *Revolution in Poetic Language*.) Roudiez significantly links the paragram to habits of reading, not writing. On the rich nuances of the prefix "para" see Carroll (xiv) who links it to the "faulty, irregular, disordered [and] improper"—qualities essential to the aesthetics of picturesque detail that I examine in chapter 10.

4. The attack on syntax, of course, does not originate with Cage. The Italian Futurists' *Parole in Libertà* (Words in Freedom) and the *zaum* or transrational language of the Russian Futurist Kruchenyck offer ready precedents in the twentieth century. An early introduction of musical elements into writing is Joshua Steele's *Prosodia Rationalis* (1779), which notates the pitch and intonation of words on a musical stave. For more on Steele see Rasula and McCaffery, *Imagining Language*, 237–39.

5. Others have seen an ethical stance in the refusal of egology. See, for instance, Gerald Bruns.

6. For this information I am indebted to M. B. Parkes' monumental study of the history of punctuation, *Pause and Effect*, p. 23.

7. The phonocentric nature of Saussure's project is made clear in the following passage: "In using the word *anagram*, I do not in any way mean to introduce the idea of writing, either in relation to Homeric poetry, or to any other ancient Indo-European poetry. *Anaphony* would be a more accurate word in the sense I intend" (quoted in Starobinski 14).

8. Accessible introductions to Prigogine and Stengers' theories are their two collaborative studies *From Being to Becoming: Time and Complexity in the Physical Sciences* (San Francisco: W. H. Freeman, 1982) and *Order Out of Chaos* (New York: Bantam Books, 1984).

## Chapter 5

1. This chapter revises, builds on, and selects from material first presented under the title "Context as Paratext: the Grammatological Genealogy of the Letter in *Finnegans Wake*" at the *Texte et Paratexte Colloque,* Université de Paris X (Nanterre), June 5, 1999.

2. For further reading on Sterne's marbled page, at odds with Schiff, I recommend De Voogd and Patterson. Bartine provides a concise survey of eighteenth-century reading practice.

3. The *Dictionary* is unpaginated.

4. *Marmi finti* can be found, for example, in *The Annunciation* by Simone Martini and Lippo Memmi—which was painted in 1333 for the altar of St. Anastasius in Sienna Cathedral and now is in the Ufizzi, Florence—but is absent in an earlier annunciation that forms part of Lorenzetti's 1320 Arezzo Polyptich. My thanks to Ann Lecercle-Sweet for referring me to Didi-Huberman's work; this paper is indebted to his reading of Quattrocento relative disfiguration.

5. This ejaculatory quality, however, would not be evoked by combed marble paper, the technique of which produces a repeated but relatively uniform pattern. I believe Schiff is correct when she indicates that, although twentieth-century editions preserve the random, spermal effect of contemporary editions, the editions that do not insert the marbling precisely between chapter breaks undermine the semantic complexities of the page and its sequencing. What she fails to point out is that although the Rinehart edition of 1950 (edited by Samuel Holt Monk) correctly places the marbled page, an unfortunate accident obtrudes its effect as the marbling patterning is of random vortices rather than the "blotchist" one-of-a-kind patterns found in the first and subsequent early editions. In a recent—and the first—Portuguese translation the marbled leaf has a stunning magnified effect of human sperm and its mixture of predominantly white, red, and tan colors is highly evocative of blood, flesh, and semen; it is moreover correctly placed between chapters. (The Portuguese title reads *A Vida e Opinioes de Tristram Shandy*, translated by Manuel Portela and published by Ediçioes Antigona, Lisbon, 1997. The page can be found between pages 328 and 329.) For a fecund account of spermatic knowledge see Henri Atlan, *Sparks of Randomness: Volume 1: Spermatic Knowledge*, trans. Lenn J. Schramm (Stanford: Stanford UP, 2011).

6. Giovanni di San Gimignano, *Summa de exemplis et similitudinibus rerum* (Venice: De Gregori, 1499).

7. Liane Lefaivre draws attention to a similar link between marble and the sexual in her comments on the romanzo d'amore, the *Hypnerotomachia Poliphili*. Interpreting the work as an Albertin treatise on Epicurean architecture, and claiming it to be "the first to have noticed that the hero makes love to architecture" (262 fn 39), Lefaivre offers this telling description of an altar to Bacchus. "The altar to Bacchus is made of darkly veined marble especially selected to express the virility of that deity, and it is carved with a great phallus 'rigidly rigorous'" (66). Aldus Manutius published the book first in 1499, with subsequent French and British editions. Lefaivre disputes the popular attribution of authorship to Francesco Colonna and presents a solid case for a reattribution to the humanist polymath Leon Battista Alberti. It should also be noted that unveined marble was also imbued with symbolic associations in the *Hypnerotomachia Poliphili*. Smooth white marble is compared to the flawless skin of a nude nymph at i1v, e6 and contrasted to the

virile associations evoked by the richly veined marble altar to Bacchus (Lefaivre 237). Indeed, the association of clear marble to purity and virginity is a familiar medieval trope that is closely linked to the Virgin Mary. "Hugh of Lincoln, for example, sees in the hewn white stone of his own cathedral something of her 'whiteness' and 'well-formedness.' Its whiteness stands for her *pudor* and its well-formedness for her *dogma*. The marble, which is 'smooth, gleaming, and snow white' is an embodiment of the 'bride' who is simple, gentle, hard working. The smoothness of the marble 'truly exemplifies' the 'simplicity' of the Virgin; its polish, her *mores;* its darkness, her *labor*" (Lefaivre 228).

8. Even the Annunciation and Incarnation fell victim to medieval misogyny, which reaches perhaps its most extreme in Ratherius of Verona's assertion that "even the Virgin Mary was a sinner for having ignited divine love" (quoted in Lefaivre 202). For more about the general medieval deployment of abstract shapes to distinguish different levels of reality in painting see Camille, 1996: 16.

9. The figural potential of marble did not escape the attention of the philosopher of the *nisi ipse intellectus*. In a richly suggestive passage in his *New Essays Concerning Human Understanding,* Leibniz compares the mind to a block of marble containing veins, rather than to that block of plain marble which philosophers term a *tabula rasa.* "For if the soul resembled these blank tablets, truths would be in us as the figure of Hercules in the marble, when the marble is wholly indifferent to the reception of this figure or some other. But if there were veins in the block which should indicate the figure of Hercules rather than other figures, this block would be more determined thereto, and Hercules would be in it as in some sense innate, although it would be needful to labor to discover these veins, to clear them by polishing, and by cutting away what prevents them from appearing" (Leibniz 45).

10. Theories of artificial insemination predate Christianity, the tenth-century Avicenna espoused it, as did Peretz of Corbeil (a contemporary of Aquinas). Perhaps the theory closest to insemination via annunciation is that of Abraham Johnson's (the pseudonym for Sir John Hill) whose satirical pamphlet *Lucina Sine Concubito* was submitted to the Royal Society in 1750. In it Hill argues for a method of accidental insemination through inhalation of reproductive seeds carried by the western wind. Johnson further claims to have tested the theory successfully on his unwitting housemaid. Penned no doubt as a satirical attack on the homunculist theory of insemination, it is cited in all seriousness by Feldman and Wolowelsky. See Emanuel Feldman and Joel B. Wolowelsky, eds. *Jewish Law and the New Reproductive Technologies* (Jersey City: Ktav, 1997): 19.

## Chapter 6

1. See Jed Rasula, "Poetry's Voice-Over," *Sound States: Innovative Poetics and Acoustical Technologies,* ed. Adalaide Morris (Chapel Hill: University of North Carolina Press, 1997) 274–316.

2. See http://cherrylfloyd-miller.blogspot.com/2006/12/whats-deal-with-flarf-some-people-have.html. Last accessed June 2011.

3. See www.pastsimple.org/ps6jlindsay.html. Last accessed 26 July 2011. On some of the poetico-political implications of mining spam and junk e-mails see Keston Sutherland, "Junk Subjectivity," *Mute: Culture and politics after the net,* www.metamute.org /en/junk-Subjectivity. Last accessed 24 July 2011.

4. I take the term from Benjamin Barber who employs it to name the current ambient culture of informatics, driven by the dominant media. See Benjamin Barber, "Culture McWorld contre démocratie: *Vers une société universelle de consommateurs,*" *Le Mode Diplomatique* 553 (1998): 14–15.

5. See Caleb Whitfoord, "Cross Readings from the Newspapers," *The New Foundling Hospital for Wit,* 6 volumes, 6th ed. (London: J. Debrett, 1786): II, 212–19. The method was first published in an earlier collection, *The Foundling Hospital for Wit,* published in 1743–49. (The later anthology first appeared in 1768–74.)

6. "The sublime sentiment, which is also the sentiment of the sublime, is, according to Kant, a strong and equivocal emotion: it carries with it both pleasure and pain. Better still, in it pleasure derives from pain. Within the subject, which comes from Augustine and Descartes and which Kant does not radically challenge, this contradiction, which some would call neurosis or masochism, develops as a conflict between the faculties of a subject, the faculty to conceive of something and the faculty to 'present' something. Knowledge exists if, first, the statement is intelligible, and second, if 'cases' can be derived from the experience which 'corresponds' to it. Beauty exists if a certain "case" (the work of art), given first by the sensibility without any conceptual determination, the sentiment of pleasure independent of any interest the work may elicit, appeals to the principle of universal consensus (which may never be attained)."

7. Kenneth Goldsmith, *6799* (New York: zingmagazine Press, 2000): ii.

8. "When I reach 40, I hope to have cleansed myself of all creativity." See Goldsmith, "Uncreativity as a Creative Practice," *Day* (a selection), (Calgary: House Press, 2001).

9. An equally relevant text as Beckett's is Arakawa and Gins' *Architectural Body,* the fundamental premise of which is that the body essentially architects a space. Read through their architectural theories, *Fidget* documents a multiplicity of personal micro "perceptual landing sites." See Madeline Gins and Arakawa, *Architectural Body. Fidget* too is surprisingly close to Helène Cixous' call for an *écriture feminine* in her 1974 text "The Laugh of the Medusa," in which women are encouraged to write their bodies into the text.

10. Quoted form Chuck Shepherd's syndicated column "News of the Weird," *ArtVoice* (Nov. 15–21 2007): 5.

11. Lyotard's theory of paganism is outlined in Jean-François Lyotard and Jean-Loup Thébaud, *Just Gaming,* trans. Wlad Godzich, Minneapolis: University of Minnesota Press, 1985. For an effective application of the pagan see Gerald L. Bruns, *On the Anarchy of Poetry and Philosophy: A Guide for the Unruly* (New York: Fordham University Press, 2006): 133–152.

12. I find it hard not to interpret Goldsmith's nutritionless writing as a wry allusion

to John Cage's earlier call (circa 1970) for edible texts (first exhibited at Stanford University Art Museum in January 1992) and a concept worthy of Charles Fourier (discussed in chapter 10: "Inks used for printing or writing should have delicious flavors. Magazines or newspapers read at breakfast should be eaten for lunch. Instead of throwing one's mail in the waste-basket, it should be saved for the dinner-guests" (see John Cage, *M, Writings '67–72* (Middletown CT: Wesleyan University Press, 1973): 115). Cage's lineation is not adhered to.

13. If we allow degrees of unreadability, then indisputably the most profoundly unreadable section of *Day* are the day's stock market statistics: "11.81 3.63 A Consul dd 1 7.19 7.19 7.19 21 88 6.13." Conveniently these can be experienced in a separate publication, published earlier than *Day* in its full form. Kenneth Goldsmith, *Day* Calgary: House Press, 2001, in a limited edition of 50 hand-numbered copies. An irony obtains from the strained relation of the content to its format: it is a handsome book printed on 25 percent white cotton watermarked paper, folded and bound in a hand-stitched modified Japanese style and contained between sturdy 1101b card covers.

14. The pertinent passage in Plato is *Republic* (608b), p. 833 in *The Collected Dialogues of Plato*, ed. Elizabeth Hamilton and Huntington Cairns (Princeton: Princeton University Press, 1989).

15. Atavistic granted but Goldsmith's transcriptive method is not manual: he employs assistants with scanners equipped with OCR software. Moreover the copyings of scribal, pre-print culture served as a profound spiritual calling.

16. "Introduction," *Avant-Garde* 5–6 (1991): 3.

17. Smollett itemizes his daily reports to the right of three columns listing respectively the date and the temperature in Réaumur's and Chateauneuf's systems. Ignoring the bordering of the columns, the opening of the register reads as follows: "Feb. 25 4 6 Wind north-west, blows fresh, weather cold. 26 4 6 Wind north-west, blows fresh, air sharp, fair weather. 27 4 6 Wind east, weather cloudy—Evening, air sharp and frosty." The register occupies pages 264–90 of volume two. This is not the place to discuss Smollett's register as a species of uncreative or conceptual writing *avant le lettre* but the similarity to Goldsmith's *The Weather* is worth pondering.

18. "Art invites us to intellectual consideration, and that not for the purpose of creating art again, but the knowing philosophically what art is" G. F. W. Hegel, *Aesthetics: Lectures on Fine Art*, trans. T. M. Knox (Oxford: Clarendon Press, 1975): I: 13. Blanchot develops Hegel's insight in his own concept of *désouevrement* or unworkability that radically repositions writing as a mode of non-productive utility. See especially Blanchot's *The Infinite Conversation*, trans. Susan Hanson (Minneapolis: University of Minnesota Press, 1993): 307 13, 351 59, and 403.

19. "For while poetry itself does not 'progress' anymore than electricity, which was just as accessible to the ancient Greeks as it is to us, the methods of transmitting it are nevertheless susceptible to progress." See Jean Cocteau, *A Call to Order*, trans. Rollo H. Myers (London: Faber and Gwyn, 1926): 160.

20. See Marcos Novak, "Next Babylon, Soft Babylon," *Architects in Cyberspace II*, in *Architectural Design* nos. 11–12 (1998).

21. Christian Bök, jacket blurb to Kenneth Goldsmith, *Sucking on Words: A Film by Simon Morris* (New York: Pal, 2007) DVD Video.

22. Baudrillard's argument (laid out in *Symbolic Exchange and Death* and specifically in chapter 6, "The Extermination of the Name of God") effectively turns Saussure's theory on its head. Instead of paragrammatically embedding the names of deities according to a law that governs the distribution of consonants and vowels in certain ancient texts, as Saussure concluded, the name is actually morcellated and volatized by chains of phonemic doublings whose enantiomorphic relation cancels meaning, thereby exterminating the name. For more on Saussure's investigations see Jean Starobinski, *Words upon Words,* trans. Olivia Emmet (New Haven: Yale University Press, 1979).

## Chapter 7

1. "The *post-s* and *posters* which proliferate today (poststructuralism, postmodernism, etc.) still surrender to the historicist urge. Everything marks an era, even the decentering of the subject: post humanism. It is as if one again wished to put a linear succession in order, to periodize, to distinguish before and after, to limit the risks of reversibility or repetition, transformation or permutation: an ideology of progress" (Derrida *Chora L Works* 324).

2. Like many fashionable architectural publications caught between competing desires of text and image, Betsky's book is irritatingly unpaginated.

3. The concept of architectural body was proposed in 2002 by the procedural architects Arakawa and Madeline Gins. See their *Architectural Body* (Tuscaloosa: University of Alabama Press, 2002).

4. B. L. Ullman draws attention to a canny congruity between Gothic architecture and its corresponding scripts. Developing out of the earlier Carolingian form and embracing especially the "picket fence" effect of Merovingian, the main features of Gothic script are angularity and broken lines *(fraktura)*; the replacement of circular stress by a polygrammic one; extreme condensation and letter-fusions (called *textura*); standard heavy shading; a marked increase in abbreviations and embellishments e.g. hooks, hair lines, and marginal pen flourishes. (For full details see B. L. Ullman, *Ancient Writing and its Influences,* [Cambridge: The MIT Press, 1969]: especially 118–25.)

5. See Steven Holl, *The Alphabet City. Pamphlet Architecture #5* (Princeton: Princeton University Press, 1980). Holl provides several examples of "E, H, O, B, L, U, T, X" and "H" shaped buildings and grid blocks. Of particular note are Albert Kahn's 1921 General Motors Building, in Detroit, which is designed as three interlocking and partly superimposed "H" types, and Benjamin Marshall's "X" shaped Edgewater Beach Apartments in Chicago. Exploration into the analogical possibilities of letter-forms and their composition out of a multitude of different beings and objects has a lengthy historical precedent. See for instance the rich gatherings contained in Hugues Demeude, *The Animated*

*Alphabet,* trans. Ruth Sharman (London: Thames and Hudson, 1996) and Massin [*sic*] *Letter and Image,* trans. Caroline Hillier and Vivien Menkes (New York: Van Nostrand Reinhold, 1970).

6. See the important essay "Towards Anarchitecture" in Evans 11–33.

7. Derrida's perdurable challenge to architectural practice is to have introduced the impossible into architectural practice via an insinuant philosopheme: the Platonic *chora.* His architectural collaboration with Peter Eisenman on the Parc de la Villette starts with a lengthy reflection by Derrida on *chora,* an intractable concept found in Plato's *Timaeus.* Although *chora* "figures the place of inscription of *all that is marked on the world,*" it is a pre-originary "place without space, before space and time" (Eisenmann 22, 91). The whole direction of the project moves far beyond the paradoxical origins that Harbison senses in Louis Kahn's Unitarian Church in Rochester, where the architecture gives the sense of "reaching back to early forms which precede anything known to us" (Harbison 11). Working to problematize the clear distinction between sensible and intelligible, *chora* is a situational space beyond all normative notions of place, and responsible for situating the variant logics of exclusion and inclusion, while remaining beyond the laws it situates. Despite "giving place" *chora* (being neither a donor-subject nor a support or origin) does not give place in the manner of an *es gibt.* Derrida calls *chora* a paralogical and metalogical super-oscillation (Eisenman 15) that operates between and above the oscillations of a double exclusion (neither-nor) and of the participational (both this and that). With the sum of its negative features (non-ontological, neither a void nor an interval, nor a determined place, a something which is not a thing, a reference without a referent, without a self-identity, and incapable of representation other than negatively), it is not surprising that *chora* does not provide the security of architectural ground or a base. It is not that *chora* is absence or the presence of absence, as Eisenman at one point seems to believe, but rather that *chora* remains conceptually intractable and unsayable. Despite Derrida's avowal "that non-representable space could give the receiver, the visitor, the possibility of thinking about architecture" (Eisenmann 35), one is still prompted to ask what factor or factors rendered the Parc de la Villette a collaborative failure. Is it the inability to translate deconstruction into architectural thinking and practice? Or is it an initially, ill conceived philosophemic contribution on Derrida's part? The patent failure of his collaboration with Eisenman on this project, a project (in its published accounts) characterized by Derrida's reticence and Eisenman's consistent misprisions, misapplications, and refusals to allow the philosopher's contribution to affect the architect's designs, stands as both a warning and a challenge to paracritical thinking. The entire collaboration can be found in Eisenman 1997. Both Cache and Solà-Morales demonstrate the impact of Deleuze's thinking on architecture.

8. Inflecting a related sentiment, architect Nigel Coates refers to the "richly stimulating chaos" brought on by the emergent forms of techno-media and communications (quoted in Glancey 16).

9. *Archigram* chronicles the work of this late 1960s British collective as told by its

members. A cross section of Libeskind's theoretical writings and architectural projects, including the Berlin Museum Extension with the Jewish Museum, can be found in his monograph *Countersign*. Hejduk's ephemeral, traveling architecture (termed "vagabond" by Antony Vidler) is briefly discussed in Vidler 207–14. The trilogy, *Mask of Medusa, Vladivostok,* and *Soundings* offer a chrestomathy of his architectural projects and theories. Hadid's work is readily available in *The Complete Work*. Her important architectural statement "Another Beginning" appears in Peter Noever.

10. As well as his famous proclamation that "architecture is in general frozen music," Schelling also cites the architecturally relevant myth of Amphion whose music causes stones to inhere and formulate the walls around Thebes (Schelling 177). This confluence of musical and the architectural is echoed in Goethe's later description of architecture as "petrified music" (a description he later modified to "silent music," *verstummte Tonkunst*). See Vidler 231 fn 30.

11. The most cogent critique of Eisenman's approach is Robin Evans, "Not to be Used for Wrapping Purposes: A Review of the Exhibition of Peter Eisenman's Fin d'Ou T Hou S" in Evans 119–51.

12. "An axonometric drawing consists of a plan which is set up truly but turned to a convenient angle. The verticals are then drawn on this and to scale. By these means, all the horizontal and all the vertical elements of the building are represented correctly and so to the same scale. *Anything which is neither truly vertical nor horizontal becomes distorted;* but an axonometric drawing, once one has learnt to disregard the distortions, can teach a very great deal about structure" (Murray 237 n. 5 emphases added). Axonometric effects, of course, are not novel; they are central to the logic of the paragram and to analytic Cubism. Like axonometry, the latter applies a structural logic chiasmatically across the normative rules of figuration and design. Within early–twentieth century literature, the most effective axonometric poetry is Gertrude Stein's *Tender Buttons*. Parapoetics, of course, would investigate the benefits of including distortion within a study of the structural elements.

13. See Ron Silliman, "The New Sentence," *The New Sentence* (New York: Roof Books, 1987): 63–93.

14. The above interpretative analysis merely laminates a theory onto texts whose disjunctive qualities suggest an analogy to axonometric diagramming. The question of how to *consciously* employ axonometry as a creative method finds a real answer in the realm of computer-constructed texts and visual poems, where on-screen deployment and display promises most effective results. The poetic possibilities of axonometric syntax, display, and semantics are not addressed in an otherwise excellent collection of articles investigating the format and political possibilities of computers and the Internet gathered by Wershler-Henry. See Darren Wershler-Henry, ed. "Cyberpoetics," *Open Letter* 10th Series no. 6, special edition (Fall 2000). Alert to the dangers of analogical thinkers, a paradisciplinary procedure might take the form that Deleuze notes in reflecting on his own use of a biological model. The dangers of merely analogical might be averted "if we re-

strict ourselves to *extracting from scientific operators a particular conceptualizable character* which itself refers to non-scientific domains, and converges with science without applying it or making it a metaphor." Gilles Deleuze, *The Time-Image,* trans. Hugh Tomlinson and Roberta Galeta (Minneapolis: University of Minnesota Press, 1989): 129. In other words vectors should not only be traced and registered as they converge and pass through common values, but they should also be tracked as disjunctive syntheses whose governing law is the law of the included middle.

15. See, for example, "Semiology and the Urban" in Leach 166–72, first presented as a lecture in May 1967, under the sponsorship of the *Institut Français,* and the Institute of the History of Architecture at the University of Naples.

16. As well as Knabb's excellent collection of Situationist texts and reports, Wigley *Constant's New Babylon: The Hyper-Architecture of Desire* and Sadler are also of specifically architectural interest.

17. "It was at Rome, on the fifteenth of October, 1764, as I sat musing amidst the ruins of the Capitol, while the barefooted fryars were singing Vespers in the temple of Jupiter, that the idea of writing the decline and fall of the City first started to my mind." Edward Gibbon, *Memoirs of my Life and Writings,* ed. Henry Morley (London: George Routledge & Sons, 1891): 151.

18. Pound's own view of the fragment might be deduced from his own Confucian beliefs that structure the relation of parts to whole. "The metaphysic of the Confucian *Chung Yung* or *Unwobbling Pivot,*" informs Peter Makin, "is that things are not heaps of contingent dust-drift, but have essential principles, which are durable; which are part of an overarching tendency or Principle in the universe and which, being a shaping and therefore good principle operative in man as in other things, a man may come to understand. This metaphysic is all about the relation between wholes and fragments. The mosaic is not its little glass and gold-leafed fragments; the Virgin shines down from the apse at Torcello when, or if, half of the fragments that make her have fallen" (235–36). The architectural pertinence of Makin's observations is obvious.

19. See George Simmel, "The Metropolis and Mental Life" in Leach 69–79.

20. It may please Betsky to know that support for his theoretical position is growing. The Italian *Città Lente* or "Slow Cities" movement, inaugurated by Paolo Saturnini, was implemented in 2000 in small towns and cities. An offshoot of Carlo Patrini's Slow Food movement, founded a decade ago to counter the proliferation of homogenous fast food outlets, *Città Lente* is committed to a preservationist policy of traditional architecture and gastronomy. As reporter Megan Williams explains Saturnini, the Mayor of Greve-in-Chianti, "is carefully constructing barricades to keep at bay the tide of homogeneity that globalization has washed into similar-sized communities around the world. From fast-food chains to cell-phone antennas to car alarms. The Small [*sic*] Cities people have said 'No thanks' to many of the trappings of modernity." It is worth comparing these sentiments with Kenneth Goldsmith's celebration of nutritionless data in his conceptual writing examined in chapter 6. It is also useful to note the recent emergence (2008)

of a "slow poetry movement" as a strategic antidote to the "fast food" poetics of Gold-smith and Flarf (also discussed in chapter 6). See Slow Poetry: An Introduction, ed. Dale Smith, *Big Bridge* 14, www.bigbridge.org./BB14?SLOWPO.HTM. Last accessed 17 May 2011.

21. "Reflection" in *Sämtliche Werke* 4:1 234–35.

## Chapter 8

1. The phenomenon is noted by Jeffrey Masten, Peter Stallybrass, and Nancy J. Vickers in their introduction to *Language Machines: Technologies of Literary and Cultural Production* (New York: Routledge for The English Institute, 1997). Full discussions of *scriptio continua* can be found in Paul Saenger, *Space between Words: The Origins of Silent Reading* (Stanford: Stanford University Press, 1997); in Malcolm B. Parkes, *Pause and Effect: An Introduction to Punctuation in the West* (University of California Press, 1993); and in Steve McCaffery, *Prior to Meaning: the Protosemantic and Poetics* (Evanston: Northwestern University Press, 2001).

2. It remains uncertain whether the origins of the labyrinth are architectural, mythic, or diagrammatic. No remains were found at Knossos, and neither Diodorus (ca. 50 BCE), nor Pliny the Elder (23–79CE) report them.

3. Most labyrinth-scholars, e.g. Mayer, Kretschmer, Spiegelberg, Picard, Palmer, Galini, and Frisk, concur that the structure takes it name from "labrys," the two-bladed or Janusian axe that was the symbol of the Cretan king, Minos. This, however, is disputed by Kern: "All we can be certain of is that the suffix *-inthos* was usually employed in place names in a language that the Greeks encountered upon migration (ca. 2000 BCE). At the very least, this suffix could be an indication of how long the word has been in use. An analysis of the rest of the word leads one to assume, with some reservations, that it is associated, somewhat mysteriously, with 'stone'" (Kern 2, 43–45).

4. The classical labyrinth, inverted and complicated as we shall see by Arakawa and Gins, requires an additional, *emotional* landing site to the three they outline (Imaging, Perceptual, and Architectural). Karen Mac Cormack makes such a proposal in her essay, "Mutual Labyrinth: a Proposal of Exchange": "In *Architectural Body* Arakawa and Gins discuss 'The mapping of "events and locatings"' so as to 'be able to reflect all manner of experience'; they propose a landing-site 'molecule' formed of 'two landing-site "atoms" [named perceptual and imaging].' I propose that an emotional landing site occurs as a(n) (special/particular?) instance of a clinamen of these atoms, so also an event marker in and of experience" (113 fn 18). Mac Cormack has discussed this matter by phone and e-mail with Madeline Gins. For the full discussion see Karen Mac Cormack, "Mutual Labyrinth" in *Architectures of Poetry,* ed. Mariá Eugenia Diaz Sánchez and Craig D. Dworkin (Amsterdam and New York: Rodopi, 2004): 109–116.

5. The desire to connect *Irrweg* to Joyce's Earwicker is teasingly tempting and if so connected, would offer a guiding bar into a new reading of *Finnegans Wake*: Finnegans Irrweg a wake in the maze of language.

6. Eco adds to the maze and labyrinth a third labyrinth type: the net or rhizome, a concept famously exploited by Gilles Deleuze and Félix Guattari in their two volume work *Capitalism and Schizophrenia*. See Eco 80–82.

7. This summary section is profoundly indebted to Simon Sadler's detailed and provocative history of Situationist architecture, *The Situationist City*.

8. Sadler sees these laboriously detailed maps as "examples of the general postwar mania for systems analysis" (88).

9. Constant's 1953 wooden reliefs mark the artifactual transition from painting through sculpture into architectural model. Developing out of Giacometti's work on ludic sites of the 1930s (illus. de Zegher 19), Constant's reliefs mark the first illustrations of his thoughts on architecture and urbanism.

10. The name "COBRA" comes from the initial letters of the three cities where the founding members lived: Copenhagen, Brussels, and Amsterdam.

11. The article first appeared in *Internationale situationniste* 3 (December) 1959, 37–40 and is reprinted in *October* 79 (Winter 1997): 109–12.

12. A curious feature of *New Babylon* is its uncustomary development and exhibition in the form of models and photographs as opposed to drawings and blue prints. Many of Constant's labyrinth designs were constructed after his return to painting in 1969.

13. Constant's vision of a spreading city suspended above a city is not in itself original. Leonardo da Vinci offered designs for a "[c]ity on two levels," while in the twentieth century Le Corbusier adopted the suspended deck structure in his own *Pilotis*. In 1958 Alison and Peter Smithson designed a pedestrian net slung over the entire old street plan of Berlin that proved influential to Constant's own design. One might even mention that the suspended guerrilla architectural phenomenon of "lateral piercing," which was employed during the Paris Commune, involved the creation of elevated passages by breaking through the walls of adjoining houses. Here, as elsewhere, I am grateful to Simon Sadler (139). Leonardo's designs can be found in Ms. B fol. 3r and 3v, and fol. 36r., now housed in Paris at l'Institut de France but more readily available in Daniel Arasse, *Leonardo da Vinci*, 163.

14. For Heidegger, contemporary scientific pursuit involves the "extinguishing of the situation" in the current life context. Heidegger tenders three characteristics of the situation: 1. a situation is "an 'event' [*ereignis*] not a 'process.'" 2. a situation is relatively closed [*Geschlossenheit*]. 3. in a situation the "I" is never "detached" or "disengaged" [*Unabgehobenheit*]—"The 'I' never needs to come into view, [for] it swims within the situation" (Heidegger 29). How does this compare to the SI's notion of a situation? In "Definitions," (included in the 1958 journal *Situationist International* 1,) the SI does not provide an entry on the situation *per se* but defines a "constructed situation" as "[a] moment of life concretely and deliberately constructed by the collective organization of a unitary ambiance and a game of events" (quoted in Knabb 45). For the Situationists the term had its immediate roots in Sartrean existentialism. "Sartre argued that life is a series of given situations which affect the individual's consciousness and will, and which

must in turn be negotiated by that individual" (quoted in Sadler 45). Debord rethinks the "situation" as simply a given toward a willful construction of "collective ambiences, ensembles of impressions determining the quality of a moment" (Sadler 46).

15. As his prefatory motto for "The New Babylonian Culture," Constant chose Rimbaud's famous sentence: "It is a matter of achieving the unknown by a derangement of all the senses" (*le dérèglement de tous les sens*).

16. Constant found one source of inspiration in the ludic models outlined in Huizinga's 1944 book *Homo Ludens: A Study of the Play Element in Culture* and perhaps Fluxus is the true heir of this presidential spirit of play. On the relationship of Fluxus to architecture, see *Fantastic Architecture,* ed. by Dick Higgins and Wolf Vostell (New York: Something Else Press, 1969).

17. John Wilton-Ely opens up the possibility that certain influences on Constant derive from Piranesi's vortical constructions; these include Ferdinando Bibiena's stage design for a prison now in the Albertina, Vienna, and Jean-Louis Desprez's *Prison* fantasies. See Wilton-Ely 89.

18. As long ago as 1921 Kasimir Malevich claimed that human being was already in a new fourth dimension of motion.

19. Tschumi embraces violence as a necessary component of architecture. "Architecture is defined by the actions it witnesses as much as by the enclosure of its walls. Murder in the Street differs from Murder in the Cathedral in the same way as love in the street differs from the Street of Love. Radically" (100). For a full discussion see "Violence of Architecture," Tschumi 121–34.

20. See his "Next Babylon, Soft Babylon," *Architects in Cyberspace II,* ed. Neil Spiller, *Architecture and Design* Vol. 68 Nos. 11–12 (Nov./Dec. 1998): 20–27.

21. The survival of the classical labyrinth in schematizations that present it as a miniaturized pattern experienced solely visually from above annul its primarily tactile and kinetic experience.

22. Quoted in Jean-François Lyotard, *Libidinal Economy,* trans. Iain Hamilton Grant (Bloomington: Indiana University Press, 1993): 264.

23. Arakawa and Gins' use of the term "architectural body" should not be confused with Liane Lefaivre's use of it in her 1997 book *Leon Battista Alberti's "Hypnerotomachia Poliphili": Recognizing the Architectural Body in the Early Italian Renaissance.*

24. See "Towards Anarchitecture," which opens Robin Evans, *Translations from Drawing to Building and Other Essays* (Cambridge, Mass.: The MIT Press, 1997): 11–34.

25. These fascinating mutations and developments are ably traced in Lefaivre 200–251.

26. This history is not without other maverick disfigurers. In *Figueras,* for instance, Salvador Dali offered a reconstructed face of Mae West into which museum visitors walked in at a surprising entry point. "[W]e cross the chin (a short flight of steps), sit down on the lips (a sofa), where we can admire the eyes (pictures on the wall) or look out through the hair (curtains framing the whole interior)." See Harbison 49–50.

27. See Colin St. John, *The Other Tradition of Modernist Architecture: The Uncompleted Project* (London: Academy Editions, 1995).

28. See Juhani Pallasmaa, *The Eyes of the Skin: Architecture and the Senses* (London: Academy Editions, 1996). For practical examples of moves toward this other tradition, I refer the reader to the sensory exercises described in Franck and implemented by Galen Cranz at Berkeley, Nadi Alhasani at the University of Pennsylvania, Kim Tanzer (Florida), and Karen Franck herself (New Jersey Institute of Technology).

29. Kant speaks of *leitfäden* (guiding threads) in the third *Critique* when discussing the gesture of aesthetic subremption as a grasping of one of such threads. For details see Jean-François Lyotard, *Lessons on the Analytic of the Sublime,* trans. Elizabeth Rottenberg (Stanford: Stanford University Press): 183.

30. They share this terminological fecundity with Deleuze and Guattari who situate the production of new concepts at the heart of the philosophical enterprise. "Simply, the time has come for us to ask what philosophy is. We have never stopped asking this question, and we already had the answer, which has not changed: philosophy is the art of forming, inventing, and fabricating concepts" (Deleuze and Guattari 2). If we lend credence to this terse assertion, then part of Arakawa and Gins' *Reversible Destiny* project is truly philosophical.

31. For a concise description of Serra's project see Harbison 14.

32. See, for example, Joseph Masheck, *Modernities: Art-Matters in the Present* (Penn State University Press, 1993): 109–12.

33. See "Four Architects on Reversible Destiny," *Reversible Destiny* 215–21.

34. They are not alone in this misprision; Derrida too makes the same mistake: "I have a very ambiguous relationship with the labyrinth. I like it, of course, but I think it is too close to the desire to find the exit door from the reappropriation. It's too classical; it's a topos" (Derrida and Eisenman 48). As I have argued the classical labyrinth is less a topos than an orchestrated itinerary along a pathway.

35. But death still has its say. Ironically, the aim of *Reversible Destiny* is to promote the death of commonplace experience.

36. Rudofsky cites the source of this image as *Nihon Chiri Fuzuoku,* a badly produced book printed in 1936. There are other examples of architectural works and terrains that I judge remarkably similar to the external appearances of some *Reversible Destiny* projects—for instance both the caravanserai and teahouse in the Iranian town of Qum (figures 149 and 150 respectively in Rudofsky's book).

37. See, for instance, Peter and Jean Medawar, *Aristotle to Zoos* (Oxford University Press, 1983): 66–67.

38. Lyotard asks: "Would the possibilities reserved for childhood remain open in every circumstance? Might they even multiply? Could the body be younger at sixty years of age than at fifteen?" (*Reversible Destiny,* 11).

## Chapter 9

1. In his *De Gloria Atheniensium* III (346f 346e) Plutarch attributes the saying to a certain Simonides. The classic study of the theory remains Rensselaer W. Lee, *Ut Pictura Poesis: The Humanistic Theory of Painting* (New York: W. W. Norton & Co., 1967).

2. "Art at the same time, in rural improvements, pervading the province of Nature, unseen and unfelt, seemed to bear a striking analogy to that species of verse, the harmony of which results from measured quantity and varied cadence, without the too studied arrangement of final syllables, or regular return of consonant sounds." William Mason, *The English Garden. A Poem in Four Books* [Book IV]. (York: Printed by A Ward, 1781): 53. For his part, Malcolm Andrews believes "[t]he discarding of strict symmetries and neat, antithetical structures is also the prosodic equivalent of garden design over the period" (10).

3. The best study of this relationship through more recent times remains Charles Altieri, *Painterly Abstraction in Modernist American Poetry* (Pennsylvania University Press, 1989). Meyly Chin Hagemann offers a more specific example of painterly influence on writing in her "Hemingway's Secret: Visual to Verbal Art" in *Journal of Modern Literature* 7:1: 87–112.

4. Nathaniel Mackey, *Discrepant Engagement: Dissonance, Cross-Culturality, and Experimental Writing* (Cambridge University Press, 1993, reprinted Tuscaloosa: University of Alabama Press, 2000).

5. Among contemporary American practitioners I would cite Susan Howe, Bruce Andrews, John Cage, Jackson Mac Low, P. Inman, and David Melnick, all of whom embrace a disjunctive (and, in the case of Howe, Mac Low and Cage, a destructive) signifying practice. Ronald Johnson's work, while not developing those aspects of roughness specified by Price and Gilpin, is broadly consonant with the overall *desideratum* of the picturesque: to see the world as if looking at a picture. I have spoken already in chapter 2 of Johnson's conception of each page in his *Radi  os* as a picture-space in temporal suspension. In his revisionary thinking of the poem's place in the large opus *ARK*, Johnson moves *Radi  os* from its initial conception as a Dymaxion Dome over the entire poem to situate it in the "The Outworks" as a surrounding garden (appropriate in the light of the Edenic subject matter of the source text and cannily apposite to picturesque theory.)

6. For instance, the picturesque reestablished the predominance of the two-dimensional intricacy that governs Anglo-Saxon and Celtic illumination. Whorls and spirals manifest too in Pound's theory of the Vorticist image and in the structure of much of Joyce's *Finnegans Wake*. In its preoccupation with the passing through details, the picturesque further endorsed what Nikolaus Pevsner describes as "the anti-corporeal intricacies of line," which he judged characteristic of the Englishness of English Art. (See *The Englishness of English Art* (London: Penguin, 1976): 137).

7. See, for instance, the following passage from Jonson's 1640 *Discoveries*: "[*Writers*] that in composition are nothing, *but what is rough, and broken;* Quae per salebras altaque saxa cadunt. And if it would come gently, they trouble it to purpose. *They would not have run without rubs,* as if that style were more strong and manly, that stroke the eare with a kind of unevenesse. These men err not by chance, but knowingly and willingly . . . ." (*Works* viii: 585). Ben Jonson, "Discoveries," *Works*, 11 volumes, ed. C. H. Herford and P. and E. Simpson (Oxford University Press, 1925–54): viii: 585. Emphases added.

8. See "Tennyson and Picturesque Poetry" in Marshall McLuhan, *The Interior Landscape: The Selected Literary Criticism of Marshall McLuhan 1943-1962*, ed. Eugene McNamara, New York: McGraw Hill, 1969: 135–55. Brian McHale, *The Obligation Toward the Difficult Whole: Postmodernist Long Poems* (Tuscaloosa: University of Alabama Press, 2004): 120–22. I should add that this renewed link to eighteenth-century proclivities is not isolated to the picturesque. The Scottish concrete poet Ian Hamilton Finlay found inspiration for his "Little Sparta" in William Shenstone's garden The Leasowes, especially its deployment of an obelisk and inscribed benches. For details see John Dixon-Hunt, *Nature Over Again: The Garden Art of Ian Hamilton Finlay* (London: Reaktion Books, 2009): 102–3.

9. Christopher Hussey extends the inceptive and terminal dates to "roughly" 1730 and 1830 (Hussey 4). William Gilpin is the first to apply the word "picturesque" specifically to landscape in his work of the late 1740s and early 1750s; see for example his *A Dialogue upon the Gardens at Stow, etc.*

10. In his 1912 notebooks of his walking tour through France, Pound draws a distinction between landscape and scenery. Sections of these notebooks found their way into the ur-cantos where Pound's attraction to the picturesque finds clear endorsement in his linking of the empirical experience of landscapes to the effects of old masters. (Much of the early *Cantos* derive from an abandoned tour guide to Provence.) See Ezra Pound, *A Walking Tour in Southern France: Ezra Pound among the Troubadours*, ed. Richard Sieburth (New York: New Directions, 1992).

11. Johns additionally discusses the seventeenth-century skepticism about the credibility of images as an accurate representation of the world. See especially 433–41.

12. Modernity's great vanguard of symmetry is Baudelaire who proffers his own antidote to picturesque irregularity in his "*Rêve Parisien,*" in which vegetation is rusticated because of its irregularity and trees are replaced by symmetrical colonnades "l'envirante monotonaire/ Du métail" (a thematic contrast caught too in Charles Reknikoff's short poem "Walk about the Subway Station"). The social implications of the symmetry emerging as a result of capitalism seemingly passed Baudelaire by—not so Southey and Ruskin (see footnote 23 below).

13. Although Gilpin devised the category of "Picturesque Beauty," the possibility of a concept of "Picturesque Sublimity" was never engaged.

14. Price's book is heavily indebted to Gilpin's own discussions of picturesque theory. As evidence I quote the near identical passage from Gilpin's: "[A] pile in a state of ruin receives the richest decorations from the various colors, which it acquires from time. It receives the stains of weather; the incrustations of moss; and the varied tints of flowery weeds" (quoted in Barbier 116). Decay, however, can produce uniformity, not a picturesque heterogeneity, as in the case of brick and mortar constructions where aging removes the modular multiplicity of a façade to convey the effect of a uniform surface. Nature in this case does "naturally" what Borromini proposed technically: the "sanding" of brick walls to produce a surface uniformity.

15. The best contemporary example of picturesque erosion in poetry is probably Armand Schwerner's *The Tablets,* a fictitious quasi-scholarly "edition" of fragments of ancient texts.

16. "Where there is close vision, space is not visual, or rather the eye itself has a haptic, nonoptical function" (Deleuze and Guattari 494).

17. See Joachin Gasquet, *Cézanne: A Memoir with Conversations* (London: Thames and Hudson, 1991): 160.

18. See for example Reynolds' three *Idler* papers 76, 79, and 82 in Vol. 2 of *The Yale Edition of the Works of Samuel Johnson* (New Haven: Yale University Press, 1963).

19. This equation of the sentence with the pictorial vanishing point brackets from consideration the philosophical complexities in attempting to localize the vanishing point. See for instance Alain Badiou's discussion in his philosophical tribute to Jacques Derrida in *Pocket Pantheon: Figures of Postwar Philosophy,* trans. David Macey (London and New York: Verso, 2009): 125–44.

20. Coolidge admits the influence of Ashbery's *Tennis Court Oath,* especially such short sections as 26 and the poem "Europe." See Coolidge's "Arrangement": 164.

21. One should also flag the selection included in that anthology of Aram Saroyan's poetry. Redolent with a stark minimalism, it matches Coolidge's compositional usage of space as a radical modifier-compromiser of the poetic line.

22. Robert Motherwell, ed., *The Dada Painters and Poets* (New York: George Wittenborn, 1951). The anthology was reprinted in 1967 and no doubt this second edition was Coolidge's source text.

23. It is Emmanuel Levinas who develops the notion of ontic proximity as constitutive of the essential condition of poetry (a parallel proximity to that of beings in that it characterizes his schema of ethics). There is also a germinal theory of the picturesque that Levinas identifies with caricature: "Thus a person bears on his face, alongside of its being with which he coincides, its own caricature, its picturesqueness" (Levinas 6). It's worth comparing Levinas' brief comment (made in "Reality and its Shadow") with Price's theory of the physiological picturesque. Price, for instance, compares a parson's daughter to her architectural surround: "There is a sort of resemblance between the good old parson's daughter and his house; her features have a little of the same irregularity, and her eyes are somewhat inclined to look across each other, like the roofs of the old parsonage" (Uvedale Price, *Essays on the Picturesque,* 3 vols. (London, 1810): III: 291). This sensed complementarity between animate and inanimate, as well as the subordination of social issues to aesthetic values drew the acrimony of nineteenth-century critics such as Ruskin (see his *Modern Painters).* In his discussion of Turner's picturesque method he distinguishes the "noble" from the "shallow" picturesque by way of the relative degree of mental impression aroused by an object's inner character. (For example, the "depth" association of picturesque ruination with social distress.) In Turner's estimate Price's and Gilpin's embrace of ruin and decay—as entirely surface aesthetic phenomena—betrays a "heartless" attitude to such socio-political ramifications in the human condition as

plight and poverty. (See John Ruskin, *The Works,* 13 vols. [New York: Thomas Y. Crowell & Co.] VI: 15–32.) Earlier in the century Robert Southey, in his 1807 *Letters from England by Don Manuela Alvarez Espriella,* voices through the character of Montesinos a chilling parallel of aesthetic landscape to the proletariat in the age of emergent mercantilism: "the new cottages of the manufacturers [i.e. laborers] are . . . upon the manufacturing pattern . . . naked and in a row." (Quoted in Raymond Williams, *Culture and Society 1780–1950* [London: Chatto and Windus, 1960]: 23–24.) Linear uniformity articulates the reduction of humans into "bodily machines for producing wealth" (ibid. 23). In the early-nineteenth century the word "terrace" takes on the chilling resonance of the proletarian uniform box. The social implications and the alleged insensitivity of picturesque theorists can be tested in this short passage: "among our own species, beggars, gypsies, and all such tattered figures as are merely picturesque, bear a close analogy in all qualities that make them so, to old hovels and mills" (Uvedale Price, *An Essay on the Picturesque, as Compared with the Sublime and the Beautiful . . .* [London, 1794]: 76). That said, it would be misleading to treat picturesque theory and its theorists as either conservative or apolitical. Two of its three central theorists (Uvedale Price and Richard Payne Knight) were both Whig Parliamentarians and both zealously mobilized the ready analogy of aesthetic to political freedom in the Whig cause. For documentation on the political implications of the picturesque see among others Sidney K. Robinson, *Inquiry into the Picturesque.* (Chicago: University of Chicago Press, 1991); John Barrell, *The Dark Side of the Landscape: Rural Poor in English Painting 1730–1840* (Cambridge: Cambridge University Press, 1986); and Dennis Cosgrave and Stephen Daniels eds., *The Iconography of the Landscape* (Cambridge: Cambridge University Press, 1980).

24. The soft belly of Romantic landscape theory reveals itself in Thomas Campbell's famous line from his now forgotten poem *The Pleasures of Hope:* "'Tis *distance* lends *enchantment* to the view!" (emphases added).

25. See chapter 8, "Anabasis," in Alain Badiou, *The Century,* trans. Alberto Toscano (London: Polity Press, 2007): 81–97. Badiou compares Celan's poems to *Anabasis* by Saint-Jean Perse.

26. See "Reality and Its Shadow" in Emmanuel Levinas, *Collected Philosophical Papers,* trans. Alphonso Lingis (Dordrecht: Martinus Nijhoff, 1987): 1–13. See also Gerald L. Bruns, *On the Anarchy of Poetry and Philosophy: A Guide for the Unruly* (New York: Fordham University Press, 2006).

## Chapter 10

1. Lucretius owes an obvious debt to the materialist ideas of Epicurus, who speaks of the *parenklisis* of the atom in his *Letter to Herodotus.* Epicurus himself is indebted to his precursors Leucippus and Democritus.

2. See as evidence Jarry's short article "The Virgin and the Mannekin-Pis," *Selected Works,* 127. The Mannekin-Pis is a famous fountain in Brussles that shows a small boy urinating (hence the title). I do not believe it coincidental that Duchamp invented his

own fountain by inverting a urinal—surely the link here of fountain and urination in both pieces suggests an influence.

3. *Rhetoric III* quoted in James Harris, *Philological Inquiries,* London, 1781: 50.

4. Such a superinducement is readily apparent in the Situationist strategy of the *détournement.* As defined in *Internationale Situationniste* No. 1 (June 1958), *détournement* is "[t]he integration of present or past artistic production into a superior construction of a milieu. In this sense there can be no situationist painting or music but only a situationist use of these means" (Knabb 45–46).

5. The nature of the Surreal image also accords with Aristotle's definition of enigma formed by "the putting together of impossible things" (quoted in Agamben *Stanzas* 155). Dada too comes close to embracing the 'pataphysical tenet of the anomaly. See Walter Serner in "The Swing about the Axis" published in the Dada magazine *Der Zeltweg* (Nov. 1919) where he claims that "[e]very rule has its exception without a doubt. In fact as a rule. Therefore take extra care: every rule is to be applied as an exception, for the rule is the exception" (quoted in *The Dada Reader: A Critical Anthology* ed. Dawn Ades [University of Chicago Press, 2006]: 58).

6. Baudelaire was surely familiar with Fourier's text when formulating his own theory of correspondences. Whether the Futurist F. T. Marinetti was familiar with Fourier when situating analogy as the central principle of Futurist poetics is less certain but the similarity is undeniable. See Marinetti's 1913 "Destruction of Syntax-Imagination without String-Words-in-Freedom," *Futurist Manifestos,* ed. Umbro Apollonio (London: Thames and Hudson, 1973): 95–106.

7. See his "Pataphysics for the year 2000," *The Illusion of the End,* trans. Chris Turner (Stanford University Press, 1994): 1–9.

8. See for instance William Anastasi with Michael Seidel, "Jarry in Joyce: A Conversation," *Joyce Studies Annual,* vol. 6 (Summer 1995): 39–58.

9. Gilles Deleuze, "An Unrecognized Precursor to Heidegger: Alfred Jarry," *Essays Critical and Clinical,* trans. Daniel W. Smith and Michael A. Greco (Minneapolis: University of Minnesota Press, 1997): 91–98.

10. Jarry's plays written through the 1890s are *Caesar Antichrist* and the Ubu trilogy: *Ubu Roi* (Ubu the King), *Ubu cocu* (Ubu Cuckolded) and *Ubu enchaîné* (Ubu Enchained).

11. Agamben argues that Schmitt wrote *Political Theology* as a direct response to the theories of sovereignty advanced by Benjamin in the *Trauerspiel* and his "Critique of Violence"; my comments are indebted to his discussion of that relationship. See Giorgio Agamben, *State of Exception,* trans. Kevin Attell (University of Chicago Press, 2005): 52–64.

## Chapter 11

1. Levinas insists on an absolute deconceptualization of reality attendant on the musical. With the centrality of rhythm to its praxis, music links to the image in designating a preeminently rhythmic as opposed to retinal ordering. "The idea of rhythm . . .

designates . . . the way the poetic order affects us, closed wholes whose elements call for one another like the syllables of a verse, but do so only insofar as they impose themselves on us, disengaging themselves from reality" (4). Musicality in both the poetic image and in music proper guarantees, in Levinas' estimate, a loss of reality, converting an object world into a non-object lamina of pure affectivity whose disincarnation of reality situates in "an ontological dimension . . . where commerce with reality is rhythm" (5). In musicality there is bewitchment and ekstasis, "the passage from oneself to anonymity" (4). Levinas' judgment on musicality points to a somber implication within Zukofsky's claim that "[t]he best way to find out about poetry is to read the poems. That way the reader becomes something of a poet himself: not because he 'contributes' to the poetry, but because he finds himself subject of its energy" (31). This concluding hortation to energy and its implicit bias toward force rather than form takes its place in a rich panoply of writers from Longinus through Marinetti, to Pound and Olson.

2. Gray's scientific interest in the orders of insects can be gleaned from his Latin manuscript found among the Stonehewer papers at Pembroke College; it is heavily indebted to Linnaeus' *Systema Naturae*. Although the passages indicate remarkable details on insect physiognomy, they do not engage the matter of insect sounds. Similarly neither Virgil in *Georgics* Book IV nor Maeterlink in *The Life of the Bee* pay consideration to the acoustic realm.

3. Lenz's Medusa head is discussed in Paul Celan's "Meridian Speech," Celan, *Collected Prose,* 37–55, especially 42.

4. "It is as though death were never dead enough, as though parallel with the duration of the living ran the eternal duration of the interval—the *meanwhile*. . . . The eternal duration in which a statue is immobilized differs radically from the eternity of the concept; it is the meanwhile, never finished, still enduring—something inhuman and monstrous" (Levinas 11).

5. Ornithologists specify eight distinct types of birdcalls: pleasure, distress, alarm, flight, flocking, and nesting. The final type, which indicates territorial defense, opens up the base politics of birdsong. Like primitive stone walls and the earliest human writing, ornithological vocalization is used to determine property boundaries. Through this essential link to territorialization, birdsong presupposes its listener to be a contractually ostracized stranger. Schafer comments on some co-optations of these sound functions in the human acoustic environment. "[T]he territorial calls of birds are reproduced in automobile horn blowing, their alarm calls are reproduced in police sirens and their pleasure calls in the beach-side radio. In the territorial calls of birds we encounter the genesis of the idea of acoustic space" (33).

6. The instrumental, technological quality of insect sound reappears in Louis MacNeice's "Autumn Journal" as the hidden telecommunicational intimations of war:

> . . . we go to our daily
> Jobs to the dull refrain of the caption 'War'

> Buzzing around us from hidden insects
> And we think 'This must be wrong, it has happened before,
> Just like this before, we must be dreaming;
> It was long ago these flies
> Buzzed like this, so why are they still bombarding
> The ears if not the eyes? (128)

7. A brief passage in a letter from Baudelaire to Alphonse de Calonne (cited by Crépet) connects the movement of the spheres as much to noise as to music. "Movement generally implies noise, to the extent that Pythagoras attributed music to the *moving* spheres" (quoted in Benjamin *Arcades Project* J90, 4: 383). Given the heavy kinetic stress in Futurist poetry, this dimension of Pythagorean thought (via Baudelaire) finds a curious avant-garde accommodation.

8. The auricular foundation of Wordsworth's poetics is evident in Book V of *The Prelude* in the famous Arabian dream passage in which the poet falls asleep and dreams of an encounter in a great desert with a Bedouin carrying in one hand a stone (that represents Euclid's *Elements)* and in the other a shell representing poetry. The shell jubilates with "[a] loud prophetic blast of harmony" (Book V line 95).

9. Deleuze is cognizant of the conjunctive nature of the stammer: "the conjunction AND is, neither a union, nor a juxtaposition, but the birth of a stammering, the outline of a broken line which always sets off at right angles, a sort of active and creative line of flight" (Deleuze and Parnet 9–10).

10. Such poetic deployment of sound, of course, runs counter to Pound's claim that the energy expressing itself in pure sound can only be expressed in music: "Energy expressing itself in pure sound, i.e. sound as distinct from articulate speech, can only be expressed in music" (376).

11. As Jerome McGann tells us, the Aeolian or windharp "represents a Kantian approach to aesthetic harmony" (38), so it's not surprising that Shelley chooses this instrument as his trope for the poetic mind. A harmony that results from a tensional poetics is, of course, a popular theorization: Nietzsche, Charles Bernstein, and Heidegger alike offer varyingly complex versions of antagonistic binaries. (New Criticism, of course, termed this harmonic tension "irony.") Derrida elucidates a different potential of stringed instruments in comments pertaining to his figural contribution to the architectural collaborative project with Peter Eisenman: "I drew a lyre which is also a sieve. In Plato's text, *chora* is compared to a sieve which separates things into the world of the sensible and intelligible" (Derrida and Eisenman 92). As well as chordal and harmonic, the full capabilities of the harp include stereotomic and segmentative possibilities, capabilities gruesomely evidenced in the use of piano wires for hanging and strangling.

12. I use the term "Auschwitz" in the synecdochal sense that Adorno established and in preference to the term "holocaust," which is a misnomer for the events and outcomes of the Nazi extermination camps. For cogent evidence of the term's historic inaccuracy

and a compelling history of the semantic migration of the term, see Agamben *Remnants* 28–31.

13. "Afterword" in *Out of Everywhere* (London: Reality Street Editions, 1996): 241.

14. Blanchot draws attention to the white spaces in Celan's poetry, referring to them as "arrests," "silences," positive indications of a void, "less a lack than a saturation, a void saturated with void" (Blanchot *Translating Tradition* 228).

15. I take this German word (meaning "speech grid" or "word mesh") from the title of a 1959 volume of Paul Celan's *Sprachgitter Aufnahme*.

16. The poem has a complicated publication history. Written in the early 1950s it first appeared in a Spanish translation in Gomringer's early collection *konstellationen* (Berne, Switzerland: Spiral Press, 1953) and was reprinted, along with the German original to facilitate comparison, in the 1963 *die konstellationen*. Emmett Williams's definitive *Anthology of Concrete Poetry* of 1967 reprints the Spanish version without commentary, as does Mary Ellen Solt's special edition of *Artes Hispanicas* Vol. 1, Nos. 3–4 (Winter/Spring 1968). Jerome Rothenberg's 1968 English translation of *die konstellationen* supplies the German version along with an English translation. The original German version was chosen for the catalogue of the 1970 exhibition of concrete poetry at the Stedelijk Museum, Amsterdam, here again without commentary and with an erroneous publication date of 1968. It might also be useful to point out that Gomringer, though born in Bolivia, has spent most of his life in Bamberg, Germany.

17. Lyotard broadens the scope of this indictment beyond the boundaries of Germany. In his explanation of the graphic form of the phrase "the jews" (without capital and in quotations), he refers to its specific reference "to all those who, wherever they are, seek to remember and to bear witness to something that is constitutively *forgotten,* not only in each individual mind, but in the very thought of the West" (*Political Writings* 141). On Heidegger's Nazism and silence around the matter of the camps see Victor Farias, *Heidegger and Nazism,* Philadelphia: Temple University Press, 1989 and Jean-François Lyotard, *Heidegger and "the jews"* (University of Minnesota Press, 1990).

18. Eugen Gomringer "from line to constellation," trans. Mike Weaver, *Journal of Hispanic Arts* Vol. 1. No. 3–4 (Winter Spring 1968): 67.

19. The word's polysemeity is also apparent in its English definition in *The Concise Oxford Dictionary*: "*n.* abstinence from speech or noise, being silent, taciturnity, nonbetrayal of secret etc., fact of not mentioning a thing, not communicating any message. *v.t.* make silent by force."

20. The architectural diagrams for the second master plan for Auschwitz, drawn up in February 1942, contain one that shows an aerial view of the camp. The prisoners' huts are aligned in rectangular patterns that invoke the shape of Gomringer's constellation. The original is in the Auschwitz-Birkenau State Museum, box 2/2, file BW 2/17, and more readily available on the cover of Giorgio Agamben's *Homo Sacer*.

21. Derrida constructs a *prosopopoeia* of philosophy that, when transposed into the context of this chapter, stages not only the possibility of a different encounter with Gom-

ringer's white silence (further linking a perceptible emptiness to illegibility) but also encapsulates the burden of Gomringer's poem in the full resonance of its historical contingency. "By means of the breach of philosophical identity, a breach which amounts to addressing truth to itself in an envelope, to hearing itself speak inside without opening its mouth or showing its teeth, the bloodiness of a disseminated writing comes to separate the lips, to violate the embouchure of philosophy, putting its tongue into movement, finally bringing it into contact with some other code, of an entirely other kind. A necessarily unique event, nonreproducible, hence illegible as such and, when it happens, inaudible in the conch, between earth and sea, without signature" (Jacques Derrida, *Margins of Philosophy*, trans. Alan Bass [University of Chicago Press, 1982]: xviii).

22. The poem is quoted and discussed in Kittler 235–36.

23. The historically close relationship between architecture and music lends further perspective on Gomringer's poem. Schelling adds to his well-known definition ("[a]rchitecture is in general frozen music") the relevant myth of Amphion whose music causes stones to inhere and formulate the walls around Thebes (177). This complex of cryogenics, music, and architectural construction brought on by the musical is absent in Goethe's own tropes for architecture, which are "expired harmony" and "petrified music." This latter phrase was later modified to "silent music" [*verstummte Tonkunst*], a term that would have been endearing to Keats. See Vidler, 231 fn 30.

24. This information was sent to me in an e-mail correspondence from Mr. Halsey on Mon. 10 Sept., 2001. The signed poem appears as item 351 in the September 2001 *Miscellany Catalogue* of Alan Halsey Books. In the same communiqué Halsey also states that the "Openings card is definitely the first & only edition. My guess at publication date is 1985/6/7. Harry had done it a while before & I found among his papers a rough version I'd sketched for him when he'd been staying in Hay, would be early 80s." Both "Silencio" and Keats's "Ode to a Nightingale" might be productively compared to the ending of the second act of Schoenberg's *Moses and Aaron* with its surprising exodus from music, in what the architect Daniel Libeskind terms "the non-musical fulfillment of the word" (27). "For an important structural reason, the logic of the libretto could not be completed by the musical score. At the end of the opera, Moses doesn't sing, he just speaks, 'Oh word, thou word,' addressing the absence of the word, and one can understand it as a 'text,' because when there is no more singing, the missing word that is uttered by Moses, the call for the word, the call for the deed, is understood clearly" (Libeskind 26). The repetition of this sentiment in "Silencio" is so apparent as to provoke the question as to whether or not Gomringer was consciously aware of the opera.

25. "Jazz," a poem by South African poet Kelwyn Sole, is a found text incorporating Nazi instructions to German dance bands issued in 1940. The following data, extracted from Sole's text, encapsulates the Aryan mandate: "so-called jazz composition 'may' contain at most 10 percent syncopation, the remainder must consist of a natural legato movement devoid of the hysterical rhythmic reversals characteristic of the music of barbarian races and conducive to dark instincts alien to the German people" (quoted in Spotts 63).

26. I believe Celan alludes to the signing of the final solution at Wannsee on 20 January, 1942 in his 1960 lecture "The Meridian": "Perhaps we can say that every poem is marked by its own '20th of January'? Perhaps the newness of poems written today is that they try most plainly to be mindful of this kind of date?" (Paul Celan, "The Meridian," *Collected Prose,* trans. Rosmarie Waldrop (Manchester: Carcanet Press, 1986): 37–55). This allusion to the Wannsee date seemingly passed by both Christopher Fynsk and Derrida, for both fail to mention it in their otherwise excellent and detailed studies of Celan and "The Meridian." See Jacques Derrida, "Shibboleth: For Paul Celan," in *Word Traces. Readings of Paul Celan,* ed. Aris Fioretos (Baltimore: Johns Hopkins University Press, 1994): 3–72 and Christopher Fynsk, "The Realities at Stake in a Poem: Celan's Bremen and Darmstadt Addresses," ibid: 159–84. Elsewhere, Celan offers a speaking voice equally emergent at a moment of death, whose words are as semantically charged as the white space in the center of Gomringer's text. This voice emits a counter-word, "a word against the grain, the word which cuts the string" (Celan 40). Celan is reporting the words of Lucile in Büchner's play, *Danton's Death,* uttered at the moment of the aristocrat Camille's execution. Lucile "who is blind against art, Lucile for whom language is tangible and like a person, Lucile is suddenly there with her 'Long live the king!'" (ibid). Denying that this cry indicates a covert allegiance to the *ancien régime,* Celan reads it as inscribing the very essence of poetry: "[T]his is not homage to any monarchy, to any yesterday worth preserving. It is homage to the majesty of the absurd which bespeaks the presence of human beings [and has] no definitive name, but I believe that this is . . . poetry" (40).

# Works Cited

Abrams, M. H. "English Romanticism: The Spirit of the Age." *Romanticism and Consciousness: Essays in Criticism*. Ed. Harold Bloom. New York: Norton, 1970. 91–119.

———. *The Mirror and the Lamp: Romantic Theory and the Critical Tradition*. New York: Norton, 1958.

Adorno, Theodor W. *Negative Dialectics*. Trans. E. B. Ashton. New York: Continuum, 2000.

Agamben, Giorgio. *The End of the Poem: Studies in Poetics*. Trans. Daniel Heller-Roazen. Stanford: Stanford UP, 1999.

———. *Homo Sacer: Sovereign Power and Bare Life*. Trans. Daniel Heller-Roazen. Stanford: Stanford UP, 1998.

———. *Infancy and History: Essays on the Destruction of Experience*. Trans. Liz Heron. London: Verso, 1993.

———. *Language and Death: The Place of Negativity*. Trans. Karen E. Pinkus and Michael Hardt. Minneapolis: U of Minnesota P, 1991.

———. *Means without End: Notes on Politics*. Trans. Vincenzo Binetti and Cesare Casarino. Minneapolis: U of Minnesota P, 2000.

———. *Nudities*. Trans. David Kishik and Stefan Pedatella. Stanford: Stanford UP, 2010.

———. *Remnants of Auschwitz: The Witness and the Archive*. Trans. Daniel Heller-Roazen. New York: Zone Books, 1999.

———. *Stanzas: Word and Phantasm in Western Culture*. Trans. Ronald L. Martinez. Minneapolis: U of Minnesota P, 1993.

Allen, Donald M., ed. *The New American Poetry*. New York: Grove Press, 1960.

Alpert, Barry. "Ronald Johnson: An Interview (1974)." *Ronald Johnson: Life and Works*. Eds. Joel Bettridge and Eric Murphy Selinger. Orono: National Poetry Foundation, 2008. 545–60.

Altieri, Charles. *Enlarging the Temple: New Directions in American Poetry during the 1960s*. London: Associated UP., 1984.

Anastasi, William. "Jarry, Joyce, Duchamp and Cage." *tout-fait: The Marcel Duchamp Studies Online Journal* Web. 5 March 2011. www.toutfait.com

Anderson, Sherwood. "The Work of Gertrude Stein." Introduction. *Geography and Plays*. By Gertrude Stein. New York: Something Else, 1968.

Andrews, Bruce. *Edge*. Washington D.C.: Arry Press for Some of Us Press, 1973.

Andrews, Malcolm. *The Search for the Picturesque*. Stanford: Stanford UP, 1986.

Apollonio, Umbero ed. *Futurist Manifestos*. Trans. Robert Brain, R. W. Flint, J. C. Higgitt, and Caroline Tisdall. London: Thames and Hudson, 1973.

Aquinas, Thomas. *Compendium Theologiae: Compendium of Theology*. Trans. Cyril Vollert. London: B. Herder, 1947.

Arakawa and Madeline Gins. *Architectural Body*. Tuscaloosa: U of Alabama P, 2002.

———. *Architecture: Sites of Reversible Destiny*. London: Academy Editions, 1994.

———. *Reversible Destiny: Arakawa/Gins*. New York: Guggenheim Museum, 1997.

Arasse, Daniel. *Leonardo da Vinci: The Rhythm of the World*. Trans. Rosetta Translations. London: Greenwich Editions, 1998.

Aronson, Ronald. *After Marxism*. New York: Guildford, 1995.

Badiou, Alain. *Handbook of Inaesthetics*. Trans. Alberto Toscano. Stanford: Stanford UP, 2005.

———. *Pocket Pantheon: Figures of Postwar Philosophy*. Trans. David Macey. London: Verso, 2009.

Ball, Hugo. "Cabaret Voltaire." Trans. Christina Mills. *The Dada Reader: A Critical Anthology*. Ed. Dawn Ades. Chicago: U of Chicago P, 2006.

———. *Flight Out of Time: A Dada Diary*. Ed. John Elderfield. Trans. Ann Raimes. New York: Viking, 1974.

Barbier, Carl Paul. *William Gilpin: His Drawings, Teachings and Theory of the Picturesque*. Oxford: Oxford UP, 1963.

Barthes, Roland. "The Death of the Author." *Critical Theory Since Plato*. Ed. Hazard Adams. New York: Harcourt, 1992. 1130–33.

———. *New Critical Essays*. Trans. Richard Howard. New York: Hill and Wang, 1980.

———. "Semiology and the Urban." *Rethinking Architecture*. Ed. Neil Leach. London: Routledge, 1997. 166–72.

Bartine, David. *Early English Reading Theory*. Columbia: U of South Carolina P, 1989.

Bataille, Georges. *Guilty*. Trans. Bruce Boon. Venice, CA: Lapis Press, 1988.

———. *Inner Experience*. Trans. Leslie Anne Boldt. Albany: State U of New York P, 1988.

———. *Visions of Excess: Selected Writings, 1927–1939*. Trans. Allan Stoekl with C. R. Lovitt and D. M. Leslie Jr. Minneapolis: U of Minnesota P, 1985.

Baudelaire, Charles. "The Salon of 1859: III. The Queen of the Faculties." *Critical Theory Since Plato*. Eds. Hazard Adams and Leroy Searle. Boston: Thomson Wadsworth, 2005. 604–6.

Baudrillard, Jean. *Baudrillard Live: Selected Interviews*. Ed. Mike Gane. London: Routledge, 1993.

———. *Symbolic Exchange and Death*. Trans. Iain Hamilton Grant. London: Sage, 1993.

Beaulieu, Derek. "*Fidgeting* with the scene of the crime." *Kenneth Goldsmith and Conceptual Poetics. Open Letter* 12.7 (Fall 2005): 58–61.

Beddoes, Thomas Lovell. *The Ivory Gate: Later Poems & Fragments*. Ed. Alan Halsey. Hastings: ReScript, 2011.

———. *The Letters*. Ed. Edmund Gosse. London: Elkin Mathew and John Lane, 1894.

Bely, Andrey. *Selected Essays of Andrey Bely*. Ed. Steven Cassedy. Berkeley: U of California P, 1985.

Benjamin, Walter. *The Arcades Project*. Trans. Howard Eiland and Kevin McLaughlin. Cambridge: Harvard UP, 1999.

——. *Illuminations*. Trans. Harry Zohn. New York: Schocken, 1969.

——. *The Origin of German Tragic Drama*. Trans. John Osborne. London: Verso, 1977.

——. *Reflections*. Trans. Edmund Jephcott. New York: Schocken, 1978.

——. *Selected Writings*. 4 vols. Belknap P of Harvard UP, 1996–2003.

Bentley, G. E., Jr. *The Stranger in Paradise: A Biography of William Blake*. New Haven: Yale UP, 2001.

Bernstein, Charles. *Content's Dream: Essays 1975–1984*. Los Angeles: Sun & Moon, 1986.

Betsky, Aaron. *Architecture Must Burn*. Corte Madera, CA: Gingko, 2000.

Blake, William. *The Complete Poetry and Prose of William Blake*. Ed. David V. Erdman. Berkeley: U of California P, 1982.

Blanchot, Maurice. "The Last One to Speak." *Translating Tradition: Paul Celan in France*. Trans. Joseph Simas. Ed. Benjamin Hollander. San Francisco: ACTS, A Journal of New Writing, 1988. 231–32.

——. *The Work of Fire*. Trans. Charlotte Mandell. Stanford: Stanford UP, 1995.

——. *The Writing of the Disaster*. Trans. Ann Smock. Lincoln: U of Nebraska P, 1986.

Bohn, Willard, ed. and trans. *The Dada Market: An Anthology of Poetry*. Carbondale: Southern Illinois UP, 1993.

Bök, Christian. "Unacknowledged Legislation." *Avant-Post: the Avant-Garde under "Post" Conditions*. Ed. Louis Armand. Prague: Litteraria Pragensia, 2006. 178–93.

——. *'Pataphysics: The Poetics of an Imaginary Science*. Evanston: Northwestern UP, 2002.

Breslin, James E. B. *From Modern to Contemporary: American Poetry, 1945–1965*. Chicago: U of Chicago P, 1984.

Brown, Norman O. *Love's Body*. New York: Random House, 1966.

Bruns, Gerald. *The Material of Poetry: Sketches for a Philosophical Poetics*. Athens, Ga.: U of Georgia P, 2005.

——. "Poethics: John Cage and Stanley Cavell at the Crossroads of Ethical Theory." *John Cage: Composed in America*. Eds. Marjorie Perloff and Charles Junkerman. Chicago: U of Chicago P, 1994. 206–25.

Bunting, Basil. "The Use of Poetry." *Writing* 12 (Summer, 1985): 36–43.

Cache, Bernard. *Earth Moves*. Trans. Anne Boyman and Michael Speaks. Cambridge: MIT P, 1995.

Cage, John. *anarchy*. Middletown: Wesleyan UP, 1988.

——. *Empty Words: Writings '73–'78*. Middletown: Wesleyan UP, 1979.

——. *For the Birds: John Cage in Conversation with Daniel Charles*. London: Marion Boyars, 1981.

——. *M. Writings '67–'72*. Middletown: Wesleyan UP, 1974.

——. *Themes & Variations*. Barrytown: Station Hill, 1982.

Calame, Claude. *The Craft of Poetic Speech in Ancient Greece*. Trans. Janice Orion. Ithaca: Cornell UP, 1995.

Calabrese, Omar. *Neo-Baroque: A Sign of the Times*. Trans. Charles Lambert. Princeton: Princeton UP, 1992.

Calvino, Italo. *The Uses of Literature: Essays*. Trans. Patrick Creagh. London: Harcourt, 1986.

Camille, Michael. *Gothic Art Visions and Revelations of the Medieval World*. London: George Weidenfeld & Nicolson, 1996.

———. *Image on the Edge: The Margins of Medieval Art*. London: Reaktion Books, 1992.

Canguilhem, Georges. *The Normal and the Pathological*. Trans. Carolyn R. Fawcett. New York: Zone, 1991.

Carroll, David. *Paraesthetics: Foucault, Lyotard, Derrida*. London: Routledge, 1987.

Carroll, Paul, d. *The Younger American Poets*. Chicago: Follett, 1968.

Celan, Paul. "The Meridian." *Collected Prose*. Trans. Rosmarie Waldrop. Manchester: Carcanet, 1986. 37–55.

Certeau, Michel de. *The Practice of Everyday Life*. Trans. Steven Rendall. Berkeley: U of California P, 1984.

———. *The Writing of History*. Trans. Tom Conley. New York: Columbia UP, 1988.

Clough, Rosa Trillo. *Futurism: the Story of a Modern Movement; A New Appraisal*. New York: Philosophical Library, 1961.

Cocteau, Jean. *A Call to Order*. Trans. Rollo H. Myers. London: Faber and Gwyer, 1926.

Collins, William. *The Poetical Works*. London: Bell and Daldy, n.d.

Conde, Yago. *Architecture of the Indeterminacy*. Trans. Paul Hammond. Barcelona: Actar, 2000.

Constant (Constant Niuewnhuis). "A Different City for a Different Life." Trans. John Shepley. *October* 79 (Winter 1997): 109–112.

———. "Inaugural Report to the Munich Conference." Trans. Stephen Wright. *Internationale Situationnists* 3. (1959)

———. "The Principle of Disorientation." *Constant's New Babylon: The Hyper-Architecture of Desire*. Mark Wigley. Trans. Robyn de Jong-Dalziel. Rotterdam: OIO, 1998. 225–26.

Cook, Peter ed. *Archigram*. Princeton: Princeton Architectural, 1999.

Coolidge, Clark. *Alien Tatters*. Berkeley: Atelos, 2000.

———. "Arrangement." *Talking Poetics from Naropa Institute*, eds. Anne Waldman and Marilyn Webb, 2 vols. Boulder and London: Shambala 1978. I: 143–169.

Damisch, Hubert. *Skyline: The Narcissistic City*. Trans. John Goodman. Stanford: Stanford UP, 2001.

Dante Alighieri. *Latin Works*. London: J. M. Dent, 1904.

Davenport, Guy. "Afterword." Ronald Johnson, *Radi os*. Berkeley: Sand Dollar, 1977.

———. *The Geography of the Imagination*. San Francisco: North Point, 1981.

Debord, Guy and Constant. "The Amsterdam Declaration." *Constant's New Babylon: The Hyper-Architecture of Desire*. Mark Wigley. Trans. Paul Hammond. Rotterdam: OIO, 1998. 87.

Debord, Guy. "Theory of the Dérive." *Situationist Anthology*. Trans. and ed. Ken Knabb. Berkeley: Bureau of Public Secrets, 1981. 50–54.

Deleuze, Gilles. *The Fold: Leibniz and the Baroque.* Trans. Tom Conley. Minneapolis: U of Minnesota P, 1993.

———. *Foucault.* Trans. Sean Hand. Minneapolis: U of Minnesota P, 1988.

———. *Negotiations: 1972–1990.* Trans. Martin Joughin. New York: Columbia UP, 1995.

———. *Pure Immanence: Essays on a Life.* Trans. Anne Boyman. New York: Zone, 2001.

Deleuze, Gilles, and Félix Guattari. *A Thousand Plateaus.* Trans. Brian Massumi. Minneapolis: U of Minnesota P, 1987.

———. *What is Philosophy?* Trans. Hugh Tomlinson and Graham Burchell. New York: Columbia UP, 1994.

Deleuze, Gilles, and Claire Parnet. *Dialogues.* Trans. Hugh Tomlinson and Barbara Habberjam. New York: Columbia UP, 1987.

Demos, T. J. "Zurich Dada: The Aesthetics of Exile." *The Dada Seminars.* Ed. Leah Dickerman. Washington: Distributed Art, 2005. 7–29.

Derrida, Jacques. *On the Name.* Trans. David Wood. Stanford: Stanford UP, 1993.

———. "Point de Folie—Maintenant l'Architecture." *Rethinking Architecture: A Reader in Cultural Theory.* Ed. Neil Leach. London and New York: Routledge, 1997.

———. *Points . . . Interviews, 1974–1994.* Trans. Peggy Kamuf & others. Stanford: Stanford UP, 1995.

———. *Speech and Phenomena.* Trans. David B. Allison. Evanston: Northwestern UP, 1973.

Derrida, Jacques, and Peter Eisenman. *Chora L Works.* Eds. Jeffrey Kipnis and Thomas Leeser. New York: Monacelli, 1997.

DeVoogd, Peter J. "Laurence Sterne, the Marbled Page, and 'the Use of Accidents.'" *Word & Image* 1:3 (July–Sept. 1985): 279–87.

Didi-Huberman, Georges. *Fran Angelico: Disemblance and Figuration.* Trans. Jane Marie Todd. Chicago: U of Chicago P, 1995.

D'Israeli, Isaac. *Curiosities of Literature.* London: George Bell, n.d. (ca. 1860).

Donne, John. *Devotions Upon Emergent Occasions together with Death's Duel.* Ann Arbor: U of Michigan P, 1959.

Dorn, Edward. *Gunslinger.* Durham, N.C.: Duke UP, 1989.

Duncan, Robert. *Fictive Certainties.* New York: New Directions, 1985.

Dworkin, Craig, ed. *The Ubuweb Anthology of Conceptual Writing,* http://www.ubu.com /concept. 29 Feb. 2012.

Dworkin, Craig, and Kenneth Goldsmith, eds. *Against Expression: An Anthology of Conceptual Writing.* Evanston: Northwestern UP, 2011.

Eco, Umberto. *The Open Work.* Trans. Anna Cancogni. Cambridge: Harvard UP, 1989.

———. *Semiotics and the Philosophy of Language.* Bloomington. Indiana UP, 1984.

———. *Serendipities: Language and Lunacy.* Trans. William Weaver. New York: Columbia UP, 1998.

Eisenman, Peter. *Diagram Diaries.* New York: Universe, 1999.

Eisenman, Peter and Jacques Derrida. *Chora L Works.* Eds. Jeffrey Kipnis and Thomas Leeser. New York: Monacelli, 1997.

Eliot, T. S. *The Complete Poems and Plays 1909–1950*. New York: Harcourt, 1971.

Ellman, Richard. *Yeats: The Man and the Masks*. New York: W. W. Norton, 1978.

Essick, Robert N. *William Blake, Printmaker*. Princeton UP, 1980.

Evans, Robin, *Translations from Drawing to Building and Other Essays*. Cambridge: MIT P, 1997.

Felstiner, John. *Paul Celan: Poet, Survivor, Jew*. New Haven: Yale UP, 1995.

Fernández-Galiano, Luis. *Fire and Memory: On Architecture and Energy*. Trans. Gina Cariño. Cambridge: MIT P, 2000.

Fiedler, Leslie. *The Collected Essays of Leslie Fiedler*. Vol. 2. New York: Stein & Day, 1971.

Fiumara, Gemma Corradi. *The Other Side of Language: a Philosophy of Listening*. Trans. Charles Lambert. London: Routledge, 1990.

Foucault, Michel. *Aesthetics, Method & Epistemology: Essential Works of Foucault, 1954–1984*. Vol. 1. Ed. James D. Faubion. New York: New Press, 1998.

Franck, Karen A. "It and I Bodies as Objects, Bodies as Subjects." *Architects in Cyberspace II*. Ed. Neil Spiller. *Architectural Design*, Vol. 68 Nos. 11/12 (Nov.–Dec. 1998): 16–19.

Fraser, Kathleen. "Line. On the Line. Lining up. Lined with. Between the Lines. Bottom Line." *The Line in Modern Poetry*. Eds. Robert Frank and Henry Sayre. Urbana: U of Illinois P, 1988. 152–74.

Fry, Paul H. *A Defense of Poetry: Reflections on the Occasion of Writing*. Stanford: Stanford UP, 1995.

Furlani, Andre. "'Yours Be the Speech': Ronald Johnson's Milton and Guy Davenport's Basho." *Ronald Johnson: Life and Works*. Eds. Joel Bettridge and Eric Murphy Selinger. Orono: National Poetry Foundation, 2008. 73–98.

Gallo, Rubén. "Fidget's Body." *Kenneth Goldsmith and Conceptual Poetics. Open Letter*, 12.7 (Fall 2005): 50–57

Geoffrey of Vinsauf. *Poetria Nova*. Trans. Margaret F. Nims. Toronto: Pontifical Institute of Mediaeval Studies, 1967.

Gilman, Sander. "The Mad Man as Artist: Medicine, History and Degenerate Art." *Journal of Contemporary History* 20.4 (October 1986), 575–97.

Glancey, Jonathan. *Nigel Coates: Body Buildings and City Scapes*. New York: Watson Gupthill, 1999.

Goldsmith, Kenneth. *Fidget*. Toronto: Coach House Books, 2000.

———. "A Week of Blogs for the Poetry Foundation." *The Consequence of Innovation: 21st Century Poetics*. Ed. Craig Dworkin. New York: Roof Books, 2008: 137–149.

Gray, Thomas. *The Complete Poems*. Eds. H. W. Starr and J. R. Hendrickson. Oxford: Oxford UP, 1966.

Gumpel, Liselotte. *"Concrete" Poetry from East and West Germany: The Language of Exemplarism and Experimentalism*. New Haven: Yale UP, 1976.

Haddid, Zaha. *The Complete Work*. New York: Rizzoli, 1998.

Harbison, Robert. *Thirteen Ways: Theoretical Investigations in Architecture*. Cambridge: MIT P, 1997.

Harris, William V. *Ancient Literacy.* Cambridge: Harvard UP, 1989.

Harvey, Robert, and Lawrence R. Schehr, eds. *Jean-François Lyotard: Time and Judgment. Yale French Studies* 99. New Haven: Yale UP, 2001.

Hassan, Ihab. *The Right Promethean Fire: Imagination, Science, and Cultural Change.* Urbana: Illinois UP, 1980.

Heidegger, Martin. *The Cambridge Companion to Heidegger.* Ed. Charles Guinon. Cambridge: Cambridge UP, 1993.

———. "Letter on Humanism." *Basic Writings.* Ed. David Farell Krell. San Francisco: Harper Collins, 1993. 213–265.

———. *Being and Time.* Trans. John Macquarrie & Edward Robinson. New York: Harper & Row, 1962.

Heine, Heinrich. *Travel Pictures.* Trans. Francis Store. London: George Bell & Sons, 1887.

Hejduk, John. *Medusa a Mask: Works 1947–1988.* New York: Rizzoli, 1985.

———. *Vladivostok: A Trilogy.* New York: Rizzoli, 1989.

———. *Soundings.* New York: Rizzoli, 1993.

Heller-Roazen, Daniel. *Echolalias: On the Forgetting of Language.* New York: Zone, 2008.

Hermand, Jost, and Michael Gilbert, eds. *German Essays on Music.* New York: Continuum, 1994.

Hetata, Sherif. "The Self and Autobiography" *PMLA* Vol. 118 no. 1 (January 2003): 123–125.

Higgins, Dick. *Horizons, the Poetics and Theory of the Intermedia.* Carbondale: Southern Illinois UP, 1984.

———. *Pattern Poetry Guide to an Unknown Literature.* Albany: State U of New York P, 1987.

Hollier, Denis. *Against Architecture: The Writings of Georges Bataille.* Trans. Betsy Wing. Cambridge: MIT P, 1989.

Home, Stewart, ed. *Plagiarism: Art as Commodity and Strategies for its Negation.* London: Aporia, 1987.

Hoy, Dan. "The Virtual Dependency of the Post-Avant and the Problematics of Flarf: What Happens when Poets Spend Too Much Time Fucking Around on the Internet." *Jacket* 29, April 2006. Web. 29 Feb 2012. http://jacketmagazine.com/29/hoy-flarf.html.

Huelsenbeck, Richard. *Memoirs of a Dada Drummer.* Ed. Hans J. Kleinschmidt. Trans. Joachim Neugroschel. New York: Viking, 1974.

Husserl, Edmund. *Cartesian Meditations.* Trans. Dorion Cairns. The Hague: Martinus Nijhoff, 1977.

Hussey, Christopher. *The Picturesque: Studies in a Point of View.* London: Putnams, 1927.

Hutcheon, Linda. *The Politics of Postmodernism.* London and New York: Routledge, 1989.

Ing, Catherine. *Elizabethan Lyrics: A Study of the Development of English Metres and their Relation to Poetic Effect.* London: Chatto & Windus, 1951.

Idel, Moshe. *The Mystical Experience of Abraham Abulafia.* Albany: SUNY, 1988.

Janacek, Gerald. *Zaum: The Transrational Poetry of Russian Futurism.* San Diego: San Diego State UP, 1999.

Jarry, Alfred. *Selected Works*. Eds. Roger Shattuck and Simon Watson Taylor. New York: Grove Books, 1965.

———. "Elements of 'Pataphysics." *What is 'Pataphysics. Evergreen Review,* 4.13 (May-June 1960): 131–32.

Jencks, Charles. *The Language of Post-Modern Architecture*. London: Academy Editions, 1978.

Jenkins, Henry. *Textual Poachers: Television Fans and Participatory Culture*. London and New York: Routledge, Chapman and Hall, 1992.

Johns, Adrian. *The Nature of the Book: Print and Knowledge in the Making*. Chicago: U of Chicago P, 1998.

Johnson, Ronald. *ARK*. Albuquerque: Living Batch, 1996.

———. "From *Hurrah for Euphony*." *Chicago Review* 42.1 (1996): 25.

———. *Radi os*. Berkeley: Sand Dollar, 1977.

Johnson, Samuel. "Preface to Pope." *Prefaces, Biographical and Critical to the Works of the English Poets*. Vol. 7. London: C. Bathurst, J. Buckland, W. Strahan et al., 1781.

Jolas, Eugene. "Elucidation of James Joyce's Monomyth: Explication of *Finnegans Wake*." *Critical Writings, 1924–1951*. Eds. Klaus H. Kiefer and Rainer Rumold. Evanston: Northwestern UP, 2009.

Jorn, Asgar. "Pataphysics—A Religion in the Making." Web. 30 May 2012. http://www.ubuweb.com/papers/jorn_pataphysics.html.

Anastasi, William. "Jarry, Joyce, Duchamp and Cage." *tout-fait: The Marcel Duchamp Studies Online Journal* Web. 5 March 2011. www.toutfait.com

Jose, Nicholas. *Ideas of The Restoration in English Literature 1660–71*. New Haven: Harvard UP, 1982.

Joyce, James. *Finnegans Wake*. London: Faber & Faber, 1950.

Kandinsky, Wassily. "On the Question of Form." *The Blaue Reiter Almanac*. Eds. Wassily Kandinsky and Franz Marc. New Documentary edition ed. Klaus Lankheit. New York: Viking, 1974. 147–87.

Kaufmann, Vincent. "Angels of Purity." Trans. John Goodman. *October* 79 (Winter 1997): 49–68.

Kearney, Richard. *Poetics of Imagining: from Husserl to Lyotard*. New York: Harper Collins Academic, 1993.

Keats, John. *The Poetical Works*. Ed. H. W. Garrod. Oxford: Oxford UP, 1958.

Kennedy, Bill, and Darren Wershler-Henry. *Apostrophe*. Toronto: ECW, 2006.

Kern, Hermann, *Through the Labyrinth: Designs and Meanings over 5,000 Years*. New York: Prestel, 2000.

Khlebnikov, Velimir, and A. Kruchenykh. "The Letter as Such." *Russian Futurism through its Manifestoes, 1912–1928*. Trans. and ed. Anna Lawton and Herbert Eagle. Ithaca: Cornell UP, 1988. 63–64.

Kierkegaard, Søren. *Either/ Or,* Vol. 1. Trans. David F. and Lillian Marvin Swenson. New York: Doubleday, 1959.

Kittler, Friedrich A. *Discourse Networks 1800 / 1900*. Trans. Michael Mettler, with Chris Cullens. Stanford UP, 1990.

Knabb, Ken ed., *Situationist International Anthology*, trans. and ed. Ken Knabb. Berkeley: Bureau of Public Secrets, 1981.

Kristeva, Julia. "Towards a Semiology of Paragrams." *The Tel Quel Reader*. Eds. Patrick ffrench and Roland-François Lack. London: Routledge, 1998. 25–49.

———. *Revolution in Poetic Language*. Trans. Margaret Waller. New York: Columbia UP, 1984.

Kruchenykh, Aleksei, "Explodity." *Russian Futurism through its Manifestoes, 1912-1928*. Trans. Anna Lawton and Herbert Eagle. Ithaca: Cornell UP, 1988. 65–66.

Lakoff, George. "Testing the Limit's of Brain Plasticity: Or, Why is There a Wall Down the Middle of the Tub?" *Reversible Destiny: Arakawa/Gins*. New York: Guggenheim Museum, 1997. 113–22.

Lang, Berel. *Heidegger's Silence*. Ithaca: Cornell UP, 1996.

Lawrence, Nicholas. "Ronald Johnson's *Radi  os*: A Report on Method" in *Ronald Johnson: Life and Work*. Eds. Joel Bettridge and Eric Murphy Selinger. Orono: National Poetry Foundation, 2008.

Leach, Neil ed. *Rethinking Architecture: A Reader in Cultural Theory*. London and New York: Routledge, 1997.

Lefaivre, Liane. *Leon Battista Alberti's "Hypnerotomachia Poliphili": Recognizing the Architectural Body in the Early Italian Renaissance*. Cambridge: MIT P, 1997.

Le Gallienne, Richard. *Prose Fancies (Second Series)*. London: John Lane, 1896.

Leibniz, Gottfried. *New Essays Concerning Human Understanding*. Trans. A. G. Langley. LaSalle: Open Court, 1949.

Leupin, Alexandre. *Barbarolexis: Medieval Writing and Sexuality*. Trans. Kate M. Cooper. Cambridge: Harvard UP, 1989.

Levin, Harry. *Refractions*. New York: Oxford UP, 1966.

Levinas, Emmanuel. "Reality and its Shadow." *Collected Philosophical Papers*. Trans. Alphonso Lingis. Dordrecht: Martinus Nijhoff, 1987. 1–13.

———. *Outside the Subject*. Trans. Michael B. Smith. Stanford: Stanford UP, 1993.

———. "Transcending Words: Concerning Word-Erasing." Trans. Didier Maleuvre. *Yale French Studies* 81 (1992): 145–150.

Libeskind, Daniel. *Countersign*. London: Academy Editions, 1991.

———. *The Space of Encounter*. New York: Universe Publishing, 2000.

Loy, Mina. *The Last Lunar Baedeker*. Ed. Roger Conover. Highlands: The Jargon Society, 1982.

Lucretius, *De Rerum Natura*. Trans. W. H. D. Rouse. Cambridge: Harvard UP, 1975.

Lynn, Greg. "Architectural Curvilinearity: the Folded, the Pliant and the Supple." *Architectural Design* Spec. issue of *Folding in Architecture* 102 (1993): 8–15.

Lyotard, Jean-François. *The Differend: Phrases in Dispute*. Trans. George Van Den Abbeele. Minneapolis: U of Minnesota P, 1988.

——. *The Lyotard Reader*. Ed. Andrew Benjamin. Oxford: Blackwell, 1989

——. *Peregrinations: Law, Form, Event*. New York: Columbia UP, 1988.

——. *Political Writings*. Trans. Bill Readings and Paul Geiman. Minneapolis: U of Minnesota P, 1993.

——. *The Postmodrn Condition: A Report on Knowledge*. Trans. Geoff Bennington and Brian Massumi. Minneapolis: U of Minnesota P, 1984.

——. *Soundproof Room: Malraux's Anti-Aesthetics*. Trans. Robert Harvey. Stanford UP, 2001.

MacNeice, Louis. *Collected Poems 1925–1948*. London: Faber and Faber, 1949.

Makin, Peter. *Pound's Cantos*. Baltimore: Johns Hopkins UP, 1985.

Mallarmé, Stephane. *Mallarmé*. Ed. and trans. Anthony Hartley. Harmondsworth: Penguin, 1965.

——. *Mallarmé in Prose*. Ed. Mar Ann Caws. New York: New Directions, 2001.

Manovich, Lev. *The Language of New Media*. Cambridge: MIT P, 2001.

Map, Walter. *Master Walter Map's Book, De Nugis Curialium (Courtiers' Trifles)*. Trans. Frederick Tupper and Marbury Bladen Ogle. New York: Macmillan, 1924.

Marx, Karl, and Frederick Engels. *Selected Works*. New York: International Publishers, 1968.

Massumi, Brian. *A User's Guide to Capitalism and Schizophrenia*. Cambridge: MIT P, 1992.

Maud, Ralph. *Charles Olson at the Harbor*. Vancouver: Talonbooks, 2008.

McCaffery, Steve. *North of Intention: Critical Essays 1973–1986*. New York: Roof Books, 1986.

——. *Prior to Meaning: The Protosemantic and Poetics*. Evanston: Northwestern UP, 2001.

McDonough, Thomas. "Fluid Spaces: Constant and the Situationist Critique of Architecture." *The Activist Drawing: Retracing Situationist Architectures from Constant's New Babylon to Beyond*. Eds. Catherine de Zegher and Mark Wigley. Cambridge: MIT P, 2001. 93–104.

McGann, Jerome. *Black Riders: The Visible Language of Modernism*. Princeton: Princeton UP, 1993.

——. *The Point is to Change It: Poetry and Criticism in the Continuing Present*. Tuscaloosa: U of Alabama P, 2007.

——. *Social Values and Poetic Acts: The Historical Judgment of Literary Works*. Cambridge: Harvard UP, 1988.

——. *The Textual Condition*. Princeton: Princeton UP, 1991.

McGee, Michael. *My Angie Dickinson*. Gran Canaria, Spain: Zasterle Press, 2007.

——. *The Flarf Files*. Web. 26 February 2011 <epc.buffalo.edu/authors/Bernstein/syllabi/readings/flarf.html>

McHale, Brian. *The Obligation Toward the Difficult Whole: Postmodern Long Poems*. Tuscaloosa: U Alabama P, 2004.

Meredith, George. "The Day of the Daughter of Hades." *Poems and Lyrics of the Joy of the Earth*. London: Macmillan, 1883.

Michel, Wilhelm. "Der Refraktär und sein Wort." *Der Kunstwart* XLII (October 1928): 1.

Moles, Abraham. *Information Theory and Esthetic Perception*. Trans. Joel E. Cohen. Urbana: U of Illinois P, 1969.

Morgan, Robert C. "A Sign of Beauty." *Uncontrollable Beauty: Towards a New Aesthetics*. Ed. Bill Beckley. New York: Allworth, 1998. 75–82.

Murray, Peter. *The Architecture of the Italian Renaissance*. London: Thames and Hudson, 1986.

Nancy, Jean-Luc. *The Inoperative Community*. Trans. Peter Connor, Lisa Garbus, Michael Holland, and Simona Sawheny. Minneapolis: U of Minnesota P, 1991.

Naumann, Francis M. *Marcel Duchamp: the Art of Making Art in the Age of Mechanical Reproduction*. Ghent and Amsterdam: Ludion, 1999.

Noever, Peter ed. *The End of Architecture?: Documents and Manifestos*. Munich: Prestel-Verlag, 1992.

*Notes & Queries*. Third series no. 6 Oct. 15, 1864.

Novak, Marcus. *Trans Terra Form: Liquid Architecture and the Loss of Inscription* Web. 17 May 2011. http://www.krcf.org/krcfhome/PRINT/nonlocated/nlonline/nonMarcos .html

O'Donovan, Joan, and Oliver O'Donovan, eds. *From Irenaeus to Grotius: A Soucebook in Christian Political Thought*. Grand Rapids: William B. Eerdmans, 1999.

O'Leary, Peter. "An Interview with Ronald Johnson 1995." *Ronald Johnson: Life and Works*. Eds. Joel Bettridge and Eric Murphy Selinger. Orono: National Poetry Foundation, 2008. 561–86.

Olson, Charles. *Charles Olson at Goddard College*. Ed. Kyle Schlesinger. New York: Cuneiform, 2011.

——. *Letters to Origin 1950–1955*. Ed. Albert Glover. London: Cape Golliard, 1969.

Pallasmaa, Juani. *The Eyes of the Skin: Architecture and the Senses*. London: Academy Editions, 1996.

Parkes, M. B. *Pause and Effect: Punctuation in the West*. Los Angeles: U of California P, 1993.

Patterson, Diana. "Tristram's Marblings and Marblers." *The Shandean* 3 (Nov. 1989): 129–32.

Perloff, Marjorie. "'Vocable Scriptsigns'": Differential Poetics in Kenneth Goldsmith's *Fidget*." *Fidget*. Toronto: Coach House Books, 2000. 89–107.

Pierssens, Michel. *The Power of Babel: A Study of Logophilia*. Trans. Carl R. Lovitt. London: Routledge & Kegan Paul, 1980.

Plutarch. *Plutarch's Morals. Theosophical Essays*. Trans. C. W. King. London: George Bell, 1908.

Poirier, Richard. *The Performing Self*. New York: Oxford UP, 1971.

Pound, Ezra. *Selected Prose 1909–1965*. New York: New Directions, 1973.

Price, Martin. "The Picturesque Moment." *From Sensibility to Romanticism: Essays Presented to Frederick A. Pottle.* Eds. F. W. Hillis and Harold Bloom. Oxford: Oxford UP, 1965.

Ranciere, Jacques. "The Politics of Literature." *Substance* 103 (2004): 10–24.

Rasula, Jed. *Syncopations: The Stress of Innovation in Contemporary American Poetry.* Tuscaloosa: U of Alabama P, 2004.

Rasula, Jed, and Steve McCaffery. *Imagining Language: An Anthology.* Cambridge: MIT P, 1998.

Ray, Mary-Ann. *Seven Partly Underground Rooms and Buildings for Water, Ice, and Midgets. Pamphlet Architecture* 20. Princeton: Princeton Architectural Press, 1997.

Read, Rob. *O Spam Poems: Selected Daily Treated Spam.* Toronto: BookThug, 2005.

Rexroth, Kenneth. *American Poetry in the Twentieth Century.* New York: Herder and Herder, 1971.

Richter, Hans. *Dada Art and Anti-art.* Translated by David Britt. New York: Abrams, 1965.

Rogers, Richard. *Architecture a Modern View.* London: Thames and Hudson, 1990.

Rossi, Aldo. *The Architecture of the City.* Trans. Diane Ghirardo and Joan Ockman. Cambridge: MIT P, 1984.

Rudofsky, Bernard. *Architecture Without Architects: A Short Introduction to Non-Pedigreed Architecture.* New York: Doubleday, 1964.

Sadler, Simon. *The Situationist City.* Cambridge: MIT P, 1998.

Sandomir, I. L. "Opus Pataphysicum Inaugural Harangue." *What is 'Pataphysics. Evergreen Review,* 4.13 (May-June 1960): 169–80.

Saussure, Ferdinand de. *Course in General Linguistics.* Trans. Wade Baskin. London: Fontana/Collins, 1974.

Schafer, R. Murray. *The Tuning of the World.* Toronto: McClelland and Stewart, 1977.

Schelling, Friedrich. *The Philosophy of Art.* Ed. and trans. Douglas W. Scott. Minneapolis: U of Minnesota P, 1989.

Schiff, Karen. "Topics in the History of Artists' Books: Tristram Shandy's Original Marbled Page." *The Journal of Artists' Books* 14 (Fall 2000): 6–11.

Schlegel, Friedrich. *Lucinde and the Fragments.* Trans. Peter Firchow. Minneapolis: U of Minnesota P, 1971.

Schnapp, Jeffrey T. "Introduction: Ball and Hammer." *Ball and Hammer: Hugo Ball's Tenderenda the Fantast.* By Hugo Ball. New Haven: Yale UP 2002. 1–21.

Schneidau, Herbert. "The Age of Interpretation and the Moment of Immediacy: Contemporary Art v. History." *ELH* 37 (June 1970).

Schuster, Joshua. "On Kenneth Goldsmith: The Avant-Garde at a Standstill." *Kenneth Goldsmith and Conceptual Poetics, Open Letter* 12.7 (Fall 2005): 102–9.

Scroggins, Mark. *Louis Zukofsky and the Poetry of Knowledge.* Tuscaloosa: U of Alabama P, 1998.

Serres, Michel. *Hermes: Literature, Science, Philosophy*. Eds. Josué V. Harari and David F. Bell. Baltimore: Johns Hopkins UP, 1982.

Sitwell, Edith, *A Poet's Notebook*. Boston: Little, Brown & Co., 1950.

Smith, John Thomas. *Nollekens and His Times*. 2 vols. London: Henry Colburn, 1828.

Snyder, Ellsworth Snyder. "Jackson's Poetry according to E." *Crayon Premier Issue: Festschrift for Jackson Mac Low's 75th Birthday*. Eds. Andrew Levy and Bob Harrison. Brooklyn N.Y. 1997. 116–17.

Solà-Morales, Ignasi, *Differences*. Trans. Graham Thompson and Sarah Whiting. Cambridge: MIT P, 1997.

———. *Differences: Topographies of Contemporary Architecture*. 1995. Trans. Graham Thompson. Cambridge: MIT P, 1997.

Spiller, Neil. *Maverick Demarcations: Architectural Works (1985-1998)*. Chichester: Wiley Academy, 2000.

Spotts, Frederic. *Hitler and the Power of Aesthetics*. New York: Overlook P, 2003.

Stafford, Barbara Maria. *Body Criticism: Imagining the Unseen in Enlightenment Art and Medicine*. Cambridge: MIT P, 1993.

Starobinski, Jean. *Words upon Words: The Anagrams of Ferdinand de Saussure*. Trans. Olivia Emmet. New Haven: Yale UP, 1979.

Steiner, Peter. *Russian Formalism: A Metapoetics*. Ithaca: Cornell UP, 1984.

Steinke, Gerhardt Edward. *The Life and Work of Hugo Ball. Founder of Dadaism*. The Hague: Mouton, 1967.

Sterne, Laurence. *The Life and Opinions of Tristram Shandy, Gentleman*. York: Printed for Ann Ward (9 volumes), 1760-67.

Stevens, Wallace. *Opus Posthumous*. New York: Alfred A. Knopf, 1972.

Tafuri, Manfredo. *Architecture and Utopia: Design and Capitalist Development*. Trans. Barbara Luiga La Penta. Cambridge: MIT P, 1976.

Taylor, Mark C. "Saving Not." *Reversible Destiny: Arakawa/Gins*. Ed. Michael Govan. New York: Guggenheim Museum, 1997. 124–39.

Tschumi, Bernard. *Architecture and Disjunction*. Cambridge: MIT P, 1996.

Tzara, Tristan. *Approximate Man and Other Writings*. Trans. Mary Ann Caws. Boston: Black Widow, 2005.

Ulmer, Gregory. *Applied Grammatology*. Baltimore: Johns Hopkins UP, 1985.

Valéry, Paul. *Leonardo Poe Mallarmé*. Trans. Malcolm Cowley and James R. Lawler. Princeton: Princeton UP, 1972.

———. "Poetry and Abstract Thought." *Critical Theory Since Plato*. Ed. Hazard Adams New York: Harcourt, 1992. 910–19.

Venegheim, Raoul. "Comments Against Urbanism." Trans. John Shepley. *October* 79 (Winter 1997): 123–128.

Vidler, Anthony. *The Architectural Uncanny: Essays in the Modern Unhomely*. Cambridge: MIT P, 1992.

von Humboldt, Wilhelm. *Linguistic Variability and Intellectual Development*. Trans. G. Buck and F. Raven. Coral Gables: U of Miami P, 1971.

Watten, Barrett, *Total Syntax*. Carbondale: Southern Illinois UP, 1985.

Webster, Michael. *Reading Visual Poetry after Futurism*. New York: Peter Lang, 1995.

Wershler-Henry, Darren ed. "Cyberpoetics." *Open Letter* 10th Series no. 6. Special edition (Fall 2000).

Whitman, Walt. *Democratic Vistas and Other Papers*. London: George Routledge and Son, 1887.

Wigley, Mark. *Constant's New Babylon: The Hyper-Architecture of Desire*. Rotterdam: 0I0, 1998.

———. "Paper, Scissors, Blur." *The Activist Drawing: Retracing Situationist Architectures from Constant's New Babylon to Beyond*. Eds. Catherine de Zegher and Mark Wigley. Cambridge: MIT P, 2001. 27–56.

———. "The Translation of Architecture: The Producer of Babel." *Deconstruction III*. London: Architectural Design. Academy Editions, 1994. 6–13.

Wilton-Ely, John. *The Mind and Art of Giovanni Battista Piranesi*. London: Thames & Hudson, 1978.

Witkovsky, Matthew S. "Chronology." *Dada*. ed. Leah Dickerman. Washington: Distributed Art Publishers, 2005. 416–59.

Wittgenstein, Ludwig. *Zettel*. Trans. G. E. M. Anscombe. Berkeley: U of California P, 1970.

———. *Philosophical Investigations*. Trans. G. E. M. Anscombe. London: Macmillan, 1953.

Woods, Lebbeus. *The New City*. New York: Simon and Schuster, 1992.

Wordsworth, William. *Poetical Works*. Ed. Edward Dowden. London: George Bell & Sons, 1892.

Yeats, William Butler. "Introduction." *Certain Noble Plays of Japan: from the Manuscripts of Ernest Fenollosa, chosen and finished by Ezra Pound, with an Introduction by William Butler Yeats*. Churchtown Dundrum: Cuala P, 1916.

Young, Karl. "Two Representative Works of the Last Decade: A Working Present for Jackson Mac Low on his 75th Birthday." *Crayon Premier Issue: Festschrift for Jackson Mac Low's 75th Birthday*. Eds. Andrew Levy and Bob Harrison. Brooklyn: Crayon, 1997. 134–39.

Youngblood, Gene. "Life in Counterculture." *Umelec* 2 (2006): 13.

Zegher, Catherine de, and Mark Wigley, eds. *The Activist Drawing: Retracing Situationist Architectures from Constant's New Babylon and Beyond*. Cambridge: MIT P, 2001.

Zukofsky, Louis. *Prepositions*. London: Rapp and Carroll, 1967.

# INDEX

*dérive*, architectural, 125; its connection to labyrinthine circuitry, 122; defined, 121; as Internet surfing, 132; in Kenneth Goldsmith's *Fidget*, 121, 142, 222n9

Derrida, Jacques, 1–2, 90, 97, 99–100, 106, 108, 169, 174, 191, 207, 225n7, 231n34, 234n19, 236n11, 239n21; on historicization, 96, 224n1; *Point de Folie* 1–2, 25, 113; "Shibboleth; For Paul Celan," 241n26; *Speech and Phenomena*, 216n9; *The Truth in Painting*, 98

Derrida, Jacques and Peter Eisenman, *Chora L Works*, 101–2

de Sade, Marquis, *Philosophy in the Bedroom*, 65, 178

de Sainte-Phalle, Niki, 70

de Saussure, Ferdinand, 29, 56, 58, 60–62, 217n2, 218n1, 224n22; alternate names chosen for theme-word, 52; *Cahiers d'anagrammes*, 94; his choice of "paragram" over "anagram," 52, 218n3 (chap. 4); discovery of his Notebooks, 52; his error, 53; his investigations into paragrams, 48, 51–53, 58–59, 218n2 (chap. 4); *Ms. fr. 3963*, 52; *Ms. fr. 3964*, 218n3 (chap. 4); phonocentric nature of his project, 219n7; his search for theme-words, 52; and the sublime, 62; on thought, 72. *See also* paragram

Descartes, René, 222n6

Desnos, Robert, as the first postmodern intellectual, 27

Desprez, Jean Louis, *Prison fantasies*, 230n17

*détournement*, defined, 236n4

De Voogd, Peter J., 220n2

DeVoto, Bernard, 216n8

de Zegher, Catherine, 132

diagram, 106; axonometric nature of, 106; its deconstructive potential, 106; writing-as, 106

*dianoia*, 90

Dickinson, Emily, 79–80

Didi-Huberman, Georges, 6, 67–69, 71, 220n4

Dioce, 112

Diodorus, 228n2

Dionysius the Areopagite, 23, 67, 70

Dirac, Paul, 195

di San Gimignano, Giovanni, *Summa de examples et similitudinibus rerum*, 69, 220n6

D'Israeli, Isaac, *Curiosities of Literature*, 175–76

dissipative structure, 110; as the new scientific paradigm of the age, 99; in Deleuzean curvilinear logic, 109

Divoire, Fernand, 12, 211n1 (chap. 1)

Dixon-Hunt, John, *Nature Over Again: The Garden Art of Ian Hamilton Finlay*, 233n8

Donne, John, "Death's Duel," 102

Dorn, Edward, *Gunslinger*, 88

Dotremont, Christian, member of COBRA, 123

Duchamp, Marcel, 73, 87, 127, 178, 235n2; aesthetic of indifference, 80; *The Large Glass*, 71; *Paysage fautif*, 70; readymades, 89–90, 92, 138

Duncan, Robert, 27–28, 30, 100; "Notebook 31," 185

Dworkin, Craig, 76, 83, 160, 228n4

Dryden, John, 190; "Alexander's Feast," 191

Eco, Umberto, 4, 45–49, 229n6; on the topology of the labyrinth, 118; *The Open Work*, 46. *See also* information theory

generated method of composition, 4, 42–43; its Zen Buddhist inspiration, 44. See also *Words nd Ends from Ez* (Mac Low)

Macneice, Louis, "Autumn Journal," 237n6; *Collected Poems*, 209

Macpherson, James, 150, 193

Maeterlink, Maurice, *The Life of Bees*, 237n2

Magnus, Albertus: on the formation of stones, 70

Majdanek, 210

Makin, Peter, 41, 227n18

Malevich, Kasimir: and the fourth dimension, 230n18

Mallarmé, Stephane, 4, 62, 89, 93–94, 161; "The Crisis of Poetry," 18; on the "essential" word, 4, 18; "Le Nénuphar blanc," 175; "Un coup de Dés Jamais N'Abolira Le Hasard," 33

Mallock, William Hurrell, *A Human Document*, 108, 216n9

Malraux, André, *Man's Fate*, 209

Mandelbrot, Benoit, 72

Manet, Edouard, *Déjeuner sur l'herbe*, 75

Mannerism, 149

Manovich, Lev, 132

Manutius, Aldus, 220n7

Map, Walter, *De Nugis Curialium*, 215n1

marbled paper, 5, 66; combed variety, 220n5; historical rise of, 64–65; as libertine gesture, 65; its optical lure, 65; its process of production, 70. See also *marmi finti*

Marinetti, Filipo Tommaso, 18, 92, 237n1; his attack on syntax, 219n4; "Destruction of Syntax-Imagination without Strings-Words-in-Freedom," 236n6; lyrical

intoxication, 197; its rationale in accord with Carlyle's for musical thinking, 197; words in freedom (*parole in liberta*), 10, 15, 80, 186, 195–99, 213n11

Markov, Victor, "The Principles of the New Art," 22

*marmi finti*, 5; and a "blotchist" tradition in painting, 68; as dissemblance and disfiguration, 5, 67–68; examples of, 220n4; as figure of insemination, 69–70; and the Incarnation, 68; links to a genealogy of semen, 67; meta-materiality, 68; as negative theology, 68

Martini, Simone, "Annunciation," 220n4

Marshall, Benjamin, 224n5

Marx, Karl: *Eighteenth Brumaire of Louis Bonaparte*, 211n1 (Intro.); Marxism, 95, 216n11

Masheck, Joseph, *Modernities: Art-Matters and the Present*, 231n32

Mason, William, *The English Garden*, 149, 232n2

Massin, *Letter and Image*, 225n5

Massini, Batschelet, 116

Masten, Jeffrey, Peter Stallybrass, and Nancy J. Vickers, *Language Machines: Technologies of Literary and Cultural Production*, 228n1

Massumi, Brian, 59

Matta-Clark, Gordon, 139

Maud, Ralph, 27, 215n5

Mauthausen, 210

maze, confused with labyrinth, 117

McCaffery, Steve: "The Elsewhere of Meaning," 213n17; "Insufficiency of Theory to Poetical Economy," 217n15; "*The Martyrology* as Paragram," 217n2, 217n17; *North of In-*